Teacher Education for Inclusion

How teachers might best be prepared to work in schools with an increasingly diverse pupil population is of concern to educational academics, professionals and governments around the world. Changes that have taken place in legislation and practice often fail to take into account how practitioners can ensure that all children and young people are able to achieve.

The focus of this international text is on innovative practices for preparing teachers to work in inclusive classrooms and schools. Drawing on both pre- and in-service training methods, the expert contributors to this book follow three major themes:

- Social and political challenges regarding teacher education – providing a historical perspective on the training of teachers, tensions in preparing teachers for inclusion, cultural issues, the relationship between educational funding and practices and collaborative measures to support a whole-school approach.
- Innovative approaches in pre-service teacher preparation – discussing a range of innovative models and approaches used in pre-service teacher education courses.
- Engaging professional development for in-service teachers – reviewing a range of innovative approaches employed to engage working teachers and help them establish curricula and pedagogy that meet the needs of all students in their classes.

Each chapter includes a list of proposed learning outcomes, a theoretical or conceptual framework to help readers develop the proposed innovation, an overview of recent research, a review of the research data available and a discussion of the international implications and challenges, summarising suggestions for a positive way forward.

Teacher Education for Inclusion: Changing paradigms and innovative approaches is essential reading for practising teacher educators, school leaders, university lecturers in education and postgraduate students.

Chris Forlin is Professor of Special and Inclusive Education at the Hong Kong Institute of Education. She has also edited *Reform, Inclusion and Teacher Education: Towards a new era of special education in the Asia-Pacific region* (Routledge, 2008).

Teacher Education for Inclusion

Changing paradigms and innovative approaches

Edited by Chris Forlin

Routledge
Taylor & Francis Group

LONDON AND NEW YORK

First published 2010
by Routledge
2 Park Square, Milton Park, Abingdon, Oxon OX14 4RN

Simultaneously published in the USA and Canada
by Routledge
270 Madison Avenue, New York, NY 10016

*Routledge is an imprint of the Taylor & Francis Group, an informa
business*

© 2010 Chris Forlin selection and editorial material; individual
chapters © the contributors

Typeset in Sabon by
HWA Text and Data Management, Tunbridge Wells
Printed and bound in Great Britain by
CPI Antony Rowe, Chippenham, Wiltshire

British Library Cataloguing in Publication Data
A catalogue record for this book is available from the British
Library

Library of Congress Cataloging-in-Publication Data
Teacher education for inclusion : changing paradigms and
innovative approaches / edited by Chris Forlin.
        p. cm.
 Includes bibliographical references and index.
 1. Inclusive education. 2. Teachers—Training of. I. Forlin, Chris.
 LC1200.T43 2010
 370.71'1—dc22   2009048672

ISBN13: 978-0-415-54876-2 (hbk)
ISBN13: 978-0-415-54877-9 (pbk)
ISBN13: 978-0-203-85087-9 (ebk)

Contents

Tables

Figures

Contributors

Adrian Ashman is Professor of Education at the University of Queensland, Australia. His research and teaching interests have focused on the areas of theory and practice in cognitive education, special and inclusive education, and intellectual disability. He recently completed his second PhD in creative writing due to his interest in that area. Email: adrian.ashman@uq.edu.au

Paul Bartolo coordinates Masters programs for Psychologists and Inclusion Coordinators and a Program for Culturally Responsive Education at the University of Malta. He led a National Focus Group for Inclusive Education, and an international EU Comenius project that produced training materials for preparing teachers to respond to student diversity (www.dtmp.org). Email: paul.a.bartolo@um.edu.mt

Dianne Chambers is a senior lecturer and coordinator of undergraduate and postgraduate Special Education programs at the University of Notre Dame, Australia (Fremantle). She is heavily involved in pre-service teacher education with a focus on preparing pre-service teachers for inclusion. Her main research interests include preparation for inclusion, assistive technology, education assistants, teaching children with moderate and severe disabilities and communication strategies for children with disabilities. Email: dchambers2@nd.edu.au

Robert Conway is Dean of the School of Education at Flinders University, Australia. His background is as a teacher in both mainstream and special education. His main research and teaching is in the area of students with behavior problems. He works with education systems to improve the management of students with behavior problems, particularly in the ways in which student management, learning and teaching can be addressed concurrently. He also has a strong interest in inclusion and in how education systems adapt learning and teaching strategies to meet the needs of all students. Email: bob.conway@flinders.edu.au

Joanne Deppeler is Associate Professor in the Faculty of Education at Monash University, Australia. Her research focus is on inclusive education reform and the professional learning of teachers. She publishes widely and contributes to the professional and policy domains at state, national and international levels. Email: Joanne.Deppeler@Education.monash.edu.au

Paul Fitch is Assistant Professor at the Department of Special Education Services and Instruction at Rowan University in New Jersey where he coordinates the Collaborative Teacher Education program. His research focuses on co-teaching models and practices for preparing teachers for inclusive education. Email: drpjfjr@optonline.net

Todd Fletcher is Associate Professor in the Department of Psychoeducational and Disability Studies at the University of Arizona, USA. He coordinates the graduate program in bilingual/multicultural special education. His research interests focus on culturally responsive practices for diverse learners in the USA and educational reform and special education policy in Latin America, in particular, Mexico. Email: toddf@u.arizona.edu

Lani Florian is Professor of social and educational inclusion at the University of Aberdeen, UK. Her research interests are in the areas of inclusive practice and pedagogy. She recently edited the *SAGE Handbook of Special Education*, and co-authored *Achievement and Inclusion in Schools*.Email: l.florian@abdn.ac.uk

Chris Forlin is Professor of special and inclusive education at the Hong Kong Institute of Education. She has published extensively on research in this area, particularly in reference to preparing teachers for inclusion. She consults internationally on curriculum and pedagogy for inclusive practice. Email: cforlin@ied.edu.hk

Ismael García Cedillo was Director of the National Project for Inclusive Education in Mexico, from 1995 to 2001. He is Professor at the Autonomous University of San Luis Potosi. His most recent publication is *Inclusive Education in Latin America and the Caribbean. The Mexican case*. Email: ismaelgace@yahoo.com.mx

Philip Garner is Professor of Education at the University of Northampton, UK. He has published extensively on aspects of special and inclusive education and children's emotional and behavioural difficulties. He is Director of the English Training and Development Agency's Professional Resource Network (IPRN) focusing on positive classroom management. Email: Philip.Garner@northampton.ac.uk

Garry Hornby was born in England and worked as a mainstream and special class teacher and educational psychologist in New Zealand. He has lectured at the Universities of Manchester, Hull and West Indies. He is now Professor of Education at the University of Canterbury College of Education in Christchurch, New Zealand. His teaching and research is in the areas of educational psychology, counseling, parental involvement, and special needs education. Email: garry.hornby@canterbury.ac.nz

Phyllis Jones taught and was an administrator in schools in the UK for fifteen years. She currently teaches low incidence teacher education programs at the University of South Florida, USA. Her teaching and research relate to issues of teacher thinking, inclusion, children with low incidence disabilities and teacher education including online pedagogy. Email: pjones7@coedu.usf.edu

Leena Kaikkonen has worked for 20 years as a teacher educator in Finland and in international projects dealing with teacher and school development. Her research interests include the development of more inclusive education. She connects this with teachers' needs to consider wider contexts and questions of vocational pedagogy, i.e. out-of-school learning environments and post-school inclusion. Email: leena.kaikkonen@jamk.fi

Pennee Kantavong is a lecturer and Associate Professor in the Faculty of Education, Khon Kaen University, Thailand. Her PhD is in International and Development Education. Her interests include development education, adult education, informal education and inclusive education. Her latest book is *A Synthesis of Education Research in Thailand* (W.J. Property, 2007). Email: pennee@kku.ac.th

Elizabeth Kozleski is Professor of Special Education at Arizona State University, USA. Her research examines the ways in which culture is negotiated and hybridized in schools and school systems through interactions among students, families and teachers (e.g., placement decisions, inclusive education), and through teacher learning in urban contexts. Email: Elizabeth.Kozleski@asu.edu

Chi-leung Lai was formerly a teacher in primary, secondary and special schools and has rich experience in teaching children with special needs. He is now working at the Hong Kong Institute of Education. He has been conducting workshops and seminars in the area of inclusion since the late 1990s and possesses valuable experience in conducting workshops for the Education Bureau in the area of 'Inclusive Education – the whole-school approach' for more than 50 schools. Email: cllai@ied.edu.hk

Tim Loreman is Associate Professor in the Faculty of Education at Concordia University College of Alberta, Canada. Prior to this he worked as a teacher in both Canada and Australia, and also as a lecturer at Monash University in Australia. His research interests are focused on the subject of inclusion, childhood, pre-service teacher education, and pedagogy. Email: tim.loreman@Concordia.ab.ca

Dinh Thi Nguyet is the inclusive education program manager at Catholic Relief Services in Vietnam. She has been an activist for the inclusive education movement for nearly 10 years. She has been involved in advocacy for policy for mainstreaming, human resource development including pre- and in-service teacher training curricula, and community support network promotion. Email: dnguyet@vn.seapro.crs.org

Elizabeth O'Gorman is a teacher educator (Ireland and Hong Kong). Her current research interest is the continuing professional development of teachers in the area of inclusive education and special educational needs with a focus on the creation of communities of practice as a response to the issues and challenges facing teachers working in this area. Email: elizabeth.ogorman@ucd.ie

Chung-yee Poon is a Teaching Fellow at the Centre for Special Needs and Studies in Inclusive Education at the Hong Kong Institute of Education. He has experience in promoting inclusive education in many local schools as well as professional training for teachers working with parents of children with special educational needs and teaching children with disabilities in Mainland China and Macau. Email: pooncy@ied.edu.hk

Richard Rose is Director of the Centre for Special Needs Education and Research at the University of Northampton, UK. He is currently working on a three-year longitudinal study into special needs provision in Ireland. His published work focuses on aspects of inclusive education. Email: richard.rose@northampton.ac.uk

Martyn Rouse is Chair of Social and Educational Inclusion at the University of Aberdeen, UK. Previously at the University of Cambridge, he has undertaken research and development on inclusion in the UK and for international agencies, including the OECD and UNICEF in Eastern Europe and the former Soviet Union. Recent publications include *Achievement and Inclusion in Schools* (Routledge), winner of the NASEN/TES Academic Book of 2008. Email: m.rouse@abdn.ac.uk

Spencer J. Salend is Professor in the Department of Educational Studies at the State University of New York at New Paltz. His research interests address inclusive educational practices, educational assessment, and students from culturally and linguistically diverse backgrounds. He is the author of *Creating Inclusive Classrooms: Effective and reflective practices,* and *Classroom Testing For All Students: Moving beyond standardized assessments.* Email: salends@newpaltz.edu

Kate Scorgie is Professor at Azusa Pacific University, USA, where she teaches educational psychology, special education, adult learning, educational leadership and motivation. Her research interests include transformational dynamics of parenting children with disabilities, participative case study pedagogy, and strategies for facilitating empathy. Email: KScorgie@apu. edu

Umesh Sharma has been working as a Senior Lecturer in the area of Special Education and Psychology at Monash University, Australia. His research focuses on teacher training for inclusive education, attitude measurement, and positive behaviour support. Email: Umesh.Sharma@Education. monash.edu.au

Kuen-fung Sin is the Director of the Centre for Special Needs and Studies in Inclusive Education at the Hong Kong Institute of Education. He has ample consultancy experience in many local research projects as well as providing professional training for teachers of children with disabilities in Mainland China and Macau. He is currently leading a project which aims to advance inclusion by organizing a wide range of professional development programs at different levels for Hong Kong teachers. The members of his team include Mei-lan Au, Fuk-chuen Ho, Kok-wai Tsang, Chung-yee Poon, Kin-hung Loo, Chi-leung Lai, Kai-wai Ng, and Ka-wai Leung.Email: kfsin@ied.edu.hk

Suwaree Sivabhaedya is Associate Professor in Educational Psychology and Assistant of the Dean for Academic in Faculty of Education, Khon Kaen University, Thailand. She specialized in the area of special education and behavior modification. She was trained in special education at Wollongong University, Australia in 2008. Email: suwrer@kku.ac.th

Roger Slee holds the Chair of Inclusive Education at the London Institute of Education. He is the Founding Editor of the *International Journal of Inclusive Education*. He has formerly held research chairs in Teaching and Learning, and Education Studies at the University of Western Australia. He was the Deputy Director General of the Education Ministry in Queensland where his major responsibilities were curriculum, strategic policy and workforce learning. His major research and teaching interests are the political economy of special education and inclusive education; disability studies; social theory and teacher education. Email: r.slee@ioe. ac.uk

Huan Song is Assistant Professor in teacher education at the Center for Teacher Education Research (Key Research Institute of Humanities and Social Science in Universities of MOE), Faculty of Education, Beijing Normal University. His teaching and research focus mainly on teacher professional development, teacher professional learning communities, action research, and teacher education. Email: reedyboy520@gmail.com

Kok-wai Tsang was a teacher in a special school and specializes in educating students with intellectual disabilities and Autistic Spectrum Disorder. She is now a Teaching Fellow in the Hong Kong Institute of Education, mainly engaged in teacher professional development in special and inclusive education. Email: tsangkw@ied.edu.hk

Federico R. Waitoller is a Doctoral Student at Arizona and the International Programs Team Leader at the Equity Alliance at Arizona State University, USA. He has published his work in the *Journal of Special Education* and in edited volumes and has presented it at national and international conferences and research forums. His scholarship focuses on educational equity in special and inclusive education. Email: Federico.Waitoller@asu.edu

Mian Wang is Associate Professor in the Special Education, Disabilities, and Risk Studies program at the Gevirtz Graduate School of Education, University of California, Santa Barbara. His research mainly focuses on child and family outcomes of early childhood education and services, family–professional partnership, positive behavior support in cultural context, teacher education, and special education policy. Email: mwang@education.ucsb.edu

Elizabeth A. West is Assistant Professor in the Area of Special Education, University of Washington, USA. Her primary mission and vision is to improve outcomes for learners with severe disabilities. She engages in several lines of research under the categories of teacher training, instructional procedures, and diversity. Her focus is on transforming communities to increase access for students with severe disabilities. Email: eawest@u.washington.edu

Editorial Board

All chapters in the text have been peer reviewed by two academics or practitioners in the field of special and inclusive education. The reviewers formed the editorial board for this text.

Foreword

Throughout the world, inclusive education is increasingly seen as a strategy for achieving 'Education for All' (EFA) in both rich and poor countries. EFA is the United Nations initiative calling for the provision of basic education for all, which resulted from the World Conference on Education for All attended by 150 governments in Jomtien, Thailand in 1990. Basic education is considered that which is essential for an individual to participate in society (UNESCO, 2007). Although it is often defined by that which is compulsory within a country, it is not restricted to age. Nor should it be confused, as it often is, with universal access to primary education, one of the six United Nations Millennium Development Goals aimed at eradicating poverty. Basic education may consist of primary education but it also goes beyond it by requiring access to a minimum standard of, for example, literacy and numeracy for everyone. This is important because not everyone receives a basic education even if they have been to primary school. Many millions of children and young people in both rich and poor countries do not have the opportunity to attend any school, and there are many more millions of adults worldwide who are illiterate. Among these groups, people with disabilities and others who are socially disenfranchised within a society are particularly vulnerable.

While EFA is widely associated with universal access to education and international concern about the millions of children not in school, equity within schooling is equally important. This is because even in countries with well-developed compulsory education systems, some children are excluded from school, and even when all children are included, some will not have positive experiences of education, or much to show for their time in school. Thus, EFA is also about equity in education. It is about the creation of forms of provision in which all learners are enabled to participate in a full range of educational experiences. This increasing awareness of the dual meaning of EFA as access to, and equity in education, is further underpinned by the conviction that equitable education systems improve social cohesion and create inclusive societies. A good quality basic education remains the key international policy under which it is believed that disparities between what people have and are able to do, can be reduced in the service of improved social cohesion and equality of opportunity.

The 48th International Conference on Education, *Inclusive Education: The Way of the Future* (UNESCO, 2008), called upon the international community 'to adopt an inclusive education approach in the design, implementation, monitoring and assessment of educational policies as a way to further accelerate the attainment of EFA goals as well as to contribute to building more inclusive societies' (p. 3). Here there is an acknowledgement that education is of universal importance because of the role that it is thought to play in both achieving a good quality of life for individuals, and in achieving economic, human and social development goals for countries. The right to education (access) as well as opportunities in education (equity) are seen as both a human right and as an important means to achieving other human rights, such as development rights. Here again, the ideas of EFA and inclusive education as great levellers of opportunity are widely accepted; but little attention has been paid to the implications of these ideas for initial teacher training and further professional learning of teachers.

Yet teachers are arguably the essential ingredients in a quality education because schools cannot do without them. Other than to note the important disparities in teacher qualifications, supply and deployment, however, the broader issues of the quality and content of teacher preparation and development are not well articulated as part of the EFA agenda. Issues pertaining to how well teachers are prepared, and the role they can play in reducing inequalities, by virtue of the way in which they undertake their work, have remained largely unexplored. It is, therefore, fitting that this timely book focuses on the concept of inclusive education in teacher education.

Inclusive education is based on the principle that local schools should provide for all children, regardless of any perceived difference, disability, or other social, emotional, cultural or linguistic difference. Historically this has been achieved by different forms of provision for different types of learners, based on the idea that some learners need something different from or additional to that which is provided to others of similar age, as many country definitions of special needs education make clear. Subsequent standards of teacher qualification and teacher education have followed this pattern by establishing standards for the preparation of teachers by categorical types of learners such as primary, secondary, bilingual and special education etc. Such qualifications, in turn, reinforce the idea of different types of teachers for different groups of learners: for example, primary or secondary, general or special education teachers. The problem is that separate teacher education programs have been identified as a barrier to inclusion, suggesting problems of equity in educational opportunity may be structurally linked to teacher education and teacher professional learning.

The challenge of inclusive education for teachers' professional learning is to develop programs of teacher education that respect and respond to human differences in ways that include rather than exclude learners in what is ordinarily available in mainstream schools and classrooms. Extending what is ordinarily available as opposed to doing something additional to or different from is a complex endeavour that requires sensitivity to differences between learners without perpetuating the stigmatising effects of marking some students as different. At a fundamental level this means shifting our gaze from most and some learners to all learners. Teachers who are able to do this have changed the way they think about the concept of inclusive education. Rather than defend the need to accommodate learner differences, they focus on extending what is not otherwise available. Their work is informed by the knowledge that it is possible to support the learning of all students. They know effective decisions about how to teach are as likely to be informed by what is being taught as much as by who is being taught.

Global disparities in educational provision and the differences in teacher qualifications and teacher education that exist within and between countries and different regions of the world clearly have particular implications in different contexts. The problem of teacher shortage in some parts of the world, particularly in parts of South Asia and sub-Saharan Africa where it is estimated that millions of new teachers are needed to meet basic EFA requirements, put different pressures on national systems of teacher education than those of countries where teaching is a high-status occupation with good salaries that match the university-level professional credentials that are required. For example, a model of teacher education that works well in Finland is not what is needed in Kenya. Yet, in the global society there are also unprecedented opportunities for teacher educators to engage with the dual meanings of EFA and inclusive education and to consider common themes. A Green Paper on *Teacher Education in Europe* (Buchberger *et al.*, 2000) found many common patterns and trends across universities in different countries that prepare teachers. Even in countries that do not require that teachers be prepared at university level, there are common trends and patterns in training. For example, the preparation of primary teachers is often more focused on practical training and less influenced by an academic tradition than that required for teachers who work at secondary levels. While the form and structure of teacher education varies both within and between countries, there are many common issues and challenges of providing a good quality basic education for everyone. One of the greatest challenges for teacher education is posed by the demands of inclusive education.

This book grew out of a set of invited papers that were initially presented in November 2008 at an international colloquium on teacher education for inclusive education hosted in Hong Kong by the Division of Special Education within the Department of Educational Psychology, Counselling and Learning

Needs at the Hong Kong Institute of Education. The colloquium focused on innovative approaches for preparing teachers to work in inclusive classrooms and schools and included papers on both programs of initial teacher education and life-long teacher professional learning. The book argues for a paradigm shift in both forms of training and calls upon teacher educators to ensure that theory and research on inclusive education is more clearly linked to the practice of teachers. While this is easier said than done, the book takes an important step forward in exploring how teacher education can and is being reformed in support of the EFA agenda and in what this means for preparing teachers for inclusive education.

Lani Florian
University of Aberdeen, Scotland

References

Buchberger, F., Campos, B. P., Kallos, D. and Stephenson, J. (2000) *Green Paper on Teacher Education in Europe: High quality teacher education for high quality education and training*, Umeå, Sweden: Thematic Network on Teacher Education in Europe.

UNESCO (2007) *Operational Definition of Basic Education: Thematic Framework*. Online. Available at: http://www.unesco.org/education/framework.pdf (accessed 30 July 2009).

UNESCO (2008) *Inclusive Education: The Way of the Future*, Geneva, 25–8 November. Online. Available at: http://www.ibe.unesco.org/en/ice/48th-session-2008/conclusions-and-recommendations.html (accessed 26 December 2008).

Preface

While the movement towards establishing more inclusive schools has been along a fairly distinctive trajectory, teacher education for inclusion has not always been as clear-cut. To ensure that teachers are appropriately prepared for working in diverse classrooms there needs to be a paradigm change in the focus of their training. Both initial teacher education (ITE) and ongoing professional learning (PL) must become more innovative and ensure that theory and research are better linked to actual practice. This book addresses this need in profound ways. The book has three distinct parts. The first part focuses on the broad issues associated with teacher education for inclusion and considers four inclusion contexts of curriculum, politics, cultural diversity, and training. The second part discusses a range of innovative practices during ITE for preparing new graduates to become productive inclusive teachers. The final part reviews a collection of innovative PL activities that support a teacher's life-long learning needs.

The first part commences with a discussion about why and how ITE should be reformed in order to better prepare teachers for inclusion. A "whole-faculty approach" is posited by Chris Forlin to facilitate the way in which an inclusive curriculum can be embedded across all discipline areas. Roger Slee then provides a critical review of the complex political economy of inclusive education and how exclusion continues to rampage though the schooling system. He subsequently invites those engaged in ITE to consider the nature and form of the environment in which they work and what kinds of knowledge, skills, and dispositions should be taught to prepare teachers for inclusion.

The issues of cultural difference are addressed by Richard Rose and Philip Garner as they explore how their university has adopted an international perspective for postgraduate courses in education. This confirms the importance of learning about inclusion from both a theoretical and practical stance which allows opportunities for in depth analysis of teachers' diverse cultural contexts. The final chapter in this first part by Chris Forlin and Dinh Thi Nguyet explores how a country with limited experience in inclusion set out to train teacher educators so that they can provide appropriate ITE in inclusive education to all new graduates.

Each chapter in the second part of the book is unique in its attempt to address a different aspect of preparing teachers for inclusion. Together these programs provide a large and eclectic collection of tried and tested innovative approaches that can be employed by teacher educators during ITE programs. All innovations have been implemented and trialled by the authors who provide realistic evaluations of their successes and the challenges they face in supporting the preparation of teachers for inclusion. Many of the authors have endeavored to personalize their writing by discussing their own experiences. This brings an incredible depth of realism to the proposed learning experiences.

Martyn Rouse commences Part II by reviewing the task for ITE and what it means to provide inclusive education. He suggests that in order to prepare teachers, inclusion must be conceptualized in such a way that all teachers see it as their responsibility. Thus ITE must equip them in all aspects of knowing, doing, and believing; by focusing on learning opportunities that reflect a sociocultural perspective. Tim Loreman similarly focuses on the need to ensure new graduates have the appropriate attitudes, skills, and knowledge to become inclusive teachers. He proffers the use of a content-infused model that aligns inclusion within all disciplines, demonstrating that this should be part of the everyday life of a teacher. While acknowledging that skill development is important, Federico Waitoller and Elizabeth Kozleski suggest that this alone is not sufficient to prepare teachers for diversity. They discuss an initiative that involves the partnering of university and schools. This enables pre-service teachers to address the key questions of identity, culture, learning, and assessment through school-based experiences that are moderated and mediated by both faculty and school staff.

It is interesting to note that a number of these innovations had their origin in the medical profession. The use of collaborative decision making, real case studies, and reflective practices were all born from medical practices and have subsequently been adopted by education. Developing a sense of empathy and a better understanding of the special educational needs of learners is one aspect of ITE that has not always been highlighted. The next four chapters all consider practical and authentic approaches for embedding these ideals within initial programs. A triad of inclusive experiences is presented firstly by Dianne Chambers and Chris Forlin as a model for providing sufficient and varied opportunities for pre-service teachers to engage with people with diverse learning needs, and to explore and develop positive personal beliefs and attitudes about inclusion. A program for fostering empathy and understanding towards parents of learners with a disability is provided next by Kate Scorgie. This innovative program involves using genuine case studies whereby pre-service teachers are invited to enter empathetically with a parent of a child with a disability using a participative pedagogical approach. Each participant becomes the parent of a virtual child and over their course of study is involved in the child's development from before birth to adolescence. Garry Hornby further explores how pre-service teachers can be prepared to work collaboratively with parents. He proposes a theoretical model for enhancing empathy and outlines the attitudes, knowledge, and skills needed by teachers during their training to achieve this. Based on the premise that positive beliefs and attitudes of teachers are critical to the success of inclusive education, Umesh Sharma proposes the use of reflective practice during ITE. He argues that using reflective practice allows teachers to become more open-minded, responsible, and committed to an inclusive philosophy. He suggests a number of components that could be employed by teacher educators.

The need for teachers to work more collaboratively has become a major feature for the 21st century. As teachers increasingly need to be able to work productively with other staff in inclusive classrooms, Mian Wang and Paul Fitch discuss a distinctive five-year ITE program that focuses on collaboration and co-teaching. The creation of collaborative learning communities is similarly the focus of the development of an e-learning program shared by Paul Bartolo. The model he describes is particularly useful as it was developed and employed across seven different countries, with all materials being produced in seven different languages; thus the intercultural context was visible and inclusive, providing opportunities for dynamic interactions.

The final chapter in this part provides an excellent conclusion by offering a flexible framework for evaluating ITE programs. Spencer Salend has considered seven critical aspects of inclusive ITE and provided a comprehensive evaluative outline that includes sample questions and potential data sources to examine and improve the effectiveness of such programs.

Part III has its focus on groundbreaking practices for the PL of practising teachers. Many of these report on models for supporting system-wide PL of teachers and provide approaches that link this to formalizing it though postgraduate studies.

Organizing PL to meet the diverse needs of teachers undertaking further study can be quite challenging. Doing so in an online environment while endeavoring to apply in practice the theory being espoused, poses even greater challenges. The first three chapters in this part discuss the use of online PL programs to upskill teachers for inclusion. Adrian Ashman commences this part with an open and honest discussion about how he attempted (and succeeded!) in employing key elements in his own teaching that guide and promote inclusive practice in schools. The online course discussed by Phyllis Jones is designed to engage teachers in learning about including students with intellectual and developmental disabilities. She employs a Blackboard environment to provide substantive content and utilizes *Elluminate* to allow virtual meeting and dialogues between teachers and their faculty.

Ismael García Cedillo and Todd Fletcher also discuss a national project that was developed in Mexico from an analysis of teacher needs and offered as a modular approach using online learning. Their model trained many teachers over an extended period of time. Using online technology demands considerable commitment and these authors all provide words of wisdom to those who wish to engage in this type of PL.

State-wide PL is similarly a challenge for education systems especially when large numbers of teachers are involved. The next four chapters discuss how universities can link with schools and other stakeholders to achieve this. Bob Conway commences by presenting two PL models that he has developed and implemented that focus on the needs of individuals and schools as they aim to support students with challenging behavior. Joanne Deppeler then outlines an alternative way for engaging teachers in postgraduate study by involving them in a project aligned with values of social justice and the goal of improving outcomes for students. Her LINC project responds to inclusive education reform by employing a collaborative inquiry approach to support teachers to understand, articulate, and change their practices. A similar philosophy was adopted by Elizabeth O'Gorman in the intensive year-long project she discusses. The process involved a full-time four-ply model that interwove the strengths of a collaborative approach between teachers, the school community, tertiary institutions, and the local department of education to promote inclusive education.

Another form of collaboration is that of involving students with SEN in decision-making. Leena Kaikkonen explores how students with SEN were involved in decisions regarding their first opportunity to participate in a vocational education course. This experience not only enabled their inclusion, but also the PL of teachers was enhanced as their attitudes become more positive and their pedagogical skills were improved.

In the move towards inclusion, teachers find they are invariably working with students who are culturally and linguistically diverse. Thus, PL must instill not only an increased understanding of multiculturalism, but also respect for cultural diversity. The last four chapters consider approaches that adopt culturally responsive practices to diversity. The initial chapter by Elizabeth West explores how by listening to the voice of teachers PL courses can be developed to support them in becoming culturally responsive in inclusive environments. Three country examples then discuss how different educators have aimed to do this. Huan Song provides an example of how inclusion in China is facilitated though the "Learning in Regular Classrooms" approach and how this aims to address the cultural difficulties they face in catering for diversity. Pennee Kantavong and Suwaree Sivabhaedya similarly review cultural challenges in Thailand when implementing PL for teachers, administrators, and parents to support the development of inclusion. Kuen-Fung Sin and his team finally consider the programs they have initiated for government teachers in Hong Kong.

While educators have espoused the need to better prepare teachers for inclusion there has been a general tardiness about providing good examples of such practice. This book admirably fills this void. Within its pages there is to be found a wealth of practical and realistic approaches that can be adopted, customized and further developed to meet the diverse sociocultural needs found across different tertiary and education systems. These ideas are all firmly grounded in theory, yet provide well-researched practical approaches for educators to embrace.

As the editor of this collection of chapters, I am both humbled by the incredible work that is being done by these educators in their support for inclusion and exhilarated by the possibilities that are laid before me. I hope that this eclectic array of programs for preparing teachers for inclusive practices will similarly impress and excite you and leave you eager to embrace some of these ideas. The authors invite your reflections, thoughts and further suggestions and encourage you to dialogue with them in changing training paradigms to better prepare teachers for embracing inclusive education.

Chris Forlin

Part I

Social and political challenges in teacher education for inclusion

Chapter 1

Reframing teacher education for inclusion

Chris Forlin

Learning outcomes

- Understand the inclusion movement and the need for appropriate teacher education.
- Knowledge about training programs for preparing teachers for inclusion.
- Information about how initial teacher education (ITE) can be reframed to address the changed training needs of teachers for inclusion.

Introduction

This chapter will focus on the major changes in teacher education that have occurred regarding preparing teachers for inclusion. It will consider how programs at universities, teacher training institutions and colleges can be reframed to prepare teachers to provide appropriate education provision for students with disabilities and other diverse learning needs as education transitions towards a more inclusive approach to schooling. The degree to which teacher education has kept pace with societal changes and community expectations in the new knowledge-based paradigm will be considered and insights will be provided into what might be required to ensure a better match between teacher education and the needs of students in today's world.

Teacher education

Teacher education has been in the frame for considerably longer than the last century; yet how much has this frame changed during this time? Societal and political changes have been vast and far reaching, as have advancements in technology, science, medicine and the humanities. Major changes have occurred in the movement towards more democratic and equitable educational opportunities and in the clientele group for mainstream schools; but what has changed in teacher education? While there is enormous diversity across the world in the needs of students and in the way they respond to their teachers and there is a general acceptance that these needs have become more intense, demanding, and more difficult to respond to placing considerable demands on teachers; there has been relatively little by way of radical changes to teacher preparation and professional development to facilitate this.

In many western countries, student expectations have made teaching very challenging, resulting in a teaching profession that is disillusioned and despondent with students becoming disenfranchized with schooling, either dropping out or making life extremely unpleasant for their teachers (Rose and Jones, 2007). In less-developed countries, many learners are receiving free education for the first time, resulting in the need to provide education for large numbers; frequently without a strongly developed infrastructure and with teachers who are poorly trained and ill equipped to deal with their diverse needs (Du Toit and Forlin, 2009).

Coupled with these changes has been a far-reaching paradigm shift in the education of students with disabilities and other special needs (Ainscow, 2003). In recent years enormous transitions in thinking, expectations and opportunities have occurred. Traditionally, students with specialized needs were educated in segregated facilities, often categorically aligned so that they could be educated with their own kind. Over the past 40 years there has been an evolution from segregated to inclusive placements, which has resulted in complex and often difficult changes in the way schools operate and in the expectations for teachers (Forlin, 2006). Inclusive education, while initially focusing on providing for students with disabilities in mainstream schools, now encompasses a much broader definition that refers to all children who may have been historically marginalized from meaningful education, who come from varied multicultural and multi-diverse backgrounds, or who are at risk of not achieving to their potential.

Even though teacher education has also exhibited changes, have these really kept up with the pace of change that is occurring and in particular in preparing teachers for the diversity of student populations to be found in mainstream schools? In preparing teachers for inclusion there are many tensions that need to be surmounted as institutions grapple with how they can allocate sufficient time to all aspects of teacher education and as they decide to which areas they will place most resources (Chong et al., 2007). One of the major time barriers would seem to be the expectation that in order to learn about inclusion this must occur in a segregated course, rather than being embedded within the regular curriculum. Not only does this involve extra time but it continues the myth that inclusion is different from regular education and that it can only be taught by specialists. How can teacher education be reframed to overcome these challenges?

The transition to inclusion

The inappropriateness of special classes for students with mild mental retardation and the efficacy of self-contained classrooms were first challenged by Dunn in 1968. Dunn proposed that the resource teacher whose role was to withdraw children with special needs for separate work should be retrained to support general educators. He proffered that their new role would be to "... develop instructional materials and lessons for implementing the prescription found to be effective for the child and to consult and work with the other educators who serve the child" (Dunn, 1968, p. 14). Dunn also noted that many of the children found in special education were from low-status backgrounds including over-representation of ethnic minorities and poor families. A clear transition in role was posited with the special education teacher functioning as part of and support for general education rather than perpetrating a segregated form of education.

Dunn's proposal was followed rapidly by another influence. In 1970 Deno was one of the first to raise the question as to whether special education needed to exist at all as a separate administrative system. His work saw the emphasis on a medical model of disability begin to shift towards a social model when he proposed that:

> The viewpoint must switch from the present fix on pathology, which points the accusing finger of cause at the child, to approaches which emphasize the fact that the problem is not in the child but in the mismatch which exists between the child's needs and the opportunities we make available to nurture his self-realization.
>
> (Deno, 1970, p. 229)

Both of these writers (Deno, 1970; Dunn, 1968) together with the civil rights movements out of the USA and the start of the normalization movement from the Scandinavian countries had an enormous impact on the development of the inclusive movement. There would seem little doubt now that inclusive education has become the catch-phrase of the 21st century. The philosophy of educating all students regardless of SEN within the mainstream environment is now firmly established as the education of choice for many jurisdictions (Winter, 2006). With such a change in philosophy regarding the education of students it follows that a traditional homogeneous approach to teaching is no longer viable. As classrooms become more heterogeneous teachers require different skills and pedagogies if they are to ensure that all students are able to access the curriculum.

Teachers' perceptions about inclusion

It would seem generally accepted that for inclusion to be effectively implemented, policy promoting inclusive schooling must be supported by teachers who have the knowledge, skills and competencies (Winter, 2006) and an appropriate positive attitude (Avramidis and Norwich, 2002) to sustain this paradigm shift. With the majority of students who were historically excluded from mainstream schooling now being able to access their local schools in most western jurisdictions and increasingly across the Asia-Pacific region and throughout developing countries, teachers are indisputably key players in enabling this, therefore their feelings, attitudes and apprehensions about inclusion must be appropriately addressed.

In 1996, a large meta-analysis of 28 studies investigating teachers' perceptions of inclusion by Scruggs and Mastropieri (1996), reported that while 65 per cent of the more than 10,000 teachers they surveyed supported the concept of inclusion only approximately 30 per cent believed they had appropriate training or skills or sufficient resources to enable them to implement it. According to a later extensive review of literature on inclusion undertaken by Avramidis and Norwich (2002), resistance to inclusion is noticeably less when teachers have obtained special education qualifications. Yet while most teacher education has changed in recent years to incorporate some content knowledge about diversity and inclusion, newly qualified teachers in many jurisdictions still suggest that they are unprepared for working in inclusive schools (Winter, 2006) and many teachers enter the profession with little understanding of inclusion (Booth *et al.*, 2003).

Teacher attitudes

The attitude of teachers towards including students with disabilities in their mainstream classes is steadfastly established in the literature as a key element in furthering inclusive practices (Sharma *et al.*, 2008). The training of teachers in preparation for inclusion is, for that reason, recognized as a critical factor in addressing attitudes and in promoting a greater commitment to inclusion. Indeed, many have argued that initial teacher preparation is the decisive factor in developing efficacious teachers who are confident in their own ability to teach all students; willing participants in the inclusive movement; and prepared to be engaged in education reform towards inclusion (Forlin, 2008).

Opportunities to engage with people with disabilities and their advocates during initial teacher training has provided an avenue for addressing negative attitudes towards people with disabilities and for encouraging a more positive position towards inclusion. Providing innovative programs that encourage and support pre-service teachers working with students with disabilities and providing opportunities for them to engage with self-advocates within the community are approaches that have been adopted successfully (Forlin, 2003). Similarly, increasing social contact with children with special needs during training has resulted in a positive influence on attitudes towards inclusion and a greater willingness to become involved with inclusion (Sharma *et al.*, 2008). While developing more positive attitudes towards inclusion though, this also has the potential to heighten pre-service teachers' concerns (Chong *et al.*, 2007).

Teacher preparation programs for inclusive education

Teacher preparation for inclusive education is usually offered either as part of initial training or as ongoing professional learning for teachers. In most jurisdictions initial training consists of either a three- or four-year undergraduate degree; a four- or five-year double degree; or a one- or two-year postgraduate degree in education. In some instances, for example in England, it may alternatively be provided within a school in collaboration with a registered training institution, as participants take an active role within a school (Booth *et al.*, 2003). Traditional teacher preparation programs entail both course work and teaching practice, whereas alternative teaching courses typically target post-degree students who seek a faster pathway into teaching; which may offer only limited on-site practice (Boe *et al.*, 2007). There are of course still some countries where teachers receive no formal training.

This difference in preparing teachers will impact significantly on the amount of time that can be dedicated to strategies for supporting students with diverse learning needs (Winter, 2006). A review of provision for special education in initial training courses in Ireland identified three models that would seem to reflect other systemic approaches; a single unit of study delivered by specialists; infused study across all curricula areas; and a combination of both. When teachers are asked about their most preferred methods for preparing them for inclusion they suggest that direct teaching experiences with children with special needs, in-service training and attending university courses are mainly favoured (Avramidis and Norwich, 2002). It is nevertheless acknowledged that while teachers may receive some formal training in preparing them for inclusion, "[m]ost teacher education is informal and unplanned, as teachers learn through experience with and from colleagues, students and others, in settings that may be both literally and metaphorically far removed from lecture rooms or classrooms" (Booth *et al.*, 2003, p. 3). This strongly supports the argument that there must be a greater link between teacher training institutions and schools themselves and greater cross-pollination between special education and other disciplines during initial training in order to better prepare teachers for the reality of the inclusive classroom.

Reframing teacher education

Booth argued in 2003 that organizations that train teachers need to reflect upon their own views and begin a "... more structured representation of what inclusion might mean for the development of a complex institution of higher education" (p. 55). At that time he considered the barriers to inclusion within teacher education institutions to be formidable and in conflict with the accountability culture and managerialism. He further proposed that this "... requires that we replace a discourse fuelled by power with rational argument and explicit discussion of values, so that the development of the institution can be based on principled action" (Booth, 2003, p. 56). There is little evidence to suggest that six years later much has changed for most institutions where disciplines continue to exist in isolation and where special education is still an additional unit of study (if available), taught in segregated classes by so-called specialists.

In order to ensure that inclusion becomes an acceptable philosophy for teacher preparation institutions, teacher education needs to be reframed. This can be done by offering a parallel to the Whole School Approach (WSA) that leads the inclusive movement in schools, by developing a Whole Faculty Approach (WFA) that mirrors, in teacher education institutions, the inter-curricular collaborations to be found within effective inclusive schools. While faculties continue to be organized into departments, divisions and narrowly defined discipline areas, and special education is taught as a separate curriculum, there is no common understanding of what constitutes an inclusive curriculum or what the aims should be in furthering this. In 1995, Hargreaves referred to this as "balkanizing". Today, the relentless fragmenting of training into disciplines perpetuates this balkanized focus on narrow and discrete curricula which continues to endorse and promote autonomy that does not allow for the development of a common inclusive agenda.

Employing a WFA would encourage a deeper questioning of normative assumptions in relation to the purpose of education in each curriculum area. It would also allow the new demands for knowledge to be articulated within a wider debate about societal and political commitments to education in order to provide more equitable educational opportunities for traditionally disadvantaged groups. The new knowledge required by teachers in the 21st century to enable them to foster inclusive schools must be grounded by a stronger understanding of the need to provide multiple outcomes from education that respond to the diverse range of intelligences to be found within the new school structures. To be successful this approach must be adopted by all discipline areas and not left to traditional special education courses to implement.

To expect to prepare teachers for inclusive practices while training institutions persist in offering a segregated curriculum-based course that sees inclusion or special education as being outside of the core syllabus is fraught with erroneous arguments and likely to maintain the exclusion of disadvantaged groups. If courses on inclusion continue to be presented in isolation then how can teachers be equipped for developing an inclusive curriculum which by its very nature is multi-diverse? While acknowledging that withdrawing all specialized units of study in special and inclusive education has the potential to lose sight of the need for some focused learning, inclusion cannot be taught in isolation and such programs must be supported by corresponding work within and across all curriculum areas. This clearly requires a WFA if it is to be successful.

While teacher preparation courses must have an appropriate curriculum it is also critical to ensure that they utilize appropriate pedagogy that wherever possible reflects the type of pedagogies to be employed in an inclusive school (Forlin, 2008). Based on an analysis of a very large data set of teachers with one to five years teaching experience ($N = 10,952$), Boe et al. (2007) set out to investigate to what extent preparation in pedagogy and practice teaching as compared with only content knowledge contributed to a highly qualified teacher status. Their results unequivocally demonstrated that teachers with extensive preparation in pedagogy (e.g. selecting curricular materials, planning effective lessons, employing a range of instructional strategies and assessing students) and practice teaching (taken within a school environment) received significantly higher levels on their full certification than those with little or no preparation in these areas. Such practice regarding learning inclusive techniques cannot occur in isolated study but must be infused within and across all discipline areas.

In addition, how can an inclusive philosophy be promoted when many universities and colleges themselves adopt an exclusive attitude towards whom they will select to train to become a teacher? As suggested by Ware (2003):

> ... if we refuse to examine the workings of privilege, entitlement, elitism and exclusion embedded in teacher education programs then it is doubtful that teacher educators can meaningfully inform the curricula and pedagogies necessary to support inclusion ... as more inclusion proponents attempt the challenge of institutional reform in their own departments and programs the cluster of attributes that contribute to the locus of exclusion embedded in society will become more readily transparent and with any luck more swiftly extinguished.
>
> (Ware, 2003, p. 161)

Policies and documents that regulate or dictate teacher education appear to embrace the concept of inclusion; although deconstruction of such documents, while confirming that they generally provide positive attempts to ensure quality of training, usually results in rhetoric of practice that enables ethical but not genuine inclusive preparation (Booth *et al.*, 2003). The development of an inclusive pedagogy within teacher training organizations requires a dual policy focus. One aspect is to ensure that curricula taught within initial teacher education courses address the needs of teachers to prepare them to cater for multicultural and multi-diverse school populations. The other requires them to adopt an inclusive stance that encourages and enables equitable systems of teacher education by enrolling pre-service teachers from minority groups and by providing appropriate accommodations for them. According to Ballard (2003) the latter would require much more than local changes as "[t]o challenge cultural ideology that created poverty and sustains institutional racism requires ... political action" (p. 74).

Conclusion

To reframe teacher education and to ensure a better match between courses at universities and colleges and the reality of teaching in multicultural and multi-diverse schools in the 21st century requires extensive dialogue around inclusion employing a WFA. Teacher education needs to be more forward thinking and focus on preparing teachers for potential challenges, rather than providing rhetorical and homogeneous curricula that perpetuate the status quo of teacher training within narrowly focused specific disciplines.

Teacher preparation for inclusion requires a more open and collaborative approach by faculty engaging amongst themselves in dialogue about the new knowledge required by teachers and how an inclusive curriculum can be offered within each discipline that will address previous disadvantage and ensure more equitable opportunities for all students. Special education must become infused within all curriculum areas and diversity accepted as the norm for preparing teachers to work in classrooms of the future.

It also requires greater collaboration with schools to make sure that training courses are actually meeting the real needs of teachers in heterogeneous classrooms. Teaching in inclusive schools is complex and multilayered. It requires teachers to be able to address cultural issues (attitudes, values, beliefs) and systemic factors (time, resources, support). In addition to having sufficient discipline knowledge it requires them to make suitable accommodations, modify curricula to meet the multiple needs of diverse learners and utilize different pedagogies to enable effective learning outcomes for all students. These must all be addressed if teacher education is to be appropriately reframed to facilitate preparation that is inclusive, contemporary, innovative, realistic and manageable for teachers in today's schools while accommodating the diverse learning needs of all students.

References

Ainscow, M. (2003) "Using teacher development to foster inclusive classroom practices", in T. Booth, K. Nes and M. Stromstad (eds), *Developing Inclusive Teacher Education*, London: RoutledgeFalmer, pp. 15–32.

Avramidis, E. and Norwich, B. (2002) "Teachers' attitudes towards integration/ inclusion: A review of the literature", *European Journal of Special Needs Education*, 17(2): 129–47.

Ballard, K. (2003) "The analysis of context: Some thoughts on teacher education, culture, colonization and inequality", in T. Booth, K. Nes and M. Stromstad (eds), *Developing Inclusive Teacher Education*, London: RoutledgeFalmer, pp. 59–77.

Boe, E. E., Shin, S. and Cook, L. H. (2007) "Does teacher preparation matter for beginning teachers in either special or general education?", *Journal of Special Education*, 41(3): 158–70.

Booth, T. (2003) "Views from the institution: Overcoming barriers to inclusive teacher education?", in T. Booth, K. Nes and M. Stromstad, *Developing Inclusive Teacher Education*, London: RoutledgeFalmer, pp. 33–58.

Booth, T., Nes, K. and Stromstad, M. (2003) *Developing Inclusive Teacher Education*, London: RoutledgeFalmer.

Chong, S., Forlin, C. and Au, M. L. (2007) "The influence of an inclusive education course on attitude change of pre-service secondary teachers in Hong Kong", *Asia Pacific Journal of Teacher Education*, 35(2): 161–79.

Deno, E. (1970) "Special education as developmental capital", *Exceptional Children*, 37(3): 229–37.

Du Toit, P. and Forlin, C. (2009) "Cultural transformation for inclusion: What is needed? A South African perspective", *School Psychology International*, 30(6): 644–66.

Dunn, L. (1968) "Special education for the mildly retarded – is much of it justifiable?", *Exceptional Children*, 35(1): 5–22.

Forlin, C. (2003) "Pre-service teacher education: Involvement of students with intellectual disabilities", *International Journal of Learning*, 10: 317–26.

Forlin, C. (2006) "Inclusive education in Australia ten years after Salamanca", *European Journal of Psychology of Education*, 21(3): 265–77.

Forlin, C. (2008) "Education reform for inclusion in Asia: What about teacher education?", in C. Forlin and M.-G. J. Lian (eds), *Reform, Inclusion & Teacher Education: Towards a New Era of Special Education in the Asia-Pacific Region*, Abingdon: Routledge, pp. 74–82.

Hargreaves, A. (1995) "Realities of teaching", in L. W. Anderson (ed.), *International Encyclopedia of Teaching and Teacher Education*, 2nd edn, New York: Pergamon, pp. 80–7.

Rose, R. and Jones, K. (2007) "The efficacy of a volunteer mentoring scheme in supporting young people at risk", *Emotional and Behavioural Difficulties*, 12(1): 3–14.

Scruggs, T. E. and Mastropieri, M. A. (1996) "Teacher perceptions of mainstreaming/ inclusion, 1958–1995: A research synthesis", *Exceptional Children*, 63: 59–74.

Sharma, U., Forlin, C. and Loreman, T. (2008) "Impact of training on pre-service teachers' attitudes and concerns about inclusive education and sentiments about persons with disabilities", *Disability & Society*, 23(7): 773–85.

Ware, L. (2003) "Understanding disability in schools", in T. Booth, K. Nes and M. Stromstad, *Developing Inclusive Teacher Education*, London: RoutledgeFalmer, pp. 146–65.

Winter, E. C. (2006) "Preparing new teachers for inclusive schools and classrooms", *Support for Learning*, 21(2): 85–91.

Chapter 2

Political economy, inclusive education and teacher education

Roger Slee

Learning outcomes

- Appreciate the ubiquity and complexity of exclusion and disadvantage.
- Understand the way in which funding models for special education needs (SEN) or inclusive education reinforce deficit notions of students and frame approaches to teaching and learning in schools.
- An awareness of the practical value of contextualizing exclusion.
- Formulate an agenda that assists in thinking of teacher education beyond special and regular education.

Introduction

It may seem a stretch to offer a discussion of political economy in a book on inclusive schooling and teacher education. After all are not inclusive education and the professional education of a teacher workforce simply a technical matter of equipping people to work with and benefit from the differences that children bring with them to the classroom? Should not our concern be with ways of adding to and organizing resources to make schools more effective for students with SEN? Therefore, should not the purpose of the book be further development of skills to enhance the performance of teachers in classrooms?

My questions are of course tactical. This chapter contends that a number of assumptions precede this predictable set of questions that ought to be identified and interrogated. This line of interrogation will undoubtedly distress those looking for off-the-shelf solutions. The conundrums presented by the aspiration for an inclusive education are, in the first instance, political and cultural. Thereafter come the more contingent set of technical questions including: how do we prepare a professional workforce (teachers, education administrators, classroom assistants, school support workers) for the changed order of schooling?

Organized into three sections, this chapter forms an invitation for those engaged in initial and continuing teacher education, and indeed the professional learning of all those involved in the education sector, to consider the nature and form of the environment that they work in and subsequently what kinds of knowledge, skills and dispositions ought to be cultivated through teacher education.

The first section of this chapter will briefly consider the complex political economy of inclusive education. This is followed by some stipulations to impose order on the conceptual minefield of inclusive education. Here I will take my cues from the work of George Orwell (1984), Basil Bernstein (1996) and Alain Touraine (2000) to argue two propositions:

- The language of 'inclusive education' has been dulled and become deliberately vague through popular, overreaching application.
- Exclusion is ubiquitous and it is anti-democratic. Inclusion is an element of a democratic education or as Tony Knight (1985) suggested 'an apprenticeship in democracy'.

Preparing teachers for inclusive education is not achieved by grafting courses of special education onto the teacher education program. The concluding part of the chapter forms no real conclusion at all. Rather it suggests some principles and frameworks for our collective consideration as we apply civil sensibilities to rebuilding teacher education to a world we inhabit rather than one that has passed and is served by the language of special education, regular education and sadly inclusive education.

Market meltdowns, redistribution and resources of hope

Researching the political economy of inclusive education may refer to a number of different kinds of studies. Commonly they have a functionalist hue comprising examinations of the way in which additional resources are allocated to support the education of students with SEN. There have been a number of studies examining the fiscal arrangements across local education authorities (Dyson et al., 2002). Others contrast the funding models of different countries (Pijl et al., 1997). This research tends to describe the history and context of the system under scrutiny and the features of the fiscal arrangements and structures of decision-making. Rarely does such work extend to considerations of impacts on curriculum and pedagogy. Moreover, the legitimacy of SEN goes unchallenged. The focus narrows to identify different ways school systems strike balances between the scarcity of public education funds and the escalating growth in the diagnosis of additional student needs.

This research is useful as it points to the perverse side effects and limitations of government decision-making and fiscal technologies and provides important baseline data to guide system efficiency. Examples include the work of Bourke et al. (2000) in New Zealand who reviewed the structure of special education and inclusive education policy and practice to demonstrate that the attempt to ease resource demand by splitting funding between a general grant for all schools and a reserve fund for additional requests broke down in a number of ways. First was the assumption that schools would deploy targeted resources to inclusive education initiatives. Second was the fact that although the gatekeepers on the reserve fund demonstrated unassailable tenacity (Wills, 2006) the general effect was a growth in both community and school-based dissatisfaction.

Research in Queensland, Australia revealed similar distortions and conflict (Slee, 2005). The funding allocation system was called ascertainment. Driven by the hunt for the level of a child's defects, the model established a gravity that pulled the range and rate of diagnosis to unmanageable levels. Given that the allocation of funds did not accrue until a child was deemed to be at the higher level of diagnosis, the overwhelming majority of diagnoses required the production of more seriously disabled Queensland children. A lack of quality assurance resulted in local distortions: individual schools or a district having significantly higher levels of a particular impairment or disorder that defied natural distribution. In a perverse undermining of policy intent, the model of distribution produced an increasing level of teacher intolerance of difference, as the demand for ascertainment became part of the disciplinary armoury for dealing with children with inattentive and behaviour difficulties.

Graham and Slee (2008) have demonstrated the unremitting escalation of special needs referrals in the normative areas of behaviour and attention disorders in the state of New South Wales.

There are a number of important points to make about this pattern of funding. First is the fact that limiting the pathological gaze to individual children produces greater levels of diagnosis and more categories for describing SEN. Tomlinson (1982) demonstrated the steady expansion of categories for special education and suggested that since students' education opportunities and outcomes did not improve as a result of interventions, professional interest may be at play.

Second, sensitivities to defectiveness are heightened and teacher tolerance of difference diminishes. It is also worth considering whether this kind of funding model builds educational capacity. Given that each new 'disabled' child in school already receiving funds results in a further resource claim may suggest that there is not a general improvement in teacher professional knowledge and skills. Certainly a disposition that positively favours inclusion is jeopardized. The way that funds are utilized is central to questions of effect. Most often the resource equates with an additional teacher aide who is enlisted as a minder and de facto teacher. There is a growing body of literature that registers concern about this drift towards residual schooling and exclusion of students with teacher aides world-wide (Keeffe and Carrington, 2007).

This kind of research is useful as it exposes distortions and faults with funding mechanisms. More importantly it reflects a narrow conception of inclusion, exclusion and of teachers' professional roles. Educating teachers to become the transmitters of a culture of inclusion is a formidable request in a climate of exclusion.

Exclusive is pervasive

We look away as we pass the excluded on our sidewalks, many of them suffering their mental illness within what has been callously spun by governments as 'care in the community'. We are relieved that the CNN images of horror from conflicts in the Congo, Afghanistan or of the unremitting suffering from the AIDS pandemic across Africa, which Stephen Lewis (2005) correctly says 'shames us all', are but fleeting intrusions on a life of plenty. There are an estimated 79 million children who do not attend school on any day worldwide (UNESCO, 2007) for whom talk of inclusion has no meaning. This is the pervasive, if distanced global backdrop that ought to register in our thinking about the project of an inclusive education.

The relationship between class and schools and the persistence of unequal educational outcomes has been a constant feature of schooling. According to Australian researchers Teese and Polesel (2003, p. 7) 'The fact that more young people rely on school for jobs or further training does not mean that school is an equally effective path for all'.

Ball (2008) considers the impact of relentless policy reforms in education in England and Wales through the late twentieth and early twenty-first centuries. Class, he argues, remains a constant feature throughout periods of great policy, demographic and infrastructural changes in education. The neoconservative policy reform agenda from Thatcher through New Labour has not resulted in an equalization of 'educational outcomes in terms of labour market access or income', he asserts, '... by many indicators they are more unequal' (Ball, 2008, p. 1). Like Bernstein before him, Ball argues that if we want to intervene in 'the persistence of educational inequality' then the school in isolation from the complex matrix of social relations is not the sole source for effecting positive and enduring reforms. He returns to Bernstein, Bourdieu and to his extensive empirical work to demonstrate how privilege, advantage and disadvantage assert themselves through the mixed markets of schooling (Ball, 2007). 'In effect class and policy and class and educational practices are being realigned' (Ball, 2003, p. 170).

Accordingly, in the now 'ambiguous nature of class reproduction' (Ball, 2003, p. 178) his research examines a cohort of English middle-class parents, displaying a mix of confidence and fear, assert their capitals to secure a purchase on their children's futures in and through the education marketplace. The now pervasive ideology of 'good parenting' (Vincent, 2000) places strain on the family to bring additional resources to assist first in the selection of better schools and second in the purchase of education accoutrements such as tutors, technology, after-school programs, cramming schools (Ball, 2008). If necessary they may secure the diagnosis of syndromes and defects to attract additional support or leverage (Slee, 2008). 'Most families on low incomes or living in poverty are by definition excluded from these possibilities' (Ball, 2003, p. 177).

Schools are not passive agents in the education marketplace; there exists a perverse reciprocity, a juggling of positional disadvantage and advantage. They reflect and refract social inequalities. Not only is choice the prerogative of some parents, schools too attempt to exert choices. The instruments of testing, inspection and league tables interplay with the intervention of private entrepreneurial interest and divisions between types of schools (e.g. city academies, student referral units) to form a hierarchy of schools and students.

As schools attempt to improve their profile to attract a suitable clientele, students with poor education prognoses present a serious risk of failure at inspection (Slee *et al.*, 1998; Gillborn and Youdell, 2000). This is illustrated in an interview with Dave Gillborn and Deborah Youdell, who:

> ... discovered the extent of the reach of the standards agenda, and the way in which schools were focussing on the 'D' students and trying to convert them into Cs. They realized the significance of their 'D to C conversion' and its link with the process of 'educational triage' which was going on, a means of apportioning scarce resources to greatest areas of need: 'it was naming what lots of people were living' and it was clear to them that the strategies for triage being operated in schools were producing exclusion for those deemed 'hopeless cases' by concentrating on candidates who could be targeted for upward conversion.
>
> (Allan and Slee 2008, p. 38)

The 'third way' discourse that calls for the building of community, inclusion and social capital, the fiscal architecture of schools increasingly apes the marketplace (Ball, 2007). Behind the language of inclusion lurks an ethos of competitive individualism. In this context the redress of disadvantage, the building of communities and the inclusion of others becomes a threat. The now voluminous literature on inclusive education seldom hints at such issues that when all is said and done are the foundations for exclusion. Inclusive education is first a political issue about the structure of opportunity, inequality and exclusions in education. It is therefore a large reform agenda for the recognition of different student identities and the redistribution of resources to increase access, participation and success for all comers. Given that schools were never meant for all comers and are certainly not structured for the successful inclusion of diverse populations, the agenda is broad and the need for leadership great.

Hope? Inclusive education: reclaiming purpose

This has certainly been a period of political, social and economic upheaval. Lessons from the General Theory (Keynes, 1936) have been resurrected to demonstrate the possibility of redistribution. Not that redistribution has been absent from policy agendas. In Australia the public purse supports what is euphemistically called private education. Because of the structure of Federal and State responsibilities in education funding, state governments are not altogether perturbed by the 'drift' from public to private schools as it represents an easing of pressure on their budgets.

The history of special education is by no means a simple text about the struggle for rights to an education for a disenfranchised group. While it was a brave and welcome protest against the exclusion of children with disabilities from education and ultimately citizenship, it was also tainted by its links to eugenics. It would seem that inclusive education too, is not an uncomplicated call for rights of access and participation. A lack of stipulation about the aspirations of those who gather under its banner together with its popularization in government discourse has dragged or drugged it (for those operating in the behaviour and attention disorders field) towards conservative ends.

For the purpose of this essay I will seek my definitions through reference to Alain Touraine's (2000) provocation: Can we live together? He says that the measure of a society's spirit is found in its juridical and educational systems. Disability discrimination legislation shows that there is a generous spirit of juridical progress. It also suggests that this is compromised by caveats and exclusions. For example the Immigration Department is excused from the requirements of disability discrimination legislation in Australia. We also know that the Purvis case in New South Wales demonstrates that no matter how enlightened the legislation is, the struggle for a heroic complainant is heavy with anguish and costly. An education that is democratic, argues Touraine, is the vehicle for social improvement and for the valuing of difference and diversity. So too for Bernstein (1996) who established inclusion as a precondition for democratic education. Inclusion, he suggested, could never mean absorption.

Tony Knight (1985) sees inclusion as a means to an end, a part of 'an apprenticeship in democracy'. Here we return to our lessons from political economy. If as Parrish (2002) demonstrates in the USA and Gillborn (2008) parallels in the UK special education services have been deployed to channel children of colour into an alternative educational track that attenuates opportunity, our aspirations for inclusion, for democracy are shattered. The job of inclusive education is to identify and dismantle exclusion.

In this respect I am not arguing for the elimination of special education in preference to placement of those deemed disabled, disordered, difficult or defective in the regular school. Rather I am suggesting that both, special and regular, have lost historical specificity and utility. We are constantly regaled by education futurists whose quest is the placement of young people, creative new learned problem solvers in the global knowledge economy in jobs we cannot yet imagine. Schools tied to backward-looking national curriculums that dance to the choreography of high stakes tests to achieve reductive targets have found that in doing so there are groups of students who need to be jettisoned. This is not a source for hope. We ask: Inclusion into what? Just as normalization was rejected by many disabled people as a form of assimilation that invited them to deny difference, inclusive education is compromised by holding the extant regular school as the model for reform.

Educating an education workforce

Inclusive teacher education is not a special education for teachers in regular schools. It demands a critical thinking about identity and difference, about privilege and disadvantage, about inclusion and exclusion that is not achieved by either the 'regular' or 'special' teacher education programs. To be sure, children will have unique needs requiring interventions and assistance in order that they achieve at levels that were once thought impossible. This presupposes some specific knowledge that ought to be a part of a teacher's education. Those who have prized and guarded this knowledge within the church of SEN must open it to challenge and reconsideration as we determine the optimal conditions (place, pedagogy and curriculum) for all children to learn in.

Let me suggest four organizing themes for inclusive teacher education.

- Understanding and dismantling exclusion – the role of the cultural vigilante.
- Reclaiming curriculum and pedagogy for teachers.
- Teachers as communitarian workers.
- Thinking about archers as well as targets.

Understanding and dismantling exclusion – the role of the cultural vigilante

If teachers are to interrupt the constancy of exclusion they ought to be acquainted with its character and operation. In this respect becoming an inclusive educator requires that they not only acquire disciplinary knowledge, pedagogic skills and inclusive dispositions, but that they know how to identify the manifest and insidious ways in which exclusion is established through and in schooling. In this respect we are all complicit and need to be able to apply the humility to subject ourselves to the practice and not just the rhetoric of reflexiveness.

The program may well assist people to acquire knowledge about different kinds of syndromes and impairments. It ought to invite the interrogation of this knowledge as aspects of today's science will ultimately be the subject of tomorrow's mirth. There may also be studies in political economy, postcolonialism, disability studies, critical race theory and so the list extends. This is the project of becoming both learned and critical: a cultural vigilante.

Reclaiming curriculum and pedagogy for teachers

It may seem redundant, but at a time when teachers are increasingly estranged from decisions about curriculum, pedagogy and assessment (Stobart, 2008) teacher education needs to enter the debate about curriculum rather than training teachers to install it. The existing curriculum for an education in pedagogy and assessment is radically incomplete. Encouraging the neophyte as well as the experienced teacher to think about the differential impacts of pedagogic choices for diverse school populations is important. Having the new breed of teachers (for many of whom Starbucks is their preferred classroom) think about space, place and pedagogy is useful. Critical learning in the area of assessment is urgently required in the age of the high-stakes test and the international educational horse-race.

Teachers as communitarian workers

Schools that are inclusive are not well served by the classroom as fortress. How do we form a disposition of co-working to build community? Extended schools have more chance of addressing the multiple complex needs of the postmodern child and teacher. A connected teacher needs to think about the architecture of their craft and workplace. How do we encourage people to form alliances of parents and professionals? How do we form teachers guided by expertise rather than expertism? What place is there for notions of special in a community?

Thinking about archers as well as targets

Sadly the policy opticians have fitted target-driven lenses that occlude a clear view of the archer. Driven by outcome measures that are all too frequently reductive and no yardstick for creativity, learnedness or problem solving, we have lost sight of the needs, broader capacities and potential of the diverse range of students who inhabit our classrooms. Perhaps the education of the inclusive teacher provides opportunity to insert a less-restrictive vision?

Conclusion?

Such is the nature of educating for more inclusive communities – there cannot be one. Inclusive education is a strategy for dismantling barriers, for exposing exclusion and for educating educators who aspire to democratic schooling. This chapter advocates for teacher educators to dedicate courses in inclusive education to building the critical capacities of their students in order that they are equipped to identify, expose and dismantle barriers to education for all students.

References

Allan, J. and Slee, R. (2008) *Doing Inclusive Education Research*, Rotterdam: Sense Publishers.

Ball, S. J. (2003) *Class Strategies and the Education Market: The Middle Classes and Social Advantage*, London: RoutledgeFalmer.

Ball, S. J. (2007) *Education Plc: Understanding Private Sector Participation in Public Sector Education*, London: Routledge.

Ball, S. J. (2008) *The Education Debate*, Bristol: Policy Press.

Bernstein, B. B. (1996) *Pedagogy, Symbolic Control and Identity: Theory, Research, Critique*, London: Taylor & Francis.

Bourke, R., Bevan-Brown, J., Carroll-Lind, J., Cullen, J., Grant, S., Kearney, A., *et al.* (2000) *Special Education 2000. Monitoring and Evaluation of the Policy.* Report to the Ministry of Education. Palmerston North, New Zealand: Massey University.

Dyson, A., Milward, A. and Crowther, D. (2002) *Decision-Making and Provision within the Framework of the SEN Code of Practice*, DFES: Stationery Office.

Gillborn, D. (2008) *Racism and Education: Coincidence or Conspiracy?* Abingdon: Routledge.

Gillborn, D. and Youdell, D. (2000) *Rationing Education: Policy, Practice, Reform, and Equity*, Buckingham: Open University Press.

Graham, L. and Slee, R. (2008) "An illusory interiority: Interrogating the discourse/s of inclusion", *Educational Philosophy and Theory*, 40(2): 277–93.

Keeffe, M. and Carrington, S. (eds) (2007) *Schools & Diversity*, 2nd edn, Sydney, Australia: Pearson Education.

Keynes, J. M. (1936) *The General Theory of Employment, Interest & Money*, London: Macmillan.

Knight, T. (1985) "An apprenticeship in democracy", *The Australian Teacher*, 11(1): 5–7.

Lewis, S. (2005) *Race against time.* Toronto: House of Anansi Press.

Orwell, G. (1984) *Why I Write*, London: Penguin Books.

Parrish, T. (2002) "Racial disparities in the identification, funding and provision of special education", in D. Losen and G. Orfield (eds), *Racial Inequality in Special Education*, Cambridge, MA: Harvard Education Press.

Pijl, S. J., Meijer, C. J. W. and Hegarty, S. (1997) *Inclusive education: A global agenda*, London: Routledge.

Slee, R. (2005) "Education and the politics of recognition: Inclusive education – an Australian snapshot", in D. Mitchell (ed.), *Contextualizing Inclusive Education*. Abingdon: Routledge, pp. 139–65.

Slee, R. (2008) "Beyond special and regular schooling? An inclusive education reform agenda" *International Studies in Sociology of Education*, 18(2): 99–116.

Slee, R., Weiner, G. and Tomlinson, S. (1998) *School Effectiveness for Whom?: Challenges to the School Effectiveness and School Improvement Movements*, London: Falmer.

Stobart, G. (2008) *Testing Times. The uses and abuses of assessment*, Abingdon: Routledge.

Teese, R. and Polesel, J. (2003) *Undemocratic Schooling: Equity and Quality in Mass Secondary Education in Australia*, Carlton: Melbourne University Publishing.

Tomlinson, S. (1982) *A Sociology of Special Education*, London: Routledge & Kegan Paul.

Touraine, A. (2000) *Can We Live Together: Equality and Difference*, Cambridge: Polity Press.

UNESCO (2007) *Education for All-International Coordination*. Online. Available at: http://portal.unesco.org/education/en/ev.php-URL_ID=52210&URL_DO=DO_TOPIC&URL_SECTION=201.html (accessed 6 December 2008).

Vincent, C. (2000) *Including Parents? Education, Citizenship, and Parental Agency*, Buckingham: Open University Press.

Wills, R. (2006) "Special education 2000: A New Zealand experiment", *International Journal of Inclusive Education*, 10(2&3): 189–99.

Chapter 3

The professional learning of teachers through experience in an international and intercultural context

Richard Rose and Philip Garner

Learning outcomes

- Understand the challenges which face many schools in providing for learners of diverse needs.
- Appreciate how one university has responded to the needs of an international group of students in respect of understanding and interpreting inclusion.
- Understand the challenges of transferability of learning across countries and cultures.

Introduction

In recent years the numbers of international students entering UK universities has increased. Figures from the UK Higher Education International Unit indicate that in 2006 international students comprised 13 per cent of all higher education students studying in the UK. This figure puts the UK third behind New Zealand and Australia in terms of the proportion of international students attending universities and other higher education establishments. When isolating figures for those undertaking advanced research degrees the figure rises to 40 per cent. The number of new applicants for study in the UK from international students in 2007 was 68,500, an increase of 7.8 per cent on the previous year. During the same period applications from potential students living in European Union (EU) countries increased by 33 per cent (EU students are not regarded as international students in the UK under agreement with European directives). The UK Government statistics indicate that international students boost the economy of the country by almost £8.5 billion a year.

Many of these international students come to the UK in order to gain qualifications in the field of education, often bringing with them a wealth of expertise from teaching in their home countries. They enter an education system which in many instances will have significant differences from those in which they have both received their own schooling and worked as teachers. Yet they arrive in the UK anticipating that they will have opportunities to acquire new skills and knowledge which will benefit their professional development on return to their homes. This immediately raises questions about their expectations on entering courses outside of their home countries and with regards to the ability of host universities to afford them the learning opportunities which will enhance their professional skills and enable them to apply new learning when they return home. It raises further issues about the transferability of learning across countries and cultures. Not least it provokes questions about the interpretation and development of inclusive schooling, which has become an international focus of debate over the past 25 years. In this chapter, consideration is given to the ways in which international students have been encouraged to consider the development of inclusive schooling and an examination of whether this approach has relevance to practice in their home countries.

Education at a time of increased globalization

In western countries the composition of school populations has changed significantly throughout the latter half of the 20th century and into the 21st. Transnational migration has had a significant impact upon many schools and this is likely to continue for the foreseeable future (Adams and Kirova, 2006). Sharma (2000) suggests that the English education system has struggled to come to terms with meeting the needs of particular groups of learners, including those from different ethnic backgrounds. He believes that teachers, the majority of whom come from well-established white English communities, have a critical role to play in educating the majority towards a knowledge, understanding and acceptance of those who come from minority groups. His views echo those expressed by Bourdieu (1984) who described how failure in school can be masked by the suggestion that it is due to individual cognitive deficit or that it is characteristic of specific student groups. Teacher expectations of students who are perceived as 'different', whether as a result of special education needs (SEN) or because of cultural or linguistic factors are often, he suggests, lower than for those who are seen as representing the 'norm'. This belief is reinforced by studies of schools and attitudes towards students described as having SEN or disabilities. Yet within current debates about inclusive schooling there is a growing corpus of evidence which suggests that in England there are schools where teachers recognize the benefits of classroom diversity and the positive impact which this may have upon the achievement of learners (Black-Hawkins *et al.*, 2007; Farrell *et al.*, 2007).

Teachers and student teachers in today's schools need to embrace teaching approaches which not only acknowledge the changing population in schools but which also create learning environments which are inclusive and welcoming to students of diverse needs and abilities. Nussbaum (1997) has emphasized the responsibility which teachers have in shaping future citizens in an inescapably plural society. She recognizes that these responsibilities will only be met if those who manage the professional development of teachers adopt curricula and teaching approaches that encourage engagement with the issues which face people living within diverse and multicultural communities. She calls for an increased emphasis upon teaching in universities which challenges stereotypes and promotes greater understanding of diversity in order "to produce adults who can function as citizens not just as some local region or group but also, more importantly, as citizens of a complex interlocking world" (Nussbaum, 1997, p. 6).

The recognition of diversity is an essential element of achieving the more equitable society that Nussbaum advocates. Cheung and Hui (2007) have emphasized that philosophical ideas around inclusion have been debated for many years within western societies but have only more recently begun to attract similar levels of attention in Asia. They suggest that there is a necessity to acknowledge that children and teachers in many parts of Asia face socio-economic and political challenges such as poor access to basic medical care, malnutrition and inadequately trained education professionals which present a barrier to progress not common in the west.

There is clearly a danger here of imposing western cultural approaches upon an education system which is confronting major challenges and where teachers and education policy makers may perceive that these are an additional burden. A history of cultural imperialism, not least through the advocacy of western education models has been a cause of tension in the past. Said (1994) stresses the importance of acknowledging and indeed celebrating the experiences of individuals within their own countries when discussing the transfer of knowledge. He suggests that it is essential that we recognize notions of a broader human community in which certain principles transcend nationality or culture as being immutable and essential for the welfare of all individuals. Yet in so doing, Said sees the necessity to recognize and respect the individual interpretation and application of ideas according to the internal cultural needs of a country. A similar view is expressed by Sen (2006) who writes:

> The presence of cultural divides raises many interesting problems. The possibility of communication is only one of them. There is the more basic issue of the individuality of each culture, and questions about whether and how this individuality can be respected and valued even though the world grows steadily smaller and more uniform.
>
> (Sen, 2006, p. 122)

Both of these writers acknowledge the necessity to reform institutions in order to provide a society which is both equitable and just.

Being located in a multicultural country in which aspects of inclusion have been debated over many years, it might be argued that universities in the UK are well placed to support international students in learning about inclusive practice. We would, however, contend that this is only likely to be true where attention is given to ensuring that a balanced approach which links practice to theory is contextualized and related to the personal experiences of students.

When students from other countries enter English universities to study education it is right that they should engage fully in a debate which pervades much of the changes taking place in schools today. Inclusion continues to be high on the agenda of education reform and development in most societies and it is, therefore, appropriate that students should have an opportunity to participate fully in discussions and access to teaching that considers issues central to the promotion of inclusive practice. It is equally important that in providing international students with opportunities to study and to experience the development of inclusive schools tutors are committed to a dialogue which may better inform how they support such students and build upon their own experiences and expertise.

International students experiencing English schools

In common with most English universities, the University of Northampton welcomes a number of international students onto its postgraduate education courses each year. In recent years these students have come from a wide range of countries, including India, China, Tanzania, Israel, Brazil, Philippines, Cameroon and Gambia as well as European countries such as Cyprus and Greece. The students undertake studies for a higher degree in education, which comprises a number of compulsory modules such as research methodology, investigating personal professional practice and dissertation preparation. They also choose from a range of optional modules which include those with a focus on early years education, education policy development and special and inclusive education.

All students are required to undertake a small-scale research project to inform the writing of a dissertation completed at the end of their studies. During the course of their studies the students have an opportunity to attend modules alongside teachers from English schools. They also participate in an intensive week of activities with teachers from Ireland on a program during which they complete a study of the Irish education system.

As a compulsory part of the course leading to the award of an MA in Education, international students are required to attend an English school for one day a week over a period of sixteen weeks. All of the students are qualified teachers and are allocated to secondary, primary or special schools which match their professional interests and expertise. Prior to the school placement the students complete a thirty-hour non-assessed module called Introduction to the English Education System.

This module provides them with an overview of the structure of schooling in England and introduces them to education legislation and policies which have shaped English schooling. Opportunities are afforded to examine and critique National Curriculum documentation, along with national strategies for literacy and numeracy and procedures for assessment. The standards, which have to be attained by trainee teachers, are examined in some detail and discussed alongside a range of literature, which debates the nature of effective teaching.

Whilst undertaking this module the students make half-day visits to primary (5–10 years), secondary (11–16 years) and special schools and a local further education college (students aged 16+). These visits are designed to assist students in contextualizing those issues addressed through lectures, seminars and workshops during the Introduction to the English Education System module. The head teachers or other senior staff within the schools visited are briefed prior to the visit about the focus of prior taught sessions and are encouraged to provide opportunities for students to see in practice those education policies and procedures discussed during these sessions.

Students also undertake a module which focuses upon current debates surrounding inclusive education. During taught sessions they consider the ways in which the assessment of students who have difficulties with learning is conducted and debate issues such as the impact of labelling. They further consider the role of special schools and the practices adopted by teachers to ensure learning by those students described as having SEN, others for whom English is an additional language and those who have experienced personal trauma through displacement from their countries of origin. Examples of provision and practice are provided from a broad range of international contexts and students are encouraged to investigate how schooling for students with additional needs is organized in their own countries.

Students enter schools for their weekly placement only after completing the Introduction module. Their role during school placement is to work alongside and under the direction of teachers in a supportive role. They are not expected to assume responsibility for teaching a whole class. As they gain in confidence and as teachers recognize the skills which students have, however, it is often the case that students manage groups of students during lessons and in some instances do take classes. During the course of the sixteen-week school placement students are required to undertake a series of tasks. These include an analysis of school curriculum documents, observations of lessons and other school activities and interviews with key members of the school staff including the SEN coordinator to gain an impression of their role and how they operate. School-based sessions are followed by structured activities in the university during which students analyse their experiences and consider the implications of these for their own development as teachers. Throughout their school placement the students maintain a reflective diary and gather a portfolio of documents, which assists them in contextualizing their school-based experiences.

Amongst the tasks required of the MA students, a consideration of the ways in which teachers adapt their teaching to ensure the participation of students who experience difficulties with learning is given some priority. They undertake observations of individual students, interview teachers and talk with teaching assistants who support learning. They also examine teachers' planning and assessment procedures and individual education plans, which are provided for students with the most complex needs.

Following each day in school the students come together to discuss their experiences amongst themselves and with course tutors. These sessions provide an opportunity to consider what they have seen and to debate the effectiveness of various teaching practices and procedures and the underpinning theories behind the approaches adopted in schools. The students are also encouraged to consider what they have learned during the school placement in the context of their home teaching situations. Issues of transferability are discussed and the merits of various teaching approaches from their personal experiences in their own countries considered alongside their observation of English classrooms.

Reflections on school-based learning

Students who undertake this course report that the school placement is a positive learning experience. They often describe the early stages of the school placement as being challenging because of the nature of the schools and the significant difference from those in which they work in their home countries. The first few days in school are often seen as a period of acclimatization during which they slowly find their way amongst the complex range of school customs and procedures, which they find alien, and at times intimidating. As they adjust to this new environment they gain in confidence and having weekly tasks to complete enables them to maintain a focus and begin to examine what they see in a critical and questioning manner. For many, particularly those who have come from countries with poor socio-economic indicators, they are initially overwhelmed by the wealth of resources that they find in English schools. However, when they focus on aspects of pedagogy and classroom management, they begin to question how classrooms are organized, the ways teachers teach and the engagement of students.

Following their school placement, students are asked to share their impressions of the experience and are questioned about their understanding of inclusion and the transferability of what they may have learned in schools to their home teaching situation. This process of debriefing is conducted through individual interviews and through the completion of reflective writing, which is focused upon the school placement.

Their reflections suggest that the development of an understanding of inclusive schooling is considerably enhanced through their experiences in school. Whilst they participate in university-based lectures, seminars and workshops focused upon the development of inclusive approaches to teaching and the theories around whole-school approaches to inclusion, their appreciation of inclusive practice remains at an abstract level. For many, their reading of the theories surrounding inclusion and their participation in taught sessions leaves them sceptical of the application of principles in practice. It is only after they see the implementation of classroom practices and school procedures aimed at addressing the diversity of the student population within schools that their appreciation of what inclusion might mean for teachers and learners becomes clear.

Through interviews and reflective diaries, students indicate that prior to their studies in England both their appreciation of special and inclusive education and their engagement with learners who experienced challenges in their learning is limited. Furthermore, there is an indication that opportunities to learn about issues of special needs or learning diversity through initial teacher education or continuing professional development are rare.

> In China I learned nothing about special education in my four years teacher training program. Although I have long years of teaching experience in a university in China and a couple of years in-service continuing professional development at home and abroad, none of my teaching, learning or research was related to special and inclusive education. When I was teaching there were students with learning difficulties in my class, but I never identified them as having difficulties. Like many other teachers with little knowledge and understanding about special and inclusive education, I regarded them as either being slow or not trying hard enough.
>
> (Chinese student)

> I had no experience with children with special needs during my teaching years in my home country (India). I had a view that children with special needs were physically disabled and, therefore, they should be placed in a special school with special teachers.
>
> (Indian student)

Many writers (Garner, 2001) have suggested that insufficient attention to special and inclusive education at both initial teacher education (ITE) and continuing professional learning (PL) levels is a major obstacle to the promotion of inclusive practice. This view has been endorsed internationally with some authors discussing the difficulties of establishing the importance of issues associated with the education of students with SEN or disabilities in an educational climate where other education demands may take priority.

Wang (2008) has demonstrated how teachers provided with focused training in relation to interventions for learners with SEN in the early years in the Asia-Pacific region has had a significant impact upon both attitudes and expectations of such students. The fact that for many of the students participating in the MA program discussed in this chapter provides a first critical examination of special and inclusive education, indicates the challenges ahead for the provision of more equitable schooling internationally.

Participation on the degree can be seen to have had an impact upon both attitudes and learning with students articulating personal change as a feature of their learning in England.

> (Prior to this course) I was not convinced that in China inclusive education should be advocated or promoted. I held attitudes, which are still shared by many Chinese (even some Chinese educators), that there are too many issues and challenges in our education system and society as a whole.
>
> (Chinese student)

> I have learned more about children as learners. I have learned to appreciate that children are different and have varied and complex needs. As school is like a representation of society where people with different contexts and backgrounds interact, it is important that children with varied needs and abilities or disabilities are put together. It is beneficial to everyone who is involved in the process of education. I believe that inclusive education is a process towards achieving a quality education for all which may be difficult to measure in a short period of time.
>
> (Indian student)

Attitudes and expectations are a regular feature of discussion amongst international students on the course. As the excerpts above demonstrate, many students believe that negative attitudes are one of the greatest obstacles to the development of equitable education systems. It is, however, worth noting that students often recognize that this remains a challenge within English schools:

> Theory and practice are very different. Despite the efforts of some people at the school I was in towards the development of inclusive practice, I was shocked to see the use of public humiliation as a disciplinary tool and the lack of compromise for some pupils with SEN, using the excuse of a lack of resources.
>
> (Brazilian student)

The instilling of positive attitudes towards learners who are seen to present challenges to the teacher has been the subject of considerable discussion

(Ellins and Porter, 2005; Ferguson, 2008). International students from the MA course are often able to reflect how they personally have reviewed their own previous conceptions of teaching and have begun to challenge previously experienced stereotypes.

> I need to look at how much I can make possible a quality education for all. I have developed a strong positive attitude towards those children with SEN. Each individual child is valuable and can make a worthwhile contribution. In our context, we have been told that children from poor or lower caste backgrounds cannot achieve much in learning. It is also the case for children with special needs. I know I must be more empathetic and patient towards all learners to achieve their maximum potential with local resources.
>
> (Indian student)

It is clear from discussions with international students that in considering the place of learners from marginalized groups they deconstruct their personal schooling experiences and discuss what they see in English classrooms in relation to their own cultural contexts. This inevitably leads to discussions of what has been seen and how much of this may be transferable to classrooms in their own countries.

> I believe that I could use all that I have learned here in Brazil. It is just a case of adjusting to a different reality but the theories are pretty much universal.
>
> (Brazilian student)

> My studies have set me thinking about the current education provision for Chinese learners. The possible contribution I could make in initial teacher education and professional development in my home context ... I understand that not all policies, theories and practices of inclusive education are transferable from one country to another. Each country has its own multidimensional factors influencing their educational priorities, which will further impact on the advancement of inclusive processes. However, my knowledge of identification, recognition and celebration of the diverse learning needs of children can be transferred.
>
> (Chinese student)

Learning from international students for reform of course provision

The testaments of students from this course give a powerful indicator of the importance of learning about inclusion through both theoretical discussions and practical school experiences. The theoretical models and philosophical debates which have dominated discourses of inclusion in western countries, have provided a useful foundation for addressing a global concern. Progress towards a more equitable education system in which young people from marginalized communities are respected and take their rightful place is most likely to be achieved when policy makers and teachers gain the ability to interpret needs within their own context. Many of those students arriving in the UK today to study for higher degrees in education will return to their countries to become the policy shapers of tomorrow. The experiences that they gain during their studies may well have a significant bearing upon how they effect change within their own communities. Encouraging them to participate in a debate that is informed not only by the ideas which they discuss in seminars and hear in lectures, but also through an active engagement in classrooms could have a bearing upon how they address issues in the future. The reflections of students on their school-based experiences indicate that a synthesis between theory and practice can be achieved and that this may have long-term benefits. Not least of these is an encouragement of students to reflect upon their own experiences and to interpret these on the basis of an understanding of their own culture – surely a more appropriate approach to the promotion of educational ideas than that which has been imposed in the past.

References

Adams, L. D. and Kirova, A. (2006) *Global Migration and Education: Schools, Children and Families,* Mahwah, NJ: Lawrence Erlbaum Associates.

Black-Hawkins, K., Florian, L. and Rouse, M. (2007) *Achievement and Inclusion in Schools,* London: Routledge.

Bourdieu, P. (1984) *Distinction: A Social Critique of the Judgement of Taste,* London: Routledge.

Cheung, H. Y. and Hui, L. H. M. (2007) "Conceptions and challenges within inclusive Asian classrooms", in S. N. Phillipson (ed.), *Learning Diversity in the Chinese Classroom,* Hong Kong: Hong Kong University Press, pp. 65–93.

Ellins, J. and Porter, J. (2005) "Departmental differences in attitudes to special educational needs in the secondary school", *British Journal of Special Education,* 32(4): 188–95.

Farrell, P., Dyson, A., Polat, F., Hitcheson, G. and Gallannaugh, F. (2007) "SEN inclusion and pupils achievement in English schools", *Journal of Research in Special Educational Needs,* 7(3): 172–8.

Ferguson, D. (2008) "International trends in inclusive education: the continuing challenge to teach each one and everyone", *European Journal of Special Needs Education,* 23(2): 109–20.

Garner, P. (2001) "Goodbye Mr Chips: Special needs, inclusive education and the deceit of initial teacher training", in T. O'Brien (ed.), *Enabling Inclusion: Blue Skies ... Dark Clouds,* London: The Stationery Office.

Nussbaum, M. (1997) *Cultivating Humanity: A Classical Defence of Reform in Liberal Education,* Cambridge, MA: Harvard University Press.

Said, E. (1994) *Culture and Imperialism,* London: Vintage.

Sen, A. (2006) *The Argumentative Indian,* London: Penguin.

Sharma, D. (2000) "Educational Issues", in A. Lau (ed.), *South Asian Children and Adolescents in Britain,* London: Whurr, pp. 157–75.

Wang, H.-Y. (2008) "Preparing teachers to work with young children with disabilities", in C. Forlin and M.-G. J. Lian (eds), *Reform, Inclusion and Teacher Education: Towards a New Era of Special Education in the Asia-Pacific Region,* Oxford: Routledge, pp. 74–82.

Chapter 4

A national strategy for supporting teacher educators to prepare teachers for inclusion

Chris Forlin and Dinh Thi Nguyet

Learning outcomes

- Understand how a developing country with limited experience in inclusive and special education can prepare for inclusion.
- Knowledge about upskilling teacher educators to prepare pre-service teachers for inclusion.
- Information on how to implement a national approach to prepare teacher educators for inclusion.

Introduction

As most education systems throughout the world embrace inclusion or transition towards it, preparing teachers for this role has become a key issue. It is readily acknowledged that teachers require appropriate skills, knowledge and dispositions if they are to successfully offer an inclusive curriculum and systems have taken a variety of approaches to support them in gaining these (Forlin, 2008). Teacher training institutions, therefore, have had to review the courses they offer to ensure that teachers are prepared to work with students from increasingly diverse backgrounds (Rose, 2007). In many instances institutions have been slow to respond to this need and newly qualified teachers continue to suggest that they are insufficiently prepared to support the needs of all students within inclusive classrooms (Forlin, 2007). One of the key issues which hinder a more inclusive curriculum approach for institutions, especially in countries which are embracing inclusion for the first time, is that teacher educators themselves are poorly equipped to take on the role of educating pre- and inservice teachers about inclusion; and that the existing curriculum is still very much focused on academic objectives rather than on a children's needs perspective.

The need to upskill teacher educators to offer an appropriate curriculum and to employ suitable pedagogies to prepare teachers for inclusion poses quite a challenge in countries where there are few academics who are themselves trained in inclusive education and who lack the necessary skills, knowledge and sentiments to undertake such a role. This chapter will outline how one country, Vietnam, took this challenge and prepared an alternative model for promoting inclusion within teacher training programs. The approach employed developing a national core curriculum framework at a system level for all training institutions to infuse into their initial teacher education (ITE) programs by utilizing an intensive country wide train-the-trainer model to support this. The chapter will commence with background information about the development of inclusive education in Vietnam so that the approach can be contextualized and readers can appreciate the philosophy behind the development of the initiative.

Educating children with disabilities in Vietnam

Education for children with disabilities in Vietnam began with the first special school for deaf children being opened in 1886, and then expanded with special schools for children with other types of disabilities during the 1970s. These schools were mainly situated in the larger cities such as Hanoi, Danang and Ho Chi Minh City and provided a segregated education for children identified with specific disabilities. In more recent years, though, there has been a strong movement towards an inclusive approach to the education of these students. Indeed, Vietnam has been considered the most inclusive country across the Asia-Pacific region in terms of the education of children and youth with disabilities (Villa *et al.*, 2003).

A move towards inclusive education

The Government of Vietnam has shown its commitment to a more inclusive education approach by clearly indicating its desire to provide educational opportunities for children with disabilities in its Education Law (National Assembly, 2005) and particularly in the development and approval of the Education For All National Action Plan 2003–2015. The Vietnam education system is still very much centralized in management, therefore, any national human resource development strategy in inclusive education relies on the direction of the Ministry of Education and Training (MOET). Even though the government of Vietnam has a commitment to providing equal opportunities in education for children with disabilities (Van Tac, 2000), setting a target of 75 per cent of children with disabilities in school by 2010 and 90 per cent by 2015 (MOET, 2001; 2006) and is promoting inclusive education as the main approach for achieving these targets, preparation of skilled teachers and other necessary resources for inclusion are still very limited. Vietnam has not adopted the model of support teachers or co-teaching, thus the task of implementing inclusive education in the classroom depends entirely on regular teachers who have received little or no training in inclusive education due to the design of existing curricula for ITE programs. This is compounded by the fact that there is no policy framework for teachers working in inclusive schools, thus it is difficult to promote programs in inclusive education in teacher training courses as they are not valued.

Teacher education in special and inclusive education in Vietnam

Teacher training in special education has been limited to date by the capacity and size of the institutions which can deliver appropriate programs. Only a few teacher training colleges and universities provide special training programs while almost none of them provide inclusive education courses either through an infusion mode or as a separate course.

By 2004, Vietnam only had four national universities (Hanoi, Ho Chi Minh, Danang, Quynhon) and three national teacher training colleges (Hanoi, Ho Chi Minh, Nhatrang) providing ITE in special education (Bergsma and Nguyen, 2004). For instance, Hanoi University offered four formal pre-service training courses with an initial total of 134 graduates and a further 117 by 2004. These were available only in special education within a four-year program either in visual impairment, hearing impairment or intellectual disability. By 2004, across the whole of Vietnam, approximately 329 teachers under the four-year program (BA level) and around 263 graduates from a three-year program (Diploma level) had been trained in special education. Noticeably there remains a huge gap in providing regular teachers with training in inclusive education either during their ITE or through latter PL programs.

Upskilling teacher educators for teaching inclusive education

With the current limitation in formal ITE programs in inclusive education, many stakeholders (either private organizations supporting inclusive education or local education agencies) have chosen the approach of PL (either through degree or certificate) for providing teachers and managers with at least some basic training about inclusion. Short professional learning courses have occurred through activities organized by the MOET, the National Institute of Education Sciences, local education agencies and international NGOs (e.g. Catholic Relief Services, 2001; Catholic Relief Services and National Institute for Education Strategy and Curriculum, 2006). This has meant that from the late 1990s until 2004, approximately 29,000 preschool and primary teachers received training for either one week or more in special and inclusive education, representing approximately 2.8 per cent of primary teachers (Bergsma and Nguyen, 2004). While this is a positive move forward in training teachers these numbers are still too small in comparison to the current need for expanding inclusive education into all preschool, primary and secondary schools in Vietnam where an estimated 944,410 teachers require upskilling (Statistical Source Office, 2008).

A curriculum framework for training institutions

Recently, the MOET in collaboration with Catholic Relief Services initiated an innovative development to support inclusion. Together they produced a national core curriculum and pedagogical framework on inclusive education for ensuring quality and equitable training programs for teacher educators at all universities and training colleges.

This was a most important initiative to ensure that all teachers in training received at least some basic knowledge about inclusion. There was, however, a major challenge in implementing this due to the relatively short supply of faculty who themselves had sufficient knowledge to provide the training. Thus measures had to be taken to initially provide appropriate training for the teacher educators in the universities and colleges which are considered key institutions for delivering and disseminating inclusive education approaches throughout the country.

Consequently, an implementation model was employed that utilized a train-the-trainer approach to prepare teacher educators from national and provincial universities and colleges across Vietnam. The training course in inclusive education had two major objectives: upskill the teacher educators themselves, and engage them in appropriate pedagogies they could then employ to embed the core curriculum framework on inclusive education into their own ITE programs.

The training course

The participants were all teacher educators from across Vietnam, representing six universities (Ho Chi Minh, Dong Thap, Quy Nhon, Da Nang, Quang Nam, and Hanoi Pedagogy University), three colleges (Hanoi Pedagogy College, Ho Chi Minh Pedagogy College, Nha Trang Pedagogy College), and one centre (Bac Can Centre for education of disadvantage children). A total of 47 teacher educators from eight cities and provinces participated in a five-day intensive 40-hour course. Of the participants, 29 held an undergraduate degree, 14 held a masters degree and two had a PhD, holding a variety of different background specializations (Table 4.1). Their experience working as a special education lecturer ranged from less than one year to only one person having more than five years' experience. The mean number of years of teaching in a training institution was 2.2 years.

Outcomes of the training model

Throughout the week all aspects of the new core curriculum framework were discussed (see Forlin, 2008, for a detailed explanation of the curriculum framework). In order to engage with the curriculum, multiple opportunities

Table 4.1 Teacher educators participating in the course

Specialty	N	%
Biology	1	2
Education for Children with Development Delay	5	11
Education for Vision Impaired Children	6	14
Educational Psychology	6	13
Foreign Language	1	2
Hearing Impaired	2	5
Literature	1	2
Mathematics	1	2
Pedagogy	5	11
Preschool Education	4	9
Psychological Education for Preschool	1	2
Special Education	10	23
Primary Education	1	2

Table 4.2 Pedagogies employed to explore inclusive education and teach the new curriculum

Monday	Tuesday	Wednesday	Thursday	Friday
Discussion	Discussion	Discussion	Discussion	Discussion
Cooperative learning	Stories	Worksheet activity	Guest speaker	Case studies – books
Problem-based learning	Cooperative learning	Group sharing	Games (barrier games)	Think aloud
Videos	Videos	Panel	Quiz	Jigsaw
Audio	Analogies	Games	Videos	Brainstorming
Role playing	Newspapers	Videos	PowerPoints	Snow ball
Being "Disabled" (blind, PI, HI)	Being deaf	PowerPoints	Worksheet activity	Cooperative learning
PPs	PowerPoints	Role playing	Brainstorming	Fish Tank
Newspapers	Posters	Analogies	Cooperative learning	Journaling
Singing	de Bono's thinking hats	Cooperative learning	Videos	Model development
Analogies	Feedback	Think pair share	Oral presentations	Posters Review & reflection
Feedback			Peer tutoring	Summarizing

were provided to learn, identify and practice the pedagogical skills needed for teaching an inclusive curriculum. Table 4.2 outlines the range of pedagogies employed.

At the commencement of the course 85 per cent of participants did not seem to understand the concept of inclusion and all but two of them did not believe that inclusive education is the most effective educational approach in meeting demands of diversity in society. Although they all agreed that children with disabilities do not learn like their non-disabled peers, a very large number of participants (88 per cent) suggested that assessment of a child's abilities and needs is not a prerequisite for teachers to plan lessons for whole-class teaching. Clearly, the participants on the course were starting from a less than supportive foundation for inclusion with very limited understanding of the concept.

On completion of the course they commented on four specific areas they had learned that they would apply in their teaching, namely, theory and knowledge; instructions and skills; inclusive education practices; and a much greater awareness about inclusion. While they had a better understanding of the concept of inclusion and a willingness to provide opportunities for their students to reflect upon and improve their attitudes using some specific strategies, they were still concerned that they needed a lot more information about inclusion and best practices for supporting children with disabilities. Table 4.3 summarizes these issues.

During the course participants discussed the way forward for Vietnam from the perspectives of whether they considered Vietnam was ready for inclusion; what foundations were already in place; what else needed to be done; and the attitudes of the community towards inclusive education.

Key outcomes from group discussions *(translated from Vietnamese)*

1 Is Vietnam ready for inclusive education?
   - There are many differences between the provinces.
   - It requires a centrally developed synchronized theory and practice approach, policy and appropriate strategy with a clear definition of inclusion and integration.
   - Professional training courses are needed for all teachers.
   - Needs to move from a charity approach to a rights-based one.
   - More preparation needed before commencing inclusive education.
2 Foundations already in place:
   - Vietnamese love people, support them.
   - There are good inclusive education models in some provinces.
   - Children with disabilities (CWDs) are included in some regular classes.

Table 4.3 Summary of key issues relating to post-assessment of the training course for teacher educators in inclusive education

Areas	Key issues they will apply	Key issues they remain concerned about
Theory and knowledge	• Attitudes, beliefs and values are very important • Updated knowledge and information of IE (i.e. diversified groups) • Different methods of student evaluation	• Special knowledge of certain disability groups e.g. visual impairment or learning disability • Profound understanding of developmental delays and its causes
Instructions and Skills	• Activity-based methodology • Problem-based teaching • Group work and collaborative learning • Using teaching aids	• Appropriate communication methods used for children with disabilities • Management of challenging bahaviours • Different methods applied to diversified groups • Need assessment of CWDs • Effective teaching or instructions
Inclusive education practices	• Change attitudes and beliefs towards PWD • Organize diversified class activities and self-learning for students • Use materials and media products for student learning • Increase exposure opportunities for students • Increase community cooperation • Promote academic sharing among training staff	• Develop IEP • Identification of CWD • Organize activities for CWD in regular class • Organizing early intervention activities in regular pre-school settings
Awareness promotion	• Build beliefs for students • Increase opportunities for students to access become PWD and involved in activities for PWD • Engage PWD in training programs	• Comprehensive support from government policies • Community attitudes towards CWDs

Note. C/PWD = children/people with disabilities

- Some universities and colleges have started inclusive education courses.
- Some teachers have received inclusive education training.
- Community support and awareness is being raised.
- Special schools are operating.
- Inclusive education is the preference of parents.

3 What is needed?
   Full preparation of all human resources including:
   - All teachers teaching preschool and primary need to be trained on basic inclusive education.
   - Benefit package for inclusive education teachers needed.
   - Infrastructure needs to be in place for supporting teachers in schools.
   - Teaching and learning materials need to be developed.
   - Greater awareness needs to be raised through the media.
   - Cooperation between health and education needed.
   - Managers need to be trained on inclusive education.
   - Belief systems need to be changed to support inclusive education.

4 Attitudes towards inclusion
   Positives:
   - Teachers willing to include CWDs.
   - Teachers need to be enthusiastic, flexible, creative, hard working.
   Negatives:
   - Teachers express fear and are worried.
   - Some do not believe in or support inclusive education.
   - Some still prefer traditional approaches such as didactic teaching and passive learning.

Forward planning for inclusive education in Vietnam

A two-level action plan to further inclusive education in Vietnam involving changes at the college and university level and across all systems was proffered.

Changes at the college and university level

- Inclusive education content should be included into all ITE curricula with immediate priority being given to preschool and primary teacher training.
- The new core curriculum framework should be applied to all courses using a range of interactive pedagogies and involving latest best-practice knowledge about teaching.
- Appropriate training materials should be developed by each training institute.

Changes at the system level

- Inclusive education training courses should be organized for upskilling all teachers.
- An awareness-raising campaign should be enacted for managers, teachers, students and the community regarding inclusive education.
- Opportunities should be made available to discuss and share experiences with other schools, centres, local and international agencies.
- Closer cooperation between all government systems is needed in order to have good implementation of inclusive education; e.g. Education, Health, Social Services and other agencies and organizations.
- Teaching practice in inclusive education needs to be strengthened and inclusive education support centres need to be developed.
- Policy requires amendment in order to support inclusion.
- The government should lead the development of a clear and transparent strategy which is comprehensive, synchronized and long lasting on inclusive education.

Conclusion

The initiative discussed in this chapter was developed in order to meet the urgent need to ensure all new teachers received some training in inclusive education, as this was being promoted by the MOET for mainstream schools. A new core curriculum framework for inclusion was developed by a collaborative process between MOET, training institutions and NGO agencies that was to be introduced nationally to all teacher training institutions. The biggest challenge was how to prepare teacher educators to implement this as they did not have the knowledge, skills and dispositions to be able to teach the proposed curriculum in a timely and effective way. Consequently, an intensive 40-hour course was provided in order to address the large task of preparing teacher educators from the many training institutions across Vietnam. These trained educators will be the resource experts for delivering inclusive education in their ITE programs and for disseminating information to other training institutions nationwide. During training the participants gained the knowledge and appropriate dispositions towards inclusion and had sufficient practice to be able to feel more confident in becoming inclusive teacher educators. However, the course went far beyond dissemination of content knowledge as it allowed for profoundly deep reflection about their own beliefs and constructive dialogue as the teacher educators grappled with an understanding of the philosophy of inclusive education; the needs of children from diverse backgrounds; the challenges faced by teachers; and their own role in furthering inclusion.

The example discussed here of how one developing country took the initiative to establish a nationwide movement towards preparing all teachers for inclusive education provides an alternative model for other jurisdictions to consider. Taking a country context such as Vietnam, the model of providing a national core curriculum for initial training programs and then training key educators with essential inclusive education knowledge and skills in order to prepare their own students, could be a useful innovation for other countries with similar management systems and at similar stages in launching inclusive education to consider. While the train-the-trainer model has received some negative response in more developed countries (Orfaly *et al.*, 2005), this approach seems to have been pertinent to the urgent needs of a developing country that is faced with the challenge of ensuring that all new teachers have some training in inclusion and that the teacher educators at universities and colleges have the capacity to provide this. This is especially pertinent in a country where training systems and programs are based on the direction of the management agency.

It was reiterated by the MOET representative that Vietnam was very concerned about people with disabilities in both society and education; that there were many children with SEN in Vietnam and that they were just one of the agencies helping the government in supporting them. It was reaffirmed that inclusion is growing in Vietnam and there are now many programs and developing policies to assist in this movement. Future direction regarding expanding inclusion in Vietnam includes the promotion of the training of all teachers; the development of policy and guidelines; increased cooperation between the ministries of health and education; enhanced support networks; and increased awareness training across the community.

One of the seven groups which the participants had formed during the week for in-depth dialogue about the curriculum framework and the application of the pedagogies, wrote a poem to summarize their involvement in the course. They used the name of each group to produce an inventive piece of work on what inclusive education meant to these teacher educators. It is clear from this the importance they were now allocating to their roles and their commitment in furthering inclusive education in Vietnam. *Note.* The capital words represent the names of their groups during the week-long training session.

> TOGETHER we smile
> HAND-IN-HAND build a house
> FUTURE shines on our life
> BELIEF flows from the achievement of the "grower"
> FORLIN sows the seed
> SHARING the pain of people with a disability
> HOPE brightens our FUTURE
> Vietnam believes in the success of our people-growing course.
> *(translated from Vietnamese)*

References

Bergsma, S. and Nguyen, T. H. (2004) *Overall Research on Human Resource Development in Inclusive Education and Early Intervention*, Hanoi: National Politics Publishing House.

Catholic Relief Services (2001) *Concept Notes – Expansion of Community Support to Children with Disabilities*, Hanoi: Internal report.

Catholic Relief Services and National Institute for Education Strategy and Curriculum (2006) *Inclusive Education for Children with Disabilities at Primary School Level*, Hanoi: Labor and Social Welfare Publishing House.

Forlin, C. (2007) "A collaborative, collegial and more cohesive approach to supporting educational reform for inclusion in Hong Kong", *Asia-Pacific Education Review*, 8(2): 1–11.

Forlin, C. (2008) "Education reform for inclusion in Asia: What about teacher education", in C. Forlin and M.-G. J. Lian (eds), *Reform, Inclusion and Teacher Education: Towards a New Era of Special Education in the Asia-Pacific Region*, Abingdon: Routledge, pp.74–82.

MOET, Ministry of Education and Training (2001) *Education Development Strategy 2001–2010*, Hanoi: Education Publishing House.

MOET, Ministry of Education and Training (2006) "Workshop report. Direction to inclusive education system. Primary Education for disadvantaged children (PEDC)", documents presented at the Conference on Towards Inclusive Education System, MOET, Hai Phong, June.

National Assembly (2005) *Law on Education*. Online. Available at: http://www.moet. gov.vn/?page=6.1&type=documents&type=documents&view= (accessed 28 August 2008).

Orfaly, R. A., Frances, J. C., Campbell, P., Whittemore, B., Joly, B. and Koh, H. (2005) "Train-the-trainer as an education model in public health preparedness", *Journal of Public Health Management and Practice*, Supplement: S123–7.

Rose, R. (2007) "Curriculum considerations in meeting special educational needs", in L. Florian (ed.), *The International Handbook of Special Education*, London: Sage, pp. 295–306.

Statistical Source Office. (2008) *General Education*. Online. Available at: http://edu. net.vn/thongke/phothong.htm (accessed 27 April 2009).

Van Tac, L. (2000) "Inclusive education – A new phase of education in Vietnam", paper presented at the International Special Education Congress, Manchester, UK, July.

Villa, R. A., Van Tac, L., Muc, P. M., Ryan, S., Thuy, N. T. M. T., Weill, C., *et al.* (2003) "Inclusion in Viet Nam: More than a decade of implementation", *Research and Practice for Persons with Severe Disabilities*, 28(1): 23–32.

Part II

Innovative approaches for initial teacher preparation

Chapter 5

Reforming initial teacher education

A necessary but not sufficient condition for developing inclusive practice

Martyn Rouse

Learning outcomes

- Understand the arguments for having a wide definition of inclusion and the reasons for underachievement and lack of participation for certain students.
- Knowledge about the reasons why some teachers think that students who have difficulties in learning should not be their responsibility.
- Appreciate how initial teacher education (ITE) can respond to these concerns.

The current international context

Extending access to quality education is part of a worldwide agenda because schooling is seen as being crucial to human, economic and social development goals and because so many children do not have access to schooling (UNESCO, 2005). There are many reasons why children do not attend school, including high levels of mobility and migration, social conflict, child labour and exploitation, poverty, gender and disability. In some parts of the world, schooling is not available because of a shortage of school places, a lack of quality teachers, or because schools are too far from where children live. Sometimes families do not send children to school because of fears about safety and security, especially of girls, or because of the cost. Such costs include fees, uniforms, transport, books and materials, and the so-called "opportunity costs" that arise when children are not economically active because they are in school. Children are more likely to attend school if they receive a high-quality education. Therefore, increasing participation in schooling is not only about increasing school places and training more teachers, it also depends on improving the quality of teaching. Central to this task is the development of ITE programs so that teachers are prepared to respond to diversity and can support inclusion.

Problems with the quality and availability of educational opportunities are not confined to the developing world. In well-schooled countries such as Scotland, with its long history of compulsory school attendance, such concerns may seem irrelevant, but even here, not all children have positive experiences of education, nor do many have much to show for their time in school when they leave. As in some other countries, the so-called "achievement gap" between those who achieve most and those who achieve least, is a major concern (OECD, 2007). The task then, is not only to improve access to schooling, but also to ensure that meaningful participation, achievement and success is available to all, not just to some (Black-Hawkins *et al.*, 2007).

This is a complex and difficult task for many reasons. One relates to deeply embedded attitudes and beliefs about human differences, how such differences are defined and about who should be responsible for responding to them. Dealing with exclusion, marginalization and underachievement is not only the right thing to do; it makes sound economic and social sense. When schools fail in their responsibility to educate all children, it leads to an education underclass and also to a social and economic underclass, which has serious economic and social consequences for society today and in the future (Belfield and Levin, 2007). The task of inclusion, therefore, is not only about children with disabilities and special education needs (SEN), it must also address broader issues of marginalization and underachievement. The development of successful inclusive schools, or schools for all, in which the learning and participation of all children is valued, is an essential task for all countries.

In response, many countries have enacted policies designed to develop their special education systems or to encourage greater inclusion of children with disabilities or difficulties. In spite of pro-inclusion policies in many countries, achieving inclusion is a daunting task and dealing with differences and diversity continues to be one of the biggest problems faced by schools today. Such problems are associated with low expectations and aspirations, intergenerational poverty and underachievement. In addition, barriers arise from inflexible or irrelevant curricula, didactic teaching methods, inappropriate systems of assessment and examinations, and inadequate preparation of, and support for, teachers.

There is a growing recognition by researchers, governments and teachers themselves, that ITE may not be preparing beginning teachers sufficiently well to meet the needs of all children in schools that are increasingly diverse (Ofsted, 2008). Whilst there are many success stories to be told about inclusion (e.g. Ainscow, 1997; Black-Hawkins *et al.*, 2007), international research suggests that one of the greatest barriers to inclusion is that many teachers feel that they are not trained to deal with inclusion, diversity, behaviour and SEN (e.g. Forlin, 2008). Teacher education, therefore, has to be reformed so that teachers are better prepared to work in inclusive ways. This has to apply to all teachers, not just some.

Reforming teacher education for inclusion: some teachers or all teachers?

It could be argued that there are two main strands to the debate about the reform of teacher education for inclusion. On the one hand, there are those who suggest that there is insufficient content knowledge about different types of difficulty in most programs. It is claimed that inclusion is difficult to achieve because new teachers do not know enough about issues such as dyslexia, autism, AD/HD or about the teaching strategies thought to be associated with these types of difficulties. The classic special education view assumes that it is not possible to include children with learning difficulties in mainstream settings because their needs are different and that it is more efficient to group children according to the nature of their disabilities or difficulties so that special pedagogical approaches can be deployed by specially trained teachers (Kauffman *et al.*, 2005). As a result, many mainstream teachers believe that they do not have these skills to do this work because there are other so-called experts to deal with these students on a one-to-one basis or in smaller more manageable groups. When special education support is conceptualized in this manner, it is a barrier to the development of inclusion because it absolves the rest of the education system from taking responsibility for all children's learning.

On the other hand, there are those (e.g. Booth and Ainscow, 2002; Slee, 2001), who argue that inclusion cannot be created through the extension of special education, which they see as part of the problem. They call for a radical approach to teaching and learning that does not depend on the identification of particular forms of disability or difficulty (Allan, 2006). In essence they propose that the barriers to learning and participation should be removed and an inclusive pedagogy be developed. This approach requires new thinking about teacher education for inclusion (Booth *et al.*, 2003; Florian and Rouse, 2009). I have suggested elsewhere (Rouse, 2008) that developing effective inclusive practice is not only about extending teachers' skills and knowledge, but it is also about doing things differently and reconsidering assumptions, attitudes and beliefs about human differences. In other words, the development of inclusion should be about "knowing", "doing", and "believing".

In many universities, the core courses in ITE only make passing reference to inclusion and students who find learning difficult in school. There may also be optional courses concentrating on the characteristics of different kinds of learners, how they should be identified and the current policy context. These courses typically focus on knowing about:

- teaching strategies related to particular types of difficulty
- particular disabilities and special needs
- how children learn

- what children need to learn
- classroom organisation and management
- where to get help when necessary
- identifying and assessing difficulties
- assessing and monitoring children's learning
- the legislative and policy context.

Such content knowledge is important, but it is insufficient to improve practice in schools, because it is not located in the broader issues of the curriculum, teaching and learning and is not available during all ITE courses. Even for those who have undertaken optional courses there may be a big gap between what they know and what they do in their classrooms. In part this is a result of the tension between what is learned in the university and what is learned in school (Hagger and McIntyre, 2006). In an attempt to bridge this gap, professional learning (PL) initiatives have been designed to link the learning of individuals with the institutional development of their schools. In other words "doing" has become an essential element of professional learning and institutional development, especially during the induction years. This may involve action research or reflective practice initiatives built around school- or classroom-based development projects and new ways of doing by:

- turning knowledge into action
- moving beyond reflective practice
- using evidence to improve practice
- learning how to work with colleagues as well as children
- becoming an "activist" professional.

Sometimes negative and deterministic attitudes held by colleagues about children's abilities and worth prevent new ways of thinking about pedagogy (Hart et al., 2004). It is nonetheless also important to consider how it might be possible for teachers to develop new ways of believing that:

- all children are worth educating
- all children can learn
- they have the capacity to make a difference to children's lives
- such work is their responsibility and not only a task for specialists.

Of course, provision varies from school to school and, therefore, any exploration of the roles and responsibilities of teachers has to acknowledge the complexity of the task. Such complexity arises from many factors including the institutional barriers to learning in the current system; the type of needs that are encountered; the professional knowledge, qualifications, status and identity of the teachers themselves (Rouse, 2008). Some special needs teachers see themselves as experts in dealing with difficulties in learning and as the only ones willing undertake this task. It is an identity built upon beliefs about specialist knowledge. In this view, their colleagues do not know how to do it, and they wouldn't want to do it even if they did know how. Inclusion involves redefining roles and can threaten teachers' identities. If responsibilities are to be shared and teachers are to take on new roles, then there have to be changes to the way inclusion is conceptualized and a realization that it can only be achieved if all teachers are supported in the development of all aspects of knowing, doing and believing. One way of understanding this task is to take the lead from Shulman (2004) who talks about the need to ensure that ITE and professional learning in all the professions should have three essential elements. He refers to these elements as the "three apprenticeships". The first is the "apprenticeship of the head", by this he means the cognitive knowledge and theoretical basis of the profession; the second is the "apprenticeship of the hand", this includes the technical and practical skills that are required to carry out the essential tasks of the role; and finally the "apprenticeship of the heart", the ethical and moral dimensions, the attitudes and beliefs, that are crucial to the particular profession and its ways of working. Thus the reform of ITE needs to be built upon the foundation of Shulman's three apprenticeships.

Background: the Scottish context

The four countries of the United Kingdom have different education systems and whilst England and Wales have many similarities, Scotland has a long history of having its own distinct system. In Scotland the government and other agencies have recognized that certain groups are particularly vulnerable to exclusion and underachievement, see for example recent reports and initiatives on autism (HMIE, 2007), dyslexia (HMIE, 2008), "looked after" children and young people (SEED, 2007), young people from Scottish travelling communities and children who do not have English as their first language. In a broad review of equality and equity in Scotland's schools, the Organisation of Economic Cooperation and Development (OECD, 2007) highlighted the chronic underachievement of a significant number of young people in spite of praising many aspects of the system and pointing out the very high levels of attainment for the highest performing 20 per cent. The report went on to claim that many attempts to improve achievement of the bottom 20 per cent have been largely unsuccessful in spite of pro-inclusion policies and anti-discrimination legislation. A series of other policy developments such as *Getting it Right for Every Child* (SEED, 2006), highlights the growing need for teachers to be better prepared to work with other adults as well as with children, not only because of the demand for better community links, but also the expectation for enhanced multi-agency collaboration and integrated children's services.

The inclusive practice project

It is in this context that the Scottish Government has funded the Inclusive Practice Project (IPP) at the University of Aberdeen. The Project reflects an ongoing interest in the School of Education to reform ITE to ensure that it is more responsive to the demands facing teachers and schools today. The reforms have involved staff in the School together with consultation of teachers, local authorities, teacher unions and former program graduates, in developing new approaches to ensure that new teachers:

1 Have a greater awareness and understanding of the education and social problems and issues that can affect students' learning.
2 Have developed strategies that can be used to support and deal with the difficulties students experience in learning.

In addition, it is expected that newly qualified teachers will have a willingness to accept the professional responsibility for developing greater participation and inclusion for all the students they teach, together with knowledge about where and how to get help, advice and support if necessary in order to develop inclusive practice.

The reformed Professional Graduate Diploma of Education (PGDE) program, which started in 2007–08 (for more details see Florian and Rouse, 2009), is informed by the Scottish Standards for ITE (GTCS, 2006) and by the importance of partnership; the idea that students become teachers by working in schools (Hagger and McIntyre, 2006). The university-based curriculum incorporates professional and theoretical knowledge as well as skills in research and refection. Eighteen weeks is spent in school experience placements supported by 18 weeks of university-based learning. The program is made up of a number of distinct but integrated elements (Professional Studies, Further Professional Studies, Learning through the Curriculum and School Experience) that cohere around a set of program aims. These aims are designed to: prepare teachers for making a contribution to the development of students within an inclusive school; to enable them to become effective teachers of the curriculum; and to attain high standards of professional practice.

As in many countries, ITE courses in Scotland involve a partnership between schools and universities and the one-year PGDE course in particular is already overloaded with content. Any reform of university-based courses must recognize the learning that occurs during students' school placement and their experiences during the induction years. Therefore, the reform of ITE has to be seen as a necessary but not sufficient condition if schools are to become more inclusive. Sustained, progressive PL that is linked to the institutional development of schools will also be required.

Major changes have been made to the structure and content of the program in which primary and secondary trainee teachers have been brought together on the professional studies element of the program. Social and educational inclusion is addressed at the heart of the program from the outset, not just an elective selected by some. It has involved significant numbers of mainstream staff. Florian (2007) identified three areas of particular attention in such reform: clearer thinking about the right to education; the need to challenge deterministic views about ability and a shift in focus from differences between learners, to learning for all. Florian's three areas (educational rights, anti-determinism and learning for all) have been embedded in the course, which is informed by the principles of learning, participation, collaboration and activism in the changing context of education. This includes the multiple overlapping layers of teaching and learning, the community of a school, and the school in the broader social and political context (Sachs, 2003). The overriding aim is to help new teachers accept the responsibility for the learning of all students and to know where to turn for help when required.

Primary and secondary teachers have much to offer and learn from each other. The program is, therefore, structured such that prospective primary and secondary teachers are taught professional studies courses together, while curriculum courses are organized by sector and subject. By combining prospective primary and secondary teachers for lectures, workshops and tutor group activities, learning opportunities can focus on the general insights of education in the practical context of classroom teaching. The emphasis is on implications for action in the classroom, such as inclusive practice. One of the most important of these is learning. While this can be conceptualized in a number of different ways, a sociocultural perspective on learning underpins the course. This is important as "sociocultural theory offers a productive way of thinking about how to understand and respond to the complexities inherent in educating diverse groups of students in different contexts" (Florian and Kershner, 2009, p.175). Florian (2007) points out that this involves understanding the interaction of a range of factors (the child, the school and broader cultural and societal factors) that produce individual differences rather than explanations that stress a single cause. Such an approach involves understanding how the relative contribution of these factors informs the responses of teachers when children experience difficulties in learning. It enables individual differences to be seen as something to be expected as a result of interactions between many different variables rather than fixed states within individuals that can be classified and categorized. Therefore, the task for teacher education is to help teachers to think about the difficulties children experience in learning as opportunities for thinking about teaching (e.g. Hart, 2000). This aspect of the task is about building confidence and broadening their repertoire of skills and strategies. It recognizes that ITE cannot produce the "finished article" and it can only prepare teachers to enter the profession. In addition, there is a need for new teachers to learn strategies for working with and through others, in part because of the changing nature of schools and because of the increase in the numbers and range of other adults working to support students in schools.

This chapter has outlined the early stages of reform to a program of initial teacher education. Whilst this is an essential precondition for the development of greater inclusion, it is not sufficient. If schools really are to be better at educating all children, then it will also be necessary to reform continuing professional learning of teachers, together with the institutional development of schools. Such an undertaking requires a massive commitment from all levels of the education system. In spite of these challenges there are sufficient examples of good practice across the world and particularly here in Scotland for us to be optimistic that we can create successful inclusive schools for all. If the Inclusive Practice Project can support new teachers in the "knowing", "being" and "doing" of inclusive education, it will be an important step in this vital task.

References

Ainscow, M. (1997) "Towards inclusive schooling", *British Journal of Special Education,* 24(1): 3–6.

Allan, J. (2006) "The repetition of exclusion", *International Journal of Inclusive Education,* 10 (2–3): 121–33.

Belfield, C. and Levin, H. (eds) (2007) *The Price We Pay: The Economic and Social Consequences of Inadequate Education,* Washington, DC: The Brookings Institution.

Black-Hawkins, K., Florian, L. and Rouse, M. (2007) *Achievement and Inclusion in Schools,* London: Routledge.

Booth, T. and Ainscow, M. (2002) *Index for Inclusion,* Bristol: CSIE.

Booth, T., Nes, K. and Stromsland, M. (eds) (2003) *Developing Inclusive Teacher Education,* London: RoutledgeFalmer.

Florian, L. (2007) "Reimagining special education", in L. Florian (ed.), *The SAGE Handbook of Special Education,* London: Sage, pp. 7–20.

Florian, L. and Kershner, R. (2009) "Inclusive pedagogy", in H. Daniels, J. Porter, J. and H. Lauder (eds), *Routledge Companion in Education,* London: Routledge, pp. 173–83.

Florian, L. and Rouse, M. (2009) "The inclusive practice project in Scotland: Teacher education for inclusive education", *Teaching and Teacher Education,* 25(4): 594–601.

Forlin, C. (2008) "Education reform for inclusion in Asia: What about teacher education?", in C. Forlin and M.-G. J. Lian (eds), *Reform, Inclusion & Teacher Education: Towards a New Era of Special Education in the Asia-Pacific Region,* Abingdon: Routledge, pp. 74–82.

GTCS (2006) *The Standard for Initial Teacher Education,* Edinburgh: General Teaching Council Scotland.

Hagger, H. and McIntyre, D. (2006) *Learning Teaching from Teachers: Realizing the Potential of School-Based Teacher Education,* Maidenhead: Open University Press.

Hart, S. (2000) *Thinking through Teaching*, London: David Fulton.

Hart, S., Dixon, A., Drummond, M. J. and McIntyre, D. (2004) *Learning Without Limits*, Maidenhead: Open University Press.

HMIE (2007) *Education for Pupils with Autism Spectrum Disorders*. Edinburgh: HMIE.

HMIE (2008) *Education for Pupils with Dyslexia*. Edinburgh: HMIE.

Kauffman, J. M., Landrum, T. J., Mock, D., Sayeski, B. and Sayeski, K. S. (2005) "Diverse knowledge and skills require a diversity of instructional groups: A position statement", *Remedial and Special Education*, 26(1): 2–6.

Ofsted (2008) *How Well New Teachers Are Prepared to Teach Pupils with Learning Difficulties and/or Disabilities*, London: Ofsted.

OECD (2007) *OECD Review of Quality and Equity of Education Outcomes in Scotland*, Paris: Organisation for Economic Co-operation and Development.

Rouse, M. (2008) "Developing inclusive practice: A role for teachers and teacher education", *Education in the North*, 16: 6–13.

Sachs, J. (2003) *The Activist Teaching Profession*, Maidenhead, UK: Open University Press.

SEED (2006) *Getting it Right for Every Child: Implementation Plan*, Edinburgh: Scottish Executive Education Department.

SEED (2007) *Looked After Children and Young People: We Can and Must Do Better*, Edinburgh: Scottish Executive Education Department.

Shulman, L. S. (2004) *The Wisdom of Practice: Essays on Teaching, Learning, and Learning to Teach*, San Francisco: Jossey-Bass.

Slee, R. (2001) "Inclusion in practice: Does practice make perfect?" *Educational Review*, 53(2): 113–23.

UNESCO (2005) *Children Out of School: Measuring Exclusion from Primary Education*, Montreal: UNESCO Institute for Statistics.

Chapter 6

A content-infused approach to pre-service teacher preparation for inclusive education

Tim Loreman

Learning outcomes

- Understand the philosophy and principles behind a content-infused approach to pre-service teacher education.
- Develop awareness of some of the inherent challenges associated with the approach.
- Become familiar with practices that can contribute to the success of this approach.

Introduction

As school authorities throughout the world place increased emphasis on providing inclusive environments, they have looked to teacher preparation institutions to provide them with staff with the attitudes, skills, and knowledge required for success. The challenge this presents is to determine how best to modify teacher preparation curriculum and pedagogy to address this reality; with the associated opportunity being to operate in ways that are creative. A content-infused approach is one non-traditional way of working that initial teacher education (ITE) courses can adopt. The term 'content-infused' is understood as meaning that the attitudes, skills, and knowledge normally taught in a single unit on inclusive or special education are spread throughout a number of units in a program, or perhaps an entire program.

Rationale for content-infusion

Research on self-contained units of study in inclusive pedagogy has demonstrated that this approach can be effective in providing pre-service teachers with the skills, knowledge, and attitudes they need in order to be successful when they enter the field (see for example Lancaster and Bain, 2007; Sharma *et al.*, 2006). In many contexts, though, educating pre-service teachers in this way may not be the most effective, efficient, or desirable option (Loreman and Earle, 2007). The units of study that universities can offer, and which students can complete, is finite. In some institutions, including a separate course in inclusive education would require the removal of some other important area of study. Further, the prevailing philosophical views of the teaching faculty and cultural environments might preclude the introduction of a separate unit of study on inclusive education. This was the case at the university where I work, where faculty wanted inclusion to be viewed as part of a teacher's regular duties and so for this and other pragmatic reasons inclusive content was infused throughout the ITE program.

Research on the efficacy of a content-infused approach to teaching about inclusive education in ITE programs is sparse, but nevertheless generally positive. It highlights both the potential for the approach to succeed, along with some areas of concern. International research by Sharma *et al.* (2008) concluded that "... both infusion and single-subject models are effective [in improving attitudes, sentiments, and concerns about inclusive education]" (p. 783). This research included data from my own university and echoed additional research by this team and others. Yerian and Grossman (1997), for example, examined pre-service teacher responses to a statement that they could easily include special education students into regular classes. Their research supported the notion that a content-infused approach can be effective in as much as this statement to some degree conveys pre-service teacher attitudes and also feelings of self-efficacy in implementing inclusive education.

The content-infused approach has also been supported by Voltz (2003) who reviewed 252 ITE institutions in the USA, finding that a 'collaborative infusion' model, similar to the content-infused approach was, in the view of department chairs, beneficial to both students and faculty. Others, such as Stayton and McCollum (2002) have argued that single-course inclusive teacher preparation models are inadequate and that models more in line with the content-infused approach should be more widely adopted. Indeed, this approach is gaining in popularity as approximately 25 per cent of all ITE institutions in the United States have adopted this model (Voltz, 2003).

Research results, however, are not all positive. Even advocates of a content-infused approach admit that there are some inherent difficulties in implementing the approach; difficulties which institutions must be cognizant of if they are to be avoided. Avramidis *et al.* (2000) argued that content-infused models are of concern because they are difficult to monitor, especially in larger ITE institutes. The department heads in Voltz's (2003) study expressed similar concerns, pointing out various areas of incongruence with university structures such as schedules, faculty expertise, and time pressures. Stayton and McCollum (2002), while supportive of a content-infused model, agreed that the approach is under-researched. As practice needs to be research-based if its continued use is to be justified in the field of education, this dearth of research needs to be addressed.

Lessons learned from a Canadian case

Two key Canadian studies of the content-infused approach have helped to inform practice and research at my university. Woloshyn and Bennett (2003) conducted a qualitative study involving 91 pre-service teachers attending a variety of teacher preparation institutions in Ontario. This study examined the beliefs and perceptions of these pre-service teachers and came to the conclusion that a content-infused approach might be the best means of allaying and addressing concerns the pre-service teachers had about their capacities to identify, assess, and program for students who have exceptionalities.

Of greater relevance is a study that examined survey responses of pre-service teachers (Loreman and Earle, 2007). This study found that while the content-infused approach to preparing pre-service teachers for inclusive education was indeed effective in terms of improving attitudes, there were some areas in which no statistically significant improvements were found, including sentiments about disability, and concerns about inclusive education. Demographic variables such as prior teaching experience and gender also had an impact.

The context: teacher education

As described in other work (see Loreman and Earle, 2007; Sharma *et al.*, 2006), my university is relatively small (approximately 1700 students) and is located in Alberta. The education program currently comprises a two-year Bachelor of Education after-degree in elementary education. The program has a positive reputation in Alberta, with graduates being highly sought-after by school jurisdictions throughout the province. Using this as a measure, the efficacy of the program in providing the field with desirable teachers would appear to be high.

Intake each year is competitive and is limited to 72, for a total of approximately 140 pre-service teachers in the program over the two years. Each intake of 72 pre-service teachers is divided equally into two cohorts of 36 with whom they take their classes, that are virtually all mandatory. The Faculty of Education is small, limited to five permanent full-time faculty members, and a number of casual instructors.

Implementing a content-infused approach

Preparing the pre-service teachers for inclusive education occurred from the inception of the program in the 1990s, however, a deliberate, coordinated approach to this was not followed until 2003 with the addition of a faculty member (myself) with a specific interest and research background in inclusive education. At this time I was asked to coordinate inclusion in the

Faculty for a two-year period, a role for which I was provided time through a reduced teaching load. During these two years I worked with faculty and casual instructors to ensure that inclusive education content was infused throughout the program, and to offer advice about pedagogy, research, and other issues. This, it was hoped, would ameliorate the need for a stand-alone subject in inclusive education.

This was possible because many of the areas of concern about a content-infused approach outlined in the literature, included difficulties in monitoring, incongruence with university structures, and pressures on time to collaborate (see Avramidis *et al.*, 2000; Stayton and McCollum, 2002; Voltz, 2003) had been addressed. In a small faculty working with a limited number of pre-service teachers, many of the issues concerning scheduling and monitoring of the approach which might be more evident in larger institutions were ameliorated. The small, collegial atmosphere combined with formal and informal leadership from a colleague with appropriate expertise resulted in an environment where all members of faculty were focused on common goals, and in addition to this were generally aware of the content, teaching methods, and assessment modes each other were engaged in. It was this smaller context, combined with a deliberate approach to ensuring inclusive content was taught throughout the program, and the conduct of research examining practice, that likely contributed to our success.

Success and change

Since the Loreman and Earle (2007) study, which demonstrated that the model was having a positive impact on attitudes, a number of changes were implemented with respect to the program. Some of these changes were enacted because our research showed that we were having little impact on sentiments towards people with disabilities, and in reducing concerns about inclusive education. Other changes were simply a function of time and professional growth. For example, teaching faculty over time developed greater expertise and became more comfortable in their roles as teachers of inclusive content, while new instructors commenced work with the understanding that they would include diversity content in their classes. Secondly, a further assignment was added to one of the mandatory subjects, and other assignments (such as writing an individual program during the technology course using school jurisdiction software) were refined. The additional assignment (modified from an idea from Umesh Sharma; see Loreman and Earle, 2007) required students to examine an area of personal concern about inclusion, and to construct a plan of action for addressing that concern which was then implemented over the course of their final practicum experience.

In addition to these assignments, a key subject which students took on Friday afternoons during their practicum, and which was facilitated by me, had been gradually modified to include a greater range of guest speakers from the field addressing topics of diversity. These included parents of children with disabilities, principals supportive of the approach, teachers, and representatives of various cultural groups. This was not, however, anything like a stand-alone subject on inclusion, but rather one aimed mainly at assisting students to reflect on many important issues and elements of their practicum experience.

Promising practices

Sharma *et al.* (2008) have suggested that perhaps rather than the mode of delivery being the most significant issue, it is more likely the content and pedagogy of a program that seems to have a greater impact on student attitudes, sentiments, and concerns about inclusive education. The following promising practices relevant to a content-infused approach can be found in the literature, and were also evident in my experience outlined above.

Leadership for content infusion

The appointment of a faculty member with appropriate expertise to coordinate the effort of infusing inclusive content is essential. Without adequate coordination, such an initiative is likely to lose momentum, direction, and impact. The coordinating faculty member needs to be someone who is capable of engaging in productive, collegial relationships with a variety of other faculty members, following a style of leadership consistent with building a professional learning community (Leadbeater, 2004). Cowley (2007), in his examination of leadership for change in the corporate world, found that the success of change initiatives was largely determined by the leaders' ability to utilize both formal and informal leadership mechanisms that were culturally appropriate to the organization.

While my position was for a two-year, finite period, it might be more helpful to appoint an inclusion coordinator as an ongoing position, consistent with a model of sustainable leadership. Sustainable leadership exercises vigilance through monitoring so that there is no decline in the environment or initiative over time (Mulford, 2008). With the abolition of the formal inclusion coordinator position, the initiative to some extent lost the deliberate, methodical tone it once had.

Small professional learning communities

One concern voiced in the literature was that larger institutions would find a content-infused approach to be unwieldy (Avramidis *et al.*, 2000). While smaller institutions have an advantage here, there are possibilities for larger universities. Faculty members in a particular program could be divided into small groups who work with an inclusion coordinator. In this instance, faculties would need to appoint multiple inclusion coordinators to work with the different groups, and schedule common and individual meeting times with those coordinators. Calkavur (2006) recommends the use of multiple small teams in implementing a change initiative, and suggests a coordinated approach for doing so which takes into account the predominant culture and issues of sustainability. It may be easier for smaller groups to become professional learning communities, sharing expertise in informal and less threatening environments (Mulford, 2008).

Regular meetings specific to the content-infusion initiative during which progress is shared with the group are necessary, and perhaps could be combined with professional development opportunities for members of faculty. Individual meetings for faculty members with the inclusion coordinator are also necessary, and should be structured in terms of reviewing the subject being taught and finding points of contact into which inclusive content can be inserted. At my university we went through our syllabi at such meetings and discussed what content could be inserted at what points in the teaching.

Curriculum decisions

The 'content' of the content-infused approach is central to success. The question needs to be asked: "What do our pre-service teachers need to know in order to be successful in an inclusive classroom?" The answer to that question will differ according to context. This task was made considerably easier for us because the Alberta Government provides all teacher preparation institutions with a list of general outcomes that teachers must meet in order to gain certification to teach in schools. In addition to that, faculty members' own knowledge of what was required to competently implement inclusion was taken into account. The exact nature of the inclusive curriculum is beyond the scope of this text, however, elaboration on these specifics can be found in the companion paper to this chapter (see Loreman, in press).

Respecting academic freedom

In a university environment it is not desirable to demand that specific content be delivered. This is another reason why the choice of the 'right person' to fill the inclusion coordinator role is so important. The inclusion coordinator, in respecting the academic freedom of the faculty member, should view their role of helping and negotiating, never as dictating. Most faculty members will want to find ways to help improve pre-service teachers' capacity to work in diverse classrooms, and in the vast majority of cases the infusion of this content will be welcome, especially where it comes with support from a coordinator with appropriate expertise.

Addressing essential areas

Although the goal of a content-infused approach is ultimately to infuse all content, the reality is that expertise in specific areas relative to inclusive education may be lacking, at least in the short-term. In this instance it might be desirable for the inclusion coordinator to address specific topics in the context of other faculty members' classes. This was a feature of our work, however, it was only short-term. In observing the inclusion coordinator, the relevant expertise was quickly developed by other faculty members, making the ongoing explicit involvement of the inclusion coordinator in this respect unnecessary.

Practical experiences

Guest speakers were one aspect of the program that were important. Pre-service teachers had the opportunity to hear about inclusion from points of view other than their professors and were able to view inclusion as a broader phenomenon. It was important to provide speakers who were positive about inclusion and who also had credibility, such as school principals, government representatives, teachers, and parents. For the same reasons, it was important to involve students in practicum experiences that were 'inclusion friendly'. New teachers tend to adopt the prevailing attitudes they encounter in schools early in their careers, and negative attitudes are difficult to change in cultures that support them. Teacher preparation institutions might consider building elements of what constitutes an inclusive environment into their criteria for selecting a practicum school. Some institutions might argue that they barely have enough willing practicum schools to meet demand, and so such a requirement might be counterproductive. To simply accept practicum schools because a quota must be filled, regardless of the standard of practice in that school, does pre-service teachers (and ultimately children) a disservice.

Engineering face-to-face contact: a dilemma

Face-to-face experiences with people with disabilities is important, and it is possible that the small amount of change evident in pre-service teachers responses on the 'sentiments' variable is the result of few opportunities to interact directly with people with disabilities (see Loreman and Earle, 2007). Forlin et al. (2001) noted an improvement in sentiments towards people with disabilities when interaction with these people was made possible. How to achieve this, however, is more or less difficult depending on context. In Canada and many other western countries, addressing the issue is not as easy as class visits to the local special school. Promoting inclusive education, while at the same time using segregated education institutions to achieve some goals, may send mixed messages to pre-service teachers. This is what we struggled with. Seemingly, the only meaningful solution relates back to practicum placements. A deliberate effort to place them in positive, inclusive environments is important, possibly in combination with increased guest speakers with disabilities throughout the program.

Making the implicit explicit

Pre-service teachers should be made explicitly aware of the content-infused approach being used. When inclusive content is being addressed in various classes, instructors should take care to point out that this is the case. This may help to allay anxieties in pre-service teachers that they are not being adequately prepared for inclusion because their program lacks the visibility of a single subject in the area. Pointing out to them where and when this content is delivered, and the administrative processes behind how this approach has come about, sends the message that inclusion is important and is a part of the normal, everyday life of a teacher.

Research informs practice

Any institution adopting a content-infused approach should consider conducting research on the efficacy of this approach. This was highly beneficial to our program and continues to inform practice. Our research included investigations of attitudes, sentiments, and concerns about inclusive education, pre-service teacher perceptions of self-efficacy, and identifying essential program outcomes for inclusion (see Loreman and Earle, 2007; Loreman, et al., 2007). Our experience was that engaging in research helped to identify points of tension and areas for improvement.

While the approach we followed was certainly imperfect, we found that a number of ingredients were germane to our success, including: leadership; engaging in small professional learning communities; deciding on appropriate curriculum; respecting academic freedom; specialist teaching of some content areas; robust practical experiences; explicit teaching of inclusive content; and researching practice.

Conclusion

This chapter has outlined the rationale behind the use of a content-infused approach to pre-service teacher preparation for inclusion and has discussed some of the advantages and challenges inherent in this approach. Suggestions for practice based on the available literature and our experience have been provided. Content-infusion of inclusive content is an effective but largely value-driven exercise still in need of greater research in a variety of contexts in order to further support the use of this promising model of teacher preparation.

References

Avramidis, E., Bayliss, P. and Burden, R. (2000) "Students teachers' attitudes towards the inclusion of children with special educational needs in the ordinary school", *Teaching and Teacher Education*, 16(3): 277–93.

Calkavur, E. (2006) "Commentary", *Reflections*, 7(2): 42–4.

Cowley, B. (2007) "Why change succeeds: An organizational self-assessment", *Organization Development Journal*, 25(2): 25–30.

Forlin, C., Jobling, A. and Carroll, A. (2001) "Preservice teachers' discomfort levels toward people with disabilities", *DISES Journal*, 4: 32–8.

Lancaster, J. and Bain A. (2007) "The design of inclusive education courses and the self-efficacy of preservice teacher education students", *International Journal of Disability, Development & Education*, 54(2): 245–56.

Leadbeater, C. (2004) *Personalisation Through Participation*, London: DEMOS.

Loreman, T. (in press) "Essential inclusive education-related outcomes for Alberta preservice teachers", *Alberta Journal of Educational Research*.

Loreman, T. and Earle, C. (2007) "The development of attitudes, sentiments, and concerns about inclusive education in a content-infused Canadian teacher preparation program", *Exceptionality Education Canada*, 17(1): 85–106.

Loreman, T., Earle, C., Sharma, U. and Forlin, C. (2007) "The development of an instrument for measuring pre-service teachers' sentiments, attitudes, and concerns about inclusive education" *International Journal of Special Education*, 22(2): 150–9.

Mulford, B. (2008) *Australian Education Review. The Leadership Challenge: Improving Learning in Schools*, Victoria, Australia: ACER Press.

Sharma, U., Forlin, C., Loreman, T. and Earle, C. (2006) "Pre-service teachers' attitudes, concerns and sentiments about inclusive education: An international comparison of the novice pre-service ", *International Journal of Special Education*, 21(2): 80–93.

Sharma, U., Forlin, C. and Loreman, T. (2008) "Impact of training on preservice teachers' attitudes and concerns about inclusive education and sentiments about persons with disabilities", *Disability & Society*, 23(7): 773–85.

Stayton, V. D. and McCollum, J. (2002). "Unifying general and special education: What does the research tell us?", *Teacher Education and Special Education*, 25(3): 211–18.

Voltz, D. L. (2003) "Collaborative infusion: An emerging approach to teacher preparation for inclusive education", *Action in Teacher Education*, 25(1): 5–13.

Woloshyn, V. and Bennett, S. (2003) "Working with students who have learning disabilities – teacher candidates speak out: Issues and concerns in preservice education and professional development", *Exceptionality Education Canada*, 13(1): 7–28.

Yerian, S. and Grossman, P. L. (1997) "Preservice teachers' perceptions of their middle level teacher education experience: A comparison of a traditional and a PDS model", *Teacher Education Quarterly*, Fall: 85–101.

Chapter 7

Inclusive professional learning schools

Federico R. Waitoller and
Elizabeth Kozleski

Learning outcomes

- Understand the role of professional learning (PL) schools and apprenticeship in preparing inclusive teachers.
- Know the importance of identity and culture in pre-service programs.

Introduction

> She is weaver, she is a creator, this Spider Woman, and she creates a web of life. It's ephemeral but enduring [...] creating themselves out of past and present, I thought. In that web that Michelle drew, everything was linked: tradition and identity, self and dreams.
>
> (Rose, 1995, pp. 365, 409)

Preparing teachers to address inclusive education has the potential to bring education equity not only for students identified with disabilities, but also for students who have been historically denied access to meaningful educational opportunities because their differences from the dominant norm are not valued. Preparing inclusive teachers, however, faces significant obstacles. Teacher education, for instance, has become an increasingly technical endeavor in which a skill-oriented curriculum is anchored by student teaching experiences that focus on the performance of these skills. Little attention is paid to the context in which teaching and learning occur so that teachers develop an understanding of the everyday cultural experiences of their students. Critical lenses are absent in most teacher education programs (Cochran-Smith *et al.*, 2004). Thus, teachers rarely have the opportunity to develop social critiques of school practices that permit critical analyses of outcomes and potentially lead to transformative changes in curriculum and instruction.

Two other obstacles inhibit the preparation of inclusive teachers. On the one hand, pre-service education programs tend to compartmentalize special and general education, creating barriers between these two fields. On the other hand, special education focuses on students' differences from a remediation perspective, resulting in teacher preparation programs that focus on skills and technical content, which overwhelm new teachers at the expense of developing critical sensibilities that question what is being done, for the benefit of whom.

In this chapter, we describe an inclusive education teacher program in development at a State University. Called the PL Initiative, it addresses the multiple issues raised in this introduction by defining inclusive education broadly, focusing on apprenticeship models of teacher learning, and addressing the identity and cultural issues that teachers must address within themselves in order to interpret and guide their students learning. In our program, pre-service teachers are placed in schools at the beginning of their program and stay in those schools throughout. Through a strong partnership, the urban professional learning schools described here offer placements to as many as 20 pre-service teachers at a time, building a community of practice around teacher learning and development that nurtures teachers and pre-service teachers simultaneously. By naming urban schools as sites for learning, the program takes the stance that it is in multicultural, multilingual schools that pre-service teachers can best take on identities as weavers of different cultures, identities, abilities, and curriculum.

In the following section, we describe PL schools and their critical role in the socialization and development of teachers. Then, we outline the theoretical and practical elements of a four-semester program organized around four themes: (a) identity, (b) culture, (c) learning, and (d) assessment.

Professional learning schools

A PL school brings together two current themes in teacher education: an apprenticeship approach to developing practitioners and professional learning communities. In an era of increased responsibility and accountability for results, all practitioners need to be socialized as career-long learners, honing their practice as students challenge them to understand more about the complex relationships between identity, culture, engagement, ability, content, context, and skill development and mastery. The best environments for realizing this are created in professional learning schools where families, children, practitioners, school leaders, and researchers work together to develop sophisticated multilayered, multidimensional approaches to learning that address and resolve some of the persistent challenges in urban schools.

Professional development school (PDS) approaches to teacher education are not new. As early as the 1980s, a variety of initiatives were established that drew their inspiration from the concept of teaching hospitals for doctor and nurse preparation (Holmes Group, 1995). From a first year of predominantly coursework and accompanying labs to multiple years of internship and residency with increasing levels of responsibility, teaching hospitals and the education of doctors holds great allure for the preparation of teachers. The PDS model has been viewed as a transformative agent for teacher education (Levine and Tachtman, 1997). Reynolds (2000) found that PDSs appear to provide a better preparation for teaching. At the end of one year of teaching, PDS graduates use more pedagogical methods and practices, are more reflective, feel better equipped to instruct ethnically and linguistically diverse student populations and are more likely to seek work in inner-city schools than their traditionally prepared peers (Cobb, 2001). A key feature of sustaining professional development school models seems to be the reciprocal relationship that university- and school-based faculties enjoy. The faculties engage joint teacher action research as well as connecting pedagogical practices with units of study for pre-service teachers and teacher practitioners. The majority of research, though, is limited almost exclusively to general education teacher preparation programs. As a result, Kozleski *et al.* suggested the following:

> When school–university partnerships and professional development schools are created, both regular and special education stakeholders must be involved. At all points in the process, including during formal contract arrangements, partnerships should include and integrate regular and special education perspectives and create an agenda of shared goals. Partnerships that connect both parties deflect the tendency to think of general and special education as occurring in segregated settings.
>
> (Kozleski *et al.*, 2003, pp. 8–9)

While PDS school approaches have proliferated, they have paralleled a similar development in the P-12 environment: schools as professional learning communities (Giles and Hargreaves, 2006). The professional learning community agenda is built on a series of assumptions around the process of change and improvement within a community. First, the change and innovation mission must be distributed throughout the organization and held by individuals in positions of both organizational and informal authority. Second, since change within organizations that provide complex sets of services to students and their families is complex, the institutional, attitudinal, technical and critical features that need to be addressed are myriad. Therefore, the change work and the change processes must be simultaneously engaged by different groups of people who converge through communication and reciprocal action.

Professional communities, then, have a culture, a shared language, a set of tools that engage data collection, analysis, interpretation and change, a process for apprenticeship, and local, specific contexts that must be navigated. When the PDS model for teacher preparation and professional learning community constructs are merged, the concept becomes a PL school where practitioners at various levels of experience, expertise, and interests come together in a common mission to improve results for children and youth. Encouraging pre-service teachers to move beyond an awareness of cultures in high needs schools to the development of habits of mind is the keystone to incorporating "an understanding of valuing of students' cultures and recognition of the need to consider those cultures in teaching practices" (Lenski *et al.*, 2005, p. 86). With an inquiry stance and sense of community, pre-service teachers are likely to feel empowered to make decisions for their students and to change the traditional cultures of teaching (Mule, 2006).

We selected three elementary schools in a local school district to work with us as PL schools. The schools were selected because of the diversity of their school population, the willingness of their faculties and school leadership to partner with university faculty, and their interest in becoming more inclusive in their practices. For each PL school, a university faculty member became a part-time member of the school. Each Thursday, university faculty work alongside the PL school faculty in classrooms, working with students, discussing practice, and building a shared understanding of inclusive education. Pre-service teachers who have enrolled in a graduate program to earn their license and teaching credentials in both general and special education apprentice in these PL schools from the first semester of their program. Each semester, the curriculum is organized around a key theme. The themes reflect the program's core principles for teacher practice: (a) identity, (b) culture, (c) learning, and (d) assessment. As pre-service teachers move through the program they develop a set of portfolio products that reflect their development in each of these areas. Because of the length limitations of this chapter, we will focus on teacher identity, describing briefly the three remaining themes.

Identity and teaching

Pre-service teachers need to understand how to provide opportunities for all children to learn and develop in ways that are healthy, respectful, supportive and challenging. As educators, they must develop an appreciation of the cultural histories and traditions that they bring with them to teaching and become conscious of the values and beliefs that filter their understanding and inform their teaching. In our program, we expect pre-service teachers to engage in an ongoing enterprise that will reshape pre-service teachers' normative assumptions about social, cultural, and intellectual capital. Through identity projects, pre-service teachers come to view themselves as actors in a reciprocal dance in which they influence and are influenced by the social reality found in urban settings. Conscious of ongoing identity development, pre-service teachers learn to scaffold instruction by webbing the everyday cultures of their students and families and the structures of formal curriculum. To do this requires understanding of developmentally effective approaches to teaching and learning that is informed by the structure of academic disciplines and the cultural contexts of their students.

The PL Initiative is interested in teacher identity as the "imagining of self in worlds of action, as social products; indeed, we begin with the premise that identity is constructed in and through activity" (Holland *et al.*, 1998, p. 5). Thus, teacher identity must be conceptualized as the work of apprenticeship. Teacher identities are neither located in the teacher nor determined by the social context. Rather identity is constantly negotiated through the activities in which pre-service teachers participate with other community members (e.g. students, parents, other colleagues). How pre-service teachers construct their identity is also shaped by what they bring to school, by how they interpret their role in the school, and what they see as the purpose of education and how they fit within this purpose.

Most policy documents and most teacher programs describe teacher development as no more than acquiring a set of skills and technicalities. From an identity perspective, however, it means to transform oneself, mediating ideals to the realities of institutional contexts, and deciding how to participate in classroom activities (Carter and Doyle, 1996). Learning skills is necessary but not sufficient to prepare teachers for developed learning environments where all differences are considered assets for learning.

The importance of identity work is that pre-service teachers learn in the present by drawing from the past and by imagining the future, creating new tools for future situations (Stard and Prusak, 2005). Thus, teachers act according to their imaginary worlds (Holland *et al.*, 1998). Teacher identities are revealed constantly in the positions and actions that teachers adopt in their daily life. Teachers' histories of experiences in similar situations, that is, their biographies, inform their expectations and actions about what can be said, who can say it, and their engagement in particular contexts. These expectations are, however, negotiated in teachers' daily practices. So, pre-service teachers' engagement in activities and discourses shapes their expectations of what it means to be an expert, and mediates how they see themselves and others.

Inclusive settings are complex contexts. Creating learning environments that provide robust education for students regardless of ability, ethnicity, gender, language, and socioeconomic status, demands a deep understanding of how teachers' biographies inform practice. Through their own biographies teachers internalize normative assumptions about difference. These assumptions undergird how teachers facilitate and constrain learning for students based on their differences. Bringing these assumptions about differences to the surface creates spaces where they can be contested and new inclusive assumptions can develop.

Learning implies becoming a different person and constructing a different identity. Teachers and students, in this way, will develop identities as learners together. When teacher identity is co-constructed with students, we may "consider teacher and student learning as two sides of the same coin" (Kelly, 2006, p. 516). There is a distinction between learning to teach and becoming a teacher (Kelly, 2006). We can understand becoming a teacher as an identity-formation process where the individual and the context surrounding them writes another page of the subjects' biography. Teachers must search out how multiple interpretations of social experience come to become part of one's identity. This is a self-empowering enterprise.

This PL school program provides experiences that support the development of robust, collaborative, and inclusive teacher identities. This is achieved by extensive and ongoing experience in inclusive classrooms and by collaborating with peers in communities of practice. Pre-service teachers focus on specific aspects of their own biographies in the first semester of their program as they concurrently build a biography of one of their students. They compare and contrast their biographies in weekly seminars, deepening their understanding of how action and reaction in the classroom is anchored by these biographies. As the semester develops, they learn to contest these identity constructions so that they can develop the concept maps and heuristics that they will need to continue to contest their own biases as they teach their students to do the same thing.

The PL school program sees everyday experiences in the classroom as a part of teachers' identity construction work; how they experience the world, how they interpret and give meaning to practice within the complex contexts of inclusive settings. In the same way that social contexts elicit certain kinds of knowledge, they also elicit certain kinds of identities (Kelly, 2006). Extensive experience working in partnering inclusive schools will create spaces for developing inclusive identities in which pre-service teachers will develop a sense of responsibility and ownership for all the students in the school, and not only for a specific grade or ability level.

The contrasting biographies are part of a series of Performance Based Assessments (PBA) that correspond to the Urban PL school outcome standards, content knowledge, and concurrent practice in the series of semester-long internships. These PBAs constitute an assessment system that assesses developing knowledge based on seminars, online learning, ongoing discussions as well as performance in schools. As pre-service teachers progress through the program, they engage specific PBAs and are guided and supported in accomplishing those assessments each semester. The PBAs are designed so that pre-service teachers can demonstrate learning around the four themes that ground the program.

Cultures in the classroom: in, of, and co-constructed

Inclusive classrooms by nature are sites where multiple cultures merge. This involves many different ways of learning, participating, communicating, and many different cognitive and material tools to solve problems. The cultural work of classrooms, though, tends to be informed by the dominant culture of the surrounding community. Thus, pre-service teachers need to understand the cultural work that occurs in schooling so that it can be transformed into an inclusive culture. The PL school initiative prepares pre-service teachers to weave difference through designing cultural responsive learning environments and collaborating with diverse families.

Therefore, PL schools are constructed as sites of cultural confluence in which the cultures that students, families, teachers, and administrators bring with them to school interact with the culture of schooling. In this semester of their program, pre-service teachers explore the cultural work of teaching and learning through observation, lesson study, focus groups with students, and tutoring sessions with individual students. They become weavers of different cultures, identities and abilities, languages and school activities. They move beyond cultural transmission models into new frontiers of cultural modeling (Lee, 2007) in which what students know and bring to school becomes the anchor for specific subject-matter learning.

Learning in and for education practice

With the foundation provided in their first two semesters, pre-service teachers focus their attention on how learning is orchestrated in classrooms in their third semester. They learn to create and sustain a learning environment that fosters positive social interaction, active engagement in learning, and self-motivation. As they accumulate experience teaching, they master the skills needed to link new concepts to a variety of prior experiences and cultural backgrounds.

The PL school initiative works with clinical teachers to ensure that they teach their pre-service teachers why and how to teach. Pre-service teachers co-teach with their clinical teachers. When a lesson is completed, the teaching pair deconstructs the experience. The pair can select from a set of heuristics that guide them through discussions. For example, one heuristic requires each member of the pair to assess their own teaching pace. They connect pace to student engagement and must use evidence from the lesson to justify their rating. First, the co-teachers discuss their own assessments, and then they assess one another. In doing so, the pre-service teachers learn how to be mindful of their own teaching and its impact on how students participate in a lesson. A variety of these heuristics scaffold reflection and use of evidence.

Assessment

In the USA, many assessment tools are built on the idea of a sequence of developmental skills. Knowledge structures are mapped based on specific cultural standards (Moss *et al.*, 2006). We use that same set of norms to distinguish performances of children who may have been enculturated into patterns of behavior far different from the ones that are familiar to mainstream US educators and psychologists. In fundamental ways, then, we might say that assessment tools are proxies for cultural capital. They shape educators' understanding about what learning is, what knowledge is valuable to have, and identify who is actively engaged in learning specific kinds of information (Moss *et al.*, 2006). As Sternberg and Grigorenko (2004) recently observed, "intelligence considered outside its cultural context, is in large measure a mythological construct" (p. 1428).

Yet, it is almost impossible to work with students without assessing. Because of the critical role that assessment plays in learning and the complexities associated with formative, summative, and diagnostic assessment, the program is structured to focus on assessment last, once pre-service teachers have found their grounding in the classroom and are better able to observe thoughtfully and use a variety of tools for assessing learner needs. Given the complexity of the assessment arena, pre-service teachers must produce a variety of products that range from micro-assessments of students in action working on a specific classroom task to at least two comprehensive child studies that demonstrate their skill in using a variety of a tools, assembling a variety of evidence, interpreting that information in ways that can guide the organization of the classroom structures and learning approaches to accommodate individual student needs.

Conclusion

In this chapter we have described an initial teacher education (ITE) program that grounds teacher learning in an apprenticeship model, that scaffolds teacher development through identity, culture, learning, and assessment so that a graduate of the program is able to design learning environments that account for the development of a learning community while acknowledging the cultural histories, intellectual experiences and psychological characteristics of each learner in that community. In doing so, we create the possibility that teachers can create inclusive education experiences that find common ground for each unique constellation of students and support their learning trajectories.

The work is complex and difficult since our approach to learning conflicts with the rigid ways that schools create and deliver curriculum. Creating professional learning schools requires that university and school faculties learn together to transform common practice into inclusive approaches to teaching and learning. We remain a work in progress, collecting evidence from our experiences to match our vision with a new reality for teacher learning.

References

Carter, K. and Doyle, W. (1996) "Personal narrative and life history in learning to teach", in J. Sikula, T. J. Buttery and E. Guyton (eds), *Handbook of Research on Teacher Education*, 2nd edn, New York: Macmillan, pp. 120–42.

Cobb, J. B. (2001) "Graduates of professional development school programs: Perceptions of the teacher as change agent", *Teacher Education Quarterly*, 28: 89–107.

Cochran-Smith, M., Davis, D. and Fries, K. (2004) "Multicultural teacher education: Research, Practice, and Policy", in J. Banks and C. Banks (eds), *Handbook of Research on Multicultural Education*, 2nd edn, San Francisco, CA: Jossey-Bass pp. 931–77.

Giles, C. and Hargreaves, A. (2006) "The sustainability of innovative schools as learning organizations and professional learning communities during standardized reform", *Educational Administration Quarterly*, 42(1): 124–56.

Holland, D., Lachicotte, W., Skinner, D. and Cain, C. (1998) *Identity and Agency in Cultural Worlds*, Cambridge: Harvard University Press.

Holmes Group (1995) *Tomorrow's Schools of Education*, East Lansing, MI: Holmes Group.

Kelly, P. (2006) "What is teacher learning? A sociocultural perspective", *Oxford Review of Education,* 32(4): 505–19.

Kozleski, E. B., Gamm, S. and Radner, B. (2003) "Looking for answers in all the right places: Urban schools and universities solve the dilemma of teacher preparation together", *Journal of Special Education Administration*, 16: 41–51.

Lee, C. D. (2007) *Culture, Literacy, and Learning*, New York: Teachers College Press.

Lenski, S. D., Crumpler, T. P., Stallworth, C. and Crawford, K. M. (2005) "Beyond awareness: Preparing culturally responsive preservice teachers", *Teacher Education Quarterly*, 32(2): 85–100.

Levine, M. and Tachtman, R. (1997) *Making Professional Development Schools Work: Politics, Practice and Policy*, New York: Teachers College Press.

Moss, P. S., Girard, B. J., Haniford, L. C., Mislevy, R. J. and Palinscar, A. S. (2006) "Validity in educational assessment", *Review of Research in Education*, 30: 109–62.

Mule, L. (2006) "Preservice teachers' inquiry in a professional development school context: Implications for the practicum", *Teaching and Teacher Education,* 205–18.

Reynolds, A. (2000) NEA Teacher Education Initiative seven-site replication study of teacher preparation: Year four cross-site and cross-year/cross-site. Technical Report. Unpublished report submitted to the National Center for Innovation, National Education Association.

Rose, M. (1995) *Possible Lives: The Promise of Public Education in America*, New York: Houghton Mifflin.

Stard, A. and Prusak, A. (2005) "Telling identities: In search of an analytical tool for investigating learning as a culturally shaped activity", *Educational Researcher*, 34(4): 14–22.

Sternberg, R. J. and Grigorenko, E. L. (2004) "Intelligence and culture: How culture shapes what intelligence means, and the implications for a science of well being", *The Royal Society*, 359: 1427–34

Chapter 8

Initial teacher education and inclusion

A triad of inclusive experiences

Dianne Chambers and Chris Forlin

Learning outcomes

- Describe attitudinal theory as it relates to pre-service teachers and inclusive education.
- Discuss the importance of addressing beliefs and attitudes towards inclusive education in an initial teacher education (ITE) program.
- Outline a range of experiences that can be undertaken to allow pre-service teachers to examine beliefs and attitudes towards inclusive education.
- Integrate a Triad of Inclusive Experiences program into ITE.

Introduction

One of the barriers to inclusive education identified by many researchers is a negative attitude of teachers towards the inclusion of students with special education needs (SEN) in a regular classroom (Mintz, 2007). The attitudes of society have a great bearing on the opportunities and experiences of people with disabilities (Bradshaw and Mundia, 2005). An appropriate time to address these attitudes for teachers is during their ITE course. This chapter reports the development of a Triad of Inclusive Experiences (TIE) program to promote positive attitudes and beliefs held by pre-service teachers about people with disabilities.

Attitudes towards inclusive education

Attitudinal theory describes the interrelatedness between beliefs, attitudes, intentions and behaviours as they relate to an object (Fishbein and Ajzen, 1972). In the case of inclusive education, the attitude towards inclusion which involves students with disabilities being educated alongside peers in regular classrooms is often what is under investigation. An attitude is a learned, evaluative response about an object or an issue, and is a cumulative result of personal beliefs. Beliefs are seen as influencing the attitudes that pre-service teachers hold in regards to inclusive education, which in turn influences intentions and behaviour. It is, therefore, important that initial teacher educators address the beliefs of their students if they wish to ensure positive attitudes towards inclusion.

The attitude theory most of interest in this case is that of expectancy-value (Fishbein and Ajzen, 1972). This theory contends that a person's attitude towards an object (in this case inclusive education) is a function of their beliefs about it and the evaluative aspects of those beliefs (evaluation of the characteristics and qualities). This theory allows us to anticipate that a change can be brought about in attitude through examination and change of beliefs and the evaluative aspects of those beliefs and through this, a change in behaviour.

Pre-service teachers interact with their own belief system in order to form consistent attitudes towards inclusive education. Attitudes are generally not 'fixed' and can be moderated through interaction with people with disabilities and further understanding of the factors surrounding inclusion, such as support of administration, attitude of teaching staff and parental interaction with the school (Richards and Clough, 2004). Once firmly established, though, negative attitudes to inclusive education can be difficult to change.

It is critical that pre-service teachers are exposed to a variety of learners with diverse learning needs to ensure that they have a full grasp of the scope of teaching requirements in the classroom (Forlin, 2008). Structured and unstructured opportunities, followed by opportunities to reflect upon these experiences, are noted as being worthwhile ways to address attitudes towards inclusion (Brownlee and Carrington, 2000).

Developing positive attitudes towards inclusive education

One approach to strengthen existing positive beliefs and address negative and possibly erroneous beliefs about people with disabilities is to ensure that pre-service teachers have suitable experiences with people with disabilities (Golder *et al.*, 2005). It is posited that this in turn will lead to a change in attitude towards the concept of the inclusion of students with disabilities in regular classrooms. Many pre-service teachers have had little or no previous contact with learners with disabilities, yet they are training to teach in increasingly diverse, regular classrooms. Research has shown that this lack of direct contact and experience can create feelings of inadequacy (Forlin, 2001).

In 2002, a forum with 36 key stakeholders (parents, teachers, community members, advocacy groups, tertiary staff, and teachers) was held in Western Australia to identify key competencies required for teachers to work in and foster inclusive school communities. One of the major outcomes of this forum was the suggestion that positive teacher attitudes and respect for others facilitates inclusion and that these could be achieved through stronger links between universities and the community.

The Triad of Inclusive Experiences program

To address the need for pre-service teachers to engage in authentic experiences with people with disabilities, the authors have, over several years, developed the TIE program (Figure 8.1). The TIE program consists of three approaches to enable pre-service teachers to gain invaluable experiences alongside people with disabilities. Aspects of this program have been implemented successfully in three different universities and have been refined and enhanced following each offering.

The TIE program was originally inspired by the idea of having community members and tertiary educators working together to find better ways to educate pre-service teachers. The program aims to 'tie' together the theory learned at university with the practice gained in the field through positive interactions with people with a range of diverse needs. The program attends to the importance of attitude change as an outcome; to the adoption of personal interactions as a pedagogy to stimulate change; and to the active involvement of people with disabilities and their families and carers in leadership and advocacy roles in the provision of learning experiences in collaboration with the university.

Throughout the TIE program people with disabilities are involved with pre-service teachers in a range of mutually beneficial activities. This has had an extremely positive impact. The very large number of agencies engaged has affirmed the success of this program. Evidence demonstrates that the TIE program is achieving valuable outcomes. The project is a positive example

Figure 8.1 The interactive nature of the Triad of Inclusive Experience

of a 'win–win' education initiative where all members of our 'community' benefit.

TIE I: Community involvement

The first of the TIE to be developed involved pre-service teachers undertaking a community placement to interact and work with people with disabilities. The placements took a number of different forms, being recreational and social in nature. This ensured that the pre-service teachers did not necessarily assume the role of caregiver or teacher, but rather the role of companion in a more equal relationship (Richards and Clough, 2004). The social focus allows pre-service teachers to view people with disabilities as people with their own interests and goals. It also promotes understanding of the difficulties faced by them and the means they have to overcome these on a daily basis. This can then be translated into potential classroom practice during feedback sessions held with the pre-service teachers.

For TIE 1 pre-service teachers must undertake a minimum of 12 hours of volunteer interactions with a person/people with a disability over a semester, which can be configured in a number of ways. For example, they may complete an hour a week for 12 weeks, two hours a week for 6 weeks, or a weekend camp. This amount of time was selected as it is sufficient to allow interaction with the person with a disability; is not overly taxing on the pre-service teachers; and can be accommodated within the semester time period. Figure 8.2 details the process that is followed for the program.

Pre-service teachers are given links to possible community organisations. They then liaise independently with the organisations to secure a placement. Some of the placements include Riding for the Disabled; recreational activities, such as bowling, shopping, and going to the movies; support for people with disabilities who wish to become volunteers in the community (Take 2 Program, Volunteering WA); and KidsCamps, for children with disabilities. It is important that good collaborative partnerships be established with organisations in the local area.

In addition to in-class discussion, the pre-service teachers are required to construct a written report or poster based on their experiences. These consist of an examination of the environment of the placements, modifications within those settings to allow the person with a disability to access the setting, links

Figure 8.2 The process for the Community Involvement Program

to literature on inclusion and a reflection on changes in their own beliefs and attitudes in regards to the inclusion of children with disabilities in regular school settings.

TIE 2: Incursion

The second of the TIE programs is an incursion which enables senior students (aged from 15 to 18 years) from local Education Support Centres or schools, which teach students with mild to moderate support needs, to experience a day in the life of a university student (see Figure 8.3). Each incursion usually involves 16–25 students from a centre and a complete year group of pre-service teachers (numbers have ranged from 35 to 255). The students visit the university campus and spend a day alongside pre-service teachers.

For most of these young adults with disabilities it is their first visit to a university campus and it opens up a new world of potential opportunities for them. They improve their social and community access skills and receive formal recognition for their involvement in the program. Similarly, this is an excellent opportunity for pre-service teachers to meet with students requiring additional support, during a positive experience. This contributes enormously to breaking down potential barriers and gives a better understanding of the education, social and emotional needs of students with disabilities. It also

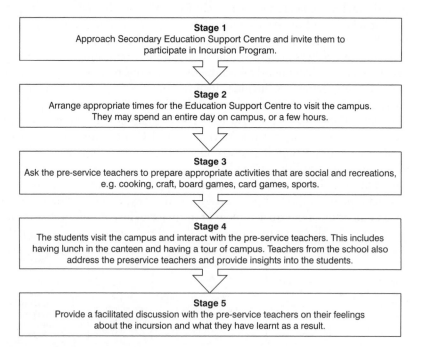

Figure 8.3 The process for an Incursion Program

allows them an opportunity to gain confidence and to overcome feelings of discomfort when interacting with people with disabilities. This program can be instigated at the same time as the community involvement (TIE 1) as it offers a different experience.

TIE 3: Authentic inquiry

The third of the TIE programs is the authentic inquiry activity. This program emerged as an outcome of the previous two aspects and as a result of the challenges being faced in implementing the community involvement program and incursion in culturally different contexts. This program provides a different experience that focuses on developing a more empathetic approach towards people with disabilities in order to foster a positive perspective about inclusive education.

Pre-service teachers working in groups of five or six set out to investigate an issue that they identify for people with disabilities in the local community (see Figure 8.4). Such investigations involve a range of issues including access to public transport and community facilities such as libraries, swimming pools, cinemas, and shopping centres. Some pre-service teachers choose to explore what support is provided by community agencies such as the Dyslexia Association, Autism Society, or the Society for the Blind. Others investigate the school options available for students with different types of disabilities including physical, vision and hearing impairments.

During their inquiry some groups choose to become 'disabled' for a day by being in a wheelchair, or blind or deaf; or to partner a person with a disability as they access the community. Throughout their investigation, while noting access and support issues, they also carefully monitor community attitudes towards people with a disability. The hidden-camera approach has enabled them to reflect in-depth on community responses to those with disabilities and to review their own values, beliefs and attitudes. A presentation to the tutorial group is given to share this information with peers.

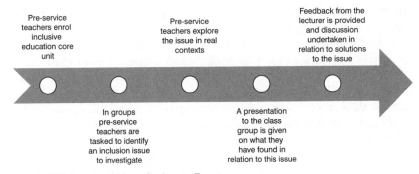

Figure 8.4 The process for an Authentic Enquiry

Evaluation of the TIE program

An integral part of the development of beliefs and attitudes towards people with disabilities is discussion of the positive and negative experiences of the TIE program participants (Turner, 2003). Changes in sentiments, attitudes and concerns about inclusion are recorded using the SACIE scale (Loreman *et al.*, 2007). Discussion that is facilitated by experienced lecturers within tutorial sessions assists in linking theory to practice (Fresko and Wertheim, 2006; Turner, 2003). Throughout engagement in any of the three elements of the TIE program, the pre-service teachers have the opportunity to describe and question their own feelings and understandings about people with disability. These sessions have resulted in some very emotive responses and personal revelations from the groups. Ongoing review of the community involvement (TIE 1) and incursion programs (TIE 2) involves all pre-service teachers, university staff, community members and participating schools being invited to reflect on their participation. This review process has resulted in changes being made to the programs.

Formal evaluation of the community involvement program is undertaken at the beginning and end of each unit of study. In addition, on completion of TIE 1, semi-structured small focus group interviews are held with participants. In 2008, pre-service teachers were overwhelmingly positive about their experiences with people with disabilities and the value of the inclusion experience for them personally. Some of their comments related to the relationships experienced: "[I learnt] a lot about getting over fear of what you might be asked to do, how to treat people with disabilities, not being afraid and understanding that you build a relationship with them". Some interesting discussion was also evident in regards to inclusion:

> I could actually see the kids interact with each other, mainstream and people with special needs, they actually learn off each other. And I thought that was a great gain for both and so I think inclusion would be a good idea.

Agencies taking part in the program are surveyed annually about their satisfaction with the volunteer assistance and overall experience of the program. As the program is constantly reviewed and changes made where appropriate, the nature of the placements also changes. For example, in the 2008 round of the program, pre-service teachers were also able to attend schools with students with disabilities as an option to community placement and assist them in recreational and social activities. This change was made as a result of feedback from pre-service teachers in previous cohorts.

Over the five years since this program was first offered in 2003, participants have provided many positive comments about their involvement. For example, "It was a real eye opener ... We need even more chances to put the theory into practice". A particularly revealing comment came from a participant who said that this is "Something that should be continued and perhaps backed up with another visit, with more difficult to deal with students".

The incursion program (TIE 2) was similarly reviewed on completion using written feedback and focus group interviews. While pre-service teachers were very anxious prior to the session, these anxieties were quickly alleviated when they realised that the students were more capable than they were expecting. In addition, pre-service teachers interviewed willing students from the schools who participated in the incursion. Although their responses were very limited, it was clear they had thoroughly enjoyed being a university student for a day.

The authentic inquiry activity (TIE 3) is reviewed by a critical analysis of the class presentations undertaken by the pre-service groups, together with focus group interviews and written feedback. As part of the presentation on the inquiry they are asked to provide a reflection on their involvement in the program in consideration of changes in their beliefs, values and attitudes. These are also recorded on a brief handout distributed to the class following a group presentation on their experiences.

Challenges and resolutions

While the TIE has proven to be a very exciting and motivating program, implementation of the different elements of the program have led to some challenges which the authors have had to resolve along their journey (Table 8.1). Taking on such an intensive program has not been easy, indeed it has been very time consuming, challenging and at times fraught with some very difficult issues to overcome. The rewards, though, have more than adequately compensated these efforts. With demonstrated positive attitude change and beliefs among pre-service teachers, which are unlikely to have been achieved through merely a lecture approach, they are considerably more focused and enthusiastic about inclusion as the way forward.

Conclusion

People with disabilities face great challenges in engaging in the full range of life opportunities, in achieving their potential for active, independent and fulfilling lives, and in contributing positively to society through their skills, talents and many abilities. Much of the discrimination and prejudice they encounter comes from the broader community's fear of the unknown, which arises from limited contact and a general lack of knowledge and understanding. The TIE program is underpinned by the belief that education plays a pivotal role in positively changing societal attitudes; that teachers are at the forefront of this process; and that teacher educators must, therefore,

Table 8.1 Challenges and resolutions when implementing the TIE program.

Challenges faced implementing the TIE	Resolutions and changes to the TIE
Ensuring that all pre-service teachers are adequately covered by insurance.	A copy of the university insurance cover had to be provided to all community groups with whom pre-service teachers were participating.
To ensure the timing of the programs coincides with pre-service teachers' timetables and study in other units.	Early planning and liaison with other faculty was essential when organising on campus whole-day incursions.
To make certain that all pre-service teachers have high and acceptable standards of ethics.	Clear expectations have to be communicated to all pre-service teachers in both written and verbal form (e.g. confidentiality, punctuality, respecting privacy, behaviour, dress code, language, etc).
That pre-service teachers have sufficient knowledge of people with disabilities if starting the TIE in the beginning of their course of study.	This continues to be an issue which is yet to be resolved.

ensure that they instill in pre-service teachers an appropriate inclusive attitude before they embark on their teaching careers.

The outcomes of the TIE program have been multifaceted for all concerned. Involvement in the TIE program has affirmed the rights, needs, potential and positive contribution of people with disabilities, their families, carers and supporting organisations. It has enriched life and education experiences and outcomes for people with disabilities, their families and carers, through engagement with the university community. As the pre-service teachers' beliefs and attitudes are challenged and modified, their intentions and behaviours relating to inclusive education also change (Ajzen, 2001). For our pre-service teachers it has led to dramatic improvements in their skills, knowledge and attitudes about inclusive education. They have learned to develop empathy with people with different needs and abilities and have demonstrated a more positive attitude towards inclusion and their role as new teachers in enabling this. For the universities involved there has been a noticeable increase in the presence of people with disabilities in the daily life of the university, helping to develop the university as a more inclusive environment. It has also raised the awareness of other teacher educators on campus about the need to consider their own discipline area and identify ways of modifying the curricula during ITE to prepare teachers for including students with a wide range of diverse learning needs in their classes.

It is clear, from the pre-service teacher feedback that involvement in the TIE program has resulted in a change of philosophy about inclusion. This includes more positive beliefs and values regarding catering for diverse classrooms and in them being better prepared to teach in diverse classrooms.

Campbell *et al.* (2003) note that the most effective way of changing societal attitudes in a favourable direction is "to combine formal instruction with structured and direct contact with people with special needs" (p. 371). Based on the feedback from the pre-service teachers and the community members who have been engaged in the TIE program it would seem to be heading in the right direction.

References

Ajzen, I. (2001) "Nature and operation of attitudes", *Annual Review of Psychology,* 52: 27–58.

Bradshaw, L. and Mundia, L. (2005) "Understanding preservice teachers' construct of disability: A metacognitive process", *Disability & Society,* 20(5): 563–74.

Brownlee, J. and Carrington, S. (2000) "Opportunities for authentic experience and reflection: A teaching program designed to change attitudes towards disability for preservice teachers", *Support for Learning,* 15(3): 99–104.

Campbell, J., Gilmore, L. and Cuskelly, M. (2003) "Changing student teachers' attitudes towards disability and inclusion", *Journal of Intellectual and Developmental Disability,* 28(4): 369–79.

Fishbein, M. and Ajzen, I. (1972) "Attitudes and opinions", *Annual Review of Psychology,* 23: 188–544.

Forlin, C. (2001) "Inclusion: Identifying potential stressors for regular class teachers", *Educational Research,* 43(3): 235–45.

Forlin, C. (2008) "Education reform for inclusion in Asia: What about teacher education", in C. Forlin and M.-G. J. Lian (eds), *Reform, Inclusion & Teacher Education: Towards a New Era of Special Education in the Asia-Pacific Region,* Abingdon: Routledge, pp. 74–82.

Fresko, B. and Wertheim, C. (2006) "Learning by mentoring: Prospective teachers as mentors to children at risk", *Mentoring and Tutoring,* 14(2): 149–61.

Golder, G., Norwich, B. and Bayliss, P. (2005) "Preparing teachers to teach pupils with special educational needs in more inclusive schools: Evaluating a PGCE development", *British Journal of Special Education,* 32(2): 92–9.

Loreman, T., Earle, C., Sharma, U. and Forlin, C. (2007) "The development of an instrument for measuring preservice teachers' sentiments, attitudes and concerns about inclusive education", *International Journal of Special Education,* 22(2): 150–9.

Mintz, J. (2007) "Attitudes of primary initial teacher training students to special educational needs and inclusion", *Support for Learning,* 22(1): 3–8.

Richards, G. and Clough, P. (2004) "ITE students' attitudes to inclusion", *Research in Education,* 72: 77–86.

Turner, N. D. (2003) "Preparing preservice teachers for inclusion in secondary classrooms", *Education,* 123(3): 491–5.

Chapter 9

Fostering empathy and understanding

A longitudinal case study pedagogy

Kate Scorgie

Learning outcomes

- Describe cognitive, affective and behavioral components of empathy and the importance of empathy training in initial teacher education (ITE) programs.
- Describe benefits of longitudinal participative case study pedagogy for fostering empathy in pre-service professionals.
- Implement a training exercise for pre-service teachers using participative case study pedagogy.

Introduction

This chapter presents a course component designed to enhance pre-service teachers' understanding of and empathy toward parents of children with disabilities and engender support for inclusion and collaboration. Pre-service teachers were given the opportunity to "walk a mile in a parent's shoes" by becoming the parent of a virtual child with a disability. Activities across eight sessions, spanning birth through early adolescence, required them to reflect on a variety of situations from the point of view of a parent of a child with a disability. Journal entries reflected increased empathy for parents and transformed perspectives of inclusion and collaboration.

> It gets so hard when you're forced to go back to the school and beg for services year after year. But, let me tell you what I wish. I wish that for just one day, Brian's teachers could understand life from my perspective ... I wish that just once, they could see him through my heart.
>
> (Mother of a son with autism)

The ability to place oneself in the shoes of another and understand how the other views the world is the essence of empathy (Slote, 2007). Empathy has been defined as the capacity to experience the thoughts and feelings of another in a way that engenders a response or action of beneficence toward the other (Eisenberg, 2002). According to this definition, empathy incorporates three attributes: (a) the ability to understand the worldview or perspective of another, a cognitive attribute; (b) the capacity to experience a feeling that is congruent with what another is feeling, an affective attribute; and (c) a choice to respond in a manner concordant with the welfare of the other, a behavioral attribute.

Empathy is enhanced when people perceive similarities between themselves and others. The perception of a shared, though not necessarily identical, experience provides the common ground upon which mutual understanding can be cultivated and empathy fostered. Levy *et al.* (2002) found that people who relate to others on broad, abstract terms tend to demonstrate greater empathy than those who hold concrete distinctions between themselves and others. Therefore, a person who affirms, "We are both parents" would be more likely to display greater empathic understanding of a parent of a child with disability than a person who states, "I am the parent of a typical child, but she is the parent of a child with Down syndrome".

The fields of psychology, social work, and the health care professions have specifically targeted empathy training as an essential component of practitioner preparation programs. To date, there has not been the same emphasis on empathy in ITE programs. When educators are unable to comprehend the perspective of another and when they are unable to understand how another thinks or feels, whether parent or child, they risk taking actions that disregard, devalue, or disallow the experience and needs of the other.

Many parents of children with disabilities decry the lack of empathetic understanding on the part of professionals. Green (2007) stated "parents of children with disabilities must raise their children within the context of powerful societal discourse that devalues adults with disabilities and, therefore, holds low expectations for the ultimate 'success' of parenting children with disabilities" (p. 151). Because of this, many parents of children with disabilities question whether they and their children are considered valued members of their communities, including schools.

Educators, as a whole, have reported feeling inadequately prepared to serve children with special needs and their families (Sharma *et al.*, 2006). Initial teacher education programs, therefore, need to employ curricula and pedagogy that foster greater understanding of the experiences of families of children with disabilities. In addition, pre-service teachers need to become aware of ways in which cultural differences may cloud their perception of the experiences and needs of diverse families (Wilgosh and Scorgie, 2006).

Context for the program

For the past several years I have been teaching a course on collaboration to pre-service teachers and counselors. The first year I taught the course, I was both surprised and troubled by the unfavorable, at times even hostile, attitudes many of my students held toward parents of children with special needs. They felt that these parents wanted teachers to "fix their child" and were ready to "drag them off to court" whenever they considered the schools failed to meet their "unrealistic demands." What left me most dismayed, however, was that after weeks of lectures, readings and classroom discussions about collaboration, students left class clinging to their original assumptions.

During the second and third years, I made several changes to the course content. I invited parents of children with disabilities to come to class and share their stories and I included articles and books written by parents as required course readings. While these changes served to elicit greater sympathy toward parents and their plight, an unhealthy distrust of parents often remained.

Through my own research with parents of children with disabilities (Scorgie and Wilgosh, 2008), I was keenly aware of the pain parents felt when they experienced difficult encounters with professionals. I found myself searching for a strategy to use with my pre-service teachers that would challenge their misconceptions and foster understanding of and empathy toward parents of children with disabilities. It was when I looked beyond my own discipline that I found a pedagogy that served my purpose.

Participative case study pedagogy

The training of health care and mental health professionals has historically utilized analytical clinical teaching practices that result in the objectification of a patient. In recent years, however, authentic case studies have been incorporated in training programs to provide pre-service professionals a more holistic and integrative understanding of their patients. Bleakley (2005) distinguished between the traditional, analytical case study, in which the case serves as an abstract specimen to be examined from a detached, objective perspective, and a more interactive case study approach situated in narrative pedagogy in which students are invited to enter empathically into a narrative account and think, not just about a patient, but "along with" the patient (p. 535). Use of participative cases allows pre-service professionals the opportunity to enter a "virtual laboratory" of human experience, where they can reflect on an event from a variety of perspectives, explore diverse constructions of meaning, and engage in solution-building that incorporates multiple frames of reference.

Kennedy (2001) found that role-playing exercises facilitated empathy in medical students who were required to assume the part of a patient within a simulated clinical setting. Similarly, Erera (1997) reported that social work students who were required to analyze audiotaped interviews with clients demonstrated greater empathic understanding of the client when they were instructed to place themselves in the client's mental framework as they listened to the interview. They were also able to generate more accurate alternate hypotheses regarding the client's situation than those who had listened to the audio tape in a more objective, clinical manner.

Participative case studies are effective tools for facilitating empathy for a number of reasons. First of all, participative cases allow one to assume vicariously the experience of another (Gallucci, 2006). Students are invited to enter into the case, to join with, or even become the case subject. Empathy is enhanced when trainees perceive similarities between the case study and actual life situations. Secondly, case studies can incorporate questions that are precisely worded to challenge assumptions and guide reflection. Thirdly, emotions and feelings can be explored through self-reflective journaling (Guiffrida, 2005). Fourthly, group processing and dialogue provide encounters with alternative perspectives which can challenge existing assumptions and allow imaginative investigation of alternate points of view. Finally, participative cases can include an outcome component in which participants propose a hypothetical course of action reflective of a philosophical perspective, such as care or justice, thus linking theory and practice (Gallucci, 2006).

Participative case studies allow a person to understand the perspective of another, to feel what another is feeling, and to respond in a manner that achieves mutual benefit. When used in ITE programs, participative case study pedagogy can enhance understanding of and empathy toward others, and create opportunities to explore innovative reform.

The Family Collaboration Portfolio Project

The Family Collaboration Portfolio Project (FCPP) was a nine-week interactive course component containing 32 activities that fall into four categories: longitudinal participative case study exercises, role-playing scenarios, reflective readings, and utilization of community and informational resources. The purpose of the participative case study component was to enable pre-service teachers to become the parent of a virtual child with a disability. The case studies, which were based on narrative interviews conducted with parents of children with disability (cf. Scorgie and Wilgosh, 2008) presented pre-service teachers with a disorienting dilemma (i.e., diagnosis of disability in a virtual child), and provided them opportunity to reflect, journal thoughts and feelings, engage in group problem solving, and plan a course of action for their child. Sixteen distinct longitudinal case study streams were developed and included diagnoses such as autism, Down syndrome, deafness, behavior disorder, cerebral palsy, spina bifida, seizure disorder, severe developmental delay and intellectual delay. Each pre-service teacher, therefore, parented a unique case study child across a developmental sequence from birth and diagnosis, through adolescence. While the other components of the FCPP were scored on a ten-point scale, case study entries were typically scored as either submitted or not submitted.

Activity 1: The first case study activity required pre-service teachers to imagine that they were expectant parents of a child to be born in a week's time. They were instructed to write a letter to their unborn child outlining their hopes and dreams for him. Small group and whole-class discussions confirmed shared parental attributes for an expected child and typical projected family life trajectory (Levy *et al.*, 2002). Anticipating that some students might be reluctant to assume the role of a parent, the activity was worded so that the participant could chose to address the letter to a sibling's or friend's expected child. When a class participant chose to do this, the remaining activities were rewritten to reflect that perspective, e.g. aunt or uncle.

Activity 2: The second activity presented a birth scenario which invited imaginative participation, e.g. "Last night, you rushed your wife to the hospital for the birth of your second child". In a number of scenarios, for example those involving Down syndrome, spina bifida or cerebral palsy, the diagnosis of disability was made at birth. Other scenarios involved infants who were placed in neonatal intensive care units for observation, or reflected typical birth accounts. Class participants were required to journal their thoughts and feelings about the scenario and devise a plan of action, e.g. "You are alone now. Write out your feelings. What do you need most at this time? What will your next few hours be like?" To enhance ownership of the virtual case child, participants were invited to name their child, which was then used to refer to the child in the remaining scenarios. After personal reflection and journaling, students gathered in small groups to share.

Activity 3: Scenario three was situated in infancy/toddlerhood. Several cases involved surgery or hospitalizations, e.g. Down syndrome and cerebral palsy, and several others included diagnoses, e.g. deafness and seizure disorder. As in previous scenarios, participants completed a reflective journal assignment and engaged in group discussion.

Activity 4: Scenario four was situated at the preschool developmental stage. In this session, diagnoses such as autism and mild intellectual delay were made. Other case studies involved difficulties networking with professionals and accessing needed services. Since the cases were based predominately on interviews with actual parents, wording was included to reflect typical parental love, support and attachment to the child as well as emotions of confusion, fear and disappointment. For example, in the case of the child diagnosed with spina bifida, a number of difficult surgical procedures were described. The participant case event, in which the parent had to decide between two possible treatment programs, contained a statement describing the parent's deep admiration for the courage and grace the child had displayed despite the plethora of difficulties encountered.

Activity 5: The fifth scenario involved challenges associated with entry into formal schooling, such as lack of support for inclusion, or the recommendation that the child be placed in a separate classroom or a school located far from the home. Themes of empowerment and disempowerment typically experienced by parents were integrated into the scenarios. Reflections were guided by questions such as: "What kind of educational experience do you wish for your child?", "What do you most want to avoid?" and "What are your greatest fears or concerns about your child's education?" During this session participants were also invited to form in-class parent groups to explore their "rights" as parents. Interestingly, it was often during this activity that class participants began to convey a sense of having experienced the "other," of becoming the very parents they most dreaded as educators.

Activity 6: Scenario six explored public perceptions of disability in a variety of settings and difficulties with friendship formation, especially as children aged. For example, the scenario of the child with spina bifida described an event in which the child's former friends began to exclude him from their circle as they gained greater interest in sport-related activities, such as soccer and basketball. Once again, pre-service teachers were invited to journal their thoughts and feelings about their scenario and problem solve in small groups.

Activity 7: Scenario seven incorporated parents' perceptions of reduced support for academic and social inclusion as their children approached adolescence. Issues of ambiguous belonging and marginalization guided reflective questions and group discussion.

Activity 8: During the eighth scenario pre-service teachers reflected on what they learned through parenting their virtual child by writing a farewell letter to their child. Reflections were guided by three focal areas: what they learned about children with disabilities, their parents, and parent–professional, or home–school, interactions.

Learning outcomes

Though the FCPP participative scenarios have been used in both graduate and undergraduate ITE classes for the past five years, the findings presented here are from three graduate classes. After the completion of the class, students were invited to submit their portfolios which included all their reflections for inclusion in the study. Forty students (8 males and 32 females) submitted portfolios. Confidentiality was assured and written permission obtained from each participant.

Across the three classes, pre-service professionals demonstrated strong attachment to their virtual child, e.g. "I really felt as though when I was writing I had a deaf child", even integrating them into their own family structures, e.g. "I went home after class the first night and told my children, you have a new brother and he's got Down syndrome". Through their journal entries participants affirmed that parents of children with disabilities often have to "fight a plethora of systems" to access services for their children, which requires them to be unyielding, "to work relentlessly and not give in". They asserted that parents' unconditional love serves as the catalyst for their determination, e.g. "I have learned to look past the angry parent, to see and hear their heart" and that all parents have the same desires for their children, e.g. "to be happy, loved and included ... to be treated with respect and fairness, to live a life as full as possible". Participants attested to having greater sensitivity to social structures that parents face, especially disempowerment, marginalization and alienation, e.g. "often disenfranchised, misunderstood" and maintained that the activities proved foundational in shaping attitudes toward collaboration, e.g. "I have new knowledge to change my way of working with parents; I will listen to them with greater respect".

Through parenting a virtual child, pre-service teachers also attested to gaining new insights about children with disabilities, such as their strength, internal resilience and courage. The virtual child experience enhanced awareness of issues of prejudice and tolerance, e.g. "I learned that many people harbor fear and anxiety ... and that stereotyping children with disabilities can be one of the most detrimental factors to a child's education and overall wellbeing" and engendered greater acceptance of and respect for others, e.g. "through you I have learned to accept all people with greater grace and tact". Overall, pre-service teachers indicated that the virtual parent experience provided them a powerful glimpse into another's world, e.g. "This has been an eye-opening experience. I learned that teachers need to put themselves in 'our' shoes".

When compared with the original parent interviews on which they were based, FCPP entries provided clear evidence of development of the cognitive and affective aspects of empathy. A question remained, however, about whether the virtual parenting experience would affect practice in schools and classrooms. Therefore, one year following their involvement in the class, teachers from two of the classes were contacted and asked a follow-up question about the impact of the virtual child scenarios on their current teaching practice. Eleven participants who had graduated and were in classrooms completed the follow-up question. All respondents reported a positive outcome; 64 per cent reported that they were more sensitive and compassionate to parents; 55 per cent reported that they actively listened to parents and their concerns; 55 per cent stated that they have a deeper commitment to collaborative parent–professional models; and several reported an instance in which they advocated directly on behalf of a parent. One teacher's comment was particularly illustrative:

> I recently sat in on a meeting with the parents of a child with Williams Syndrome ... As I sat there I recall taking on the role of the parent, much like I did with my virtual child. As I did this, I became aware that some of the professionals were nearly audacious in their interactions with the parents. I made it my objective to find out what the parents wished for

their child, and opened the lines of communication ... Being able to take on that mental role during that meeting, I believe, required some prior practice. The virtual child experience offered that practice.

Implications for practice

Longitudinal participative case study pedagogy gives pre-service teachers the opportunity to (a) encounter the life experience and situational perspective of another, (b) experience thoughts and feelings congruent with the other, and (c) evaluate the beneficence of a course of action with respect to multiple viewpoints. Case study reflection questions can be specifically designed to challenge prevailing assumptions and generate innovative courses of action. In addition, small-group discussions provide a venue for joint construction of meaning and collaborative solution-building with a focus on optimal outcome.

Longitudinal participative case study pedagogy, such as used in the FCPP, has the potential to effect change in attitude and behavior, potential precursors to policy change. The FCPP participants affirmed that they had shifted from thinking of parents of children with disability as more different from themselves, to more similar to themselves, as they experienced shared emotions of anxiety, devastation, love and devotion in response to the various scenarios. In addition, they began to more fully recognize that systems, including schools, incorporate dynamics of power and privilege, and that ambiguous belonging carries with it the ache of devaluation and marginalization. They also understood that scattered throughout seemingly intransigent systems were caring professionals who valued all children and celebrated their strengths, whose attitudes and behavior they aspired to emulate in their own professional lives. These insights alone became, for many, catalysts for changed perspectives.

Understanding of and empathy toward others is foundational to creating inclusive schools and communities. Empathic teachers are more likely to affirm and value diverse families, and to model collaborative parent–professional partnerships. Though the use of the longitudinal case study activities was limited by the number of participants and setting in which it was situated, pre-service teachers affirmed that the opportunity to "walk in a parent's shoes" generated greater awareness of, and sensitivity to, the issues children with disabilities and their parents faced as they navigated the education system. As one participant wrote, "I am keenly aware now of what it feels like to be on the 'other' side of the table. I only hope that the many lessons I learned will greatly impact my teaching. Prior to this project, I was terrified of teaching children with disabilities. Now I welcome the opportunity!"

References

Bleakley, A. (2005) "Stories as data, data as stories: Making sense of narrative inquiry in clinical education", *Medical Education*, 39: 534–40.

Eisenberg, N. (2002) "Empathy-related emotional responses, altruism, and their socialization", in R. J. Davidson and A. Harrington (eds), *Vision of Compassion: Western Scientists and Tibetan Buddhists Examine Human Nature*, London: Oxford University Press, pp. 131–64.

Erera, P. I. (1997) "Empathy training for helping professionals: Model and evaluation", *Journal of Social Work Education*, 33: 245–60.

Gallucci, K. (2006) "Learning concepts with cases", *Journal of College Science Teaching*, 36(2): 16–20.

Green, S. E. (2007) "'We're tired, not sad!: Benefits and burdens of mothering a child with a disability", *Social Science and Medicine*, 64: 150–63.

Guiffrida, D. A. (2005) "The emergence model: An alternative pedagogy for facilitating self-reflection and theoretical fit in counseling students", *Counselor Education and Supervision*, 44: 201–13.

Kennedy, M. (2001) "Teaching communication skills to medical students: Unexpected attitudes and outcomes", *Teaching in Higher Education*, 6(1): 119–23.

Levy, S. R., Freitas, A. L. and Salovey, P. (2002) "Construing action abstractly and blurring social distinctions: Implications for perceiving homogeneity among, but also empathizing with and helping others", *Journal of Personality and Social Psychology*, 83(5): 1224–38.

Scorgie, K. and Wilgosh, L. (2008) "Reflections on an uncommon journey: A follow-up study of life management of six mothers of children with diverse disabilities", *International Journal of Special Education*, 23(1): 103–14.

Sharma, U., Forlin, C., Loreman, T. and Earle, C. (2006) "Preservice teachers' attitudes, concerns and sentiments about inclusive education: An international comparison of the novice preservice teacher", *International Journal of Special Education*, 21(2): 80–93.

Slote, M. (2007) *The Ethics of Care and Empathy*, Abingdon, UK: Routledge.

Wilgosh, L. and Scorgie, K. (2006) "Theoretical model for conceptualizing cross-cultural applications and intervention strategies for parents of children with disabilities", *Journal of Policy and Practice in Intellectual Disabilities*, 3(4): 211–18.

Chapter 10

Preparing teachers to work with parents and families of learners with SEN in inclusive schools

Garry Hornby

Learning outcomes

- Understand the rationale for the importance of parental involvement.
- Learn a framework for effective working with parents and families.
- Discuss the attitudes, knowledge and skills necessary for working with parents.

Introduction

After working with parents as a mainstream and special class teacher, educational psychologist, researcher and teacher educator, as well a being a parent of two teenage sons, I have come to believe that a collaborative working relationship between teachers and parents is a key factor in providing the optimum education for all children, whether or not they have special education needs (SEN). I consider that developing the interpersonal skills, attitudes and knowledge needed for working effectively with parents and families is essential for all teachers in inclusive schools.

My interest in the benefits of teachers working closely with parents emerged when I was teaching adolescents with moderate learning difficulties in a secondary school special class in New Zealand 35 years ago. This experience highlighted the importance of having good working relationships with parents and stimulated my interest in learning more about this aspect of the teacher's role. Subsequently training and working as an educational psychologist I became involved in conducting workshops for parents of children with various SEN, which led to my involvement in the establishment of a parent-to-parent scheme in New Zealand that has subsequently developed into a national support network for parents of children with SEN (see Hornby, 2000).

Over these years I have conducted workshops with parents and taught courses with pre-service and inservice teachers on working with parents of children with SEN in many countries including England, Ireland, New Zealand, Barbados, Portugal and India. In this chapter I have drawn on these experiences, along with theory and research on parental involvement, in order to present a framework designed to help pre-service teachers develop the attitudes, knowledge and skills considered essential for working effectively with parents of children with SEN in inclusive schools.

Theory and research

Involving parents in the education of their children has been regarded as an important element of effective education for at least 40 years. There is now an extensive research literature indicating that parental involvement is advantageous for children of all ages (Desforges and Abouchaar, 2003; Epstein, 2001). The effectiveness of parental involvement in facilitating children's academic achievement has been reported by several reviews of the literature (Fan and Chen, 2001; Jeynes, 2005, 2007; Pomerantz, *et al.*, 2007). Other benefits of parental involvement which emerge from these reviews include: improved parent–teacher relationships, teacher morale and school climate; improved school attendance, attitudes, behavior and mental health of children; and increased parental confidence, satisfaction and parents' interest in their own education.

Despite widespread acknowledgement of these potential benefits, there are clear gaps between the rhetoric on parental involvement found in the literature and typical practices of working with parents which are found in schools. Henderson and Berla (1994) summarize the situation succinctly when they state, "The benefits of effective collaborations and how to do them are well documented across all the age ranges of schooling. Still they are not in widespread practice" (p. 18).

There are many reasons for the gap between what is said and what is done in the name of parental involvement and these can be conceptualized as barriers to teachers working effectively with parents. The various barriers can be categorized into three areas: individual parent and family factors, parent–teacher factors, and broader societal factors (Hornby, 2000). Individual parent and family factors include issues to do with parents' class, ethnicity and gender, as well as parents' beliefs about their involvement, their current life context and their perceptions of invitations for involvement from children and schools. Parent–teacher factors include issues regarding differing agendas, language and attitudes between parents and teachers. Societal factors include various historical and demographic issues plus the economics and politics of education, one important aspect of which is provision for the training of pre-service and inservice teachers on working with parents, which is the focus of this chapter.

Framework for determining content of training needed

It is considered that, in order to work effectively with parents of children with SEN in inclusive schools, pre-service teachers need to develop specific attitudes, knowledge and skills. A framework is elaborated below for determining these.

Attitudes needed to work effectively with parents

The attitudes that teachers need in order to work effectively with parents of children with SEN are ones that will help them develop productive partnerships. To bring this about teachers need to communicate to parents the attitudes of genuineness, respect and empathy, as suggested by Rogers (1980 cited in Hornby, 2000). They must be *genuine* in their relationships with parents. That is, they should come across as real people with their own strengths and weaknesses. For example, they should always be prepared to say that they "don't know" when this is the case. Hiding behind a professional facade of competence is not in anyone's interest. Teachers also need to show *respect* for parents. Parents' opinions and requests should always be given serious consideration. In the final analysis parents' wishes should be respected even if they run counter to the views of teachers, since it is parents who have the long-term responsibility for their children. Most importantly, teachers need to develop *empathy* with parents. They should try to see the child and family's situation from the point of view of the parents. If teachers can develop an empathic understanding of the parent's position then it is much more likely that a productive parent–professional partnership will evolve.

Another important attitude that teachers need to have is hopeful but realistic views about the likely progress and eventual prognosis of the children with whom they work. Parents need teachers to be optimistic but objective about their children's development. They need teachers to be people of integrity who will not shy away from being open and honest with them but will do this with sensitivity. In addition, teachers need to communicate the attitude that every situation can be improved, even if perhaps not all of the problems experienced by children or parents can be completely solved.

Knowledge needed to work effectively with parents

Fortunately, in the past 20 years, there has been a substantial growth in the number of publications on parental involvement and there is now a large number of books and articles on the topic which provide information for pre-service teachers. One aim of this chapter is to highlight the knowledge required by pre-service teachers to work effectively with parents that is over and above that which they require for effectively teaching children. There are several aspects of this additional knowledge.

First, teachers need to have a good understanding of parents' perspectives, that is, they must be able to see and appreciate parents' points of view. Teachers must also be aware of family dynamics and be able to view all students within the context of their families (see Scorgie, 2010). In addition, teachers need to know specifically what they can do to help parents of children with various types of SEN. Teachers also need to have adequate knowledge of how to work effectively with parents who present particular difficulties or challenges (Hornby, 2000). Teachers need to be knowledgeable about the range of services and other resources that are available to parents. They need to be sufficiently aware of the beliefs and customs of the ethnic groups with which they work to be able to adapt their interventions so that they are culturally appropriate. Finally, teachers must have a good knowledge of strategies and techniques for working effectively with parents.

Skills needed to work effectively with parents

In addition to communicating appropriate attitudes and possessing relevant knowledge, in order to work effectively with parents, teachers need to develop a high level of relevant interpersonal skills. A theoretical framework is proposed in order to determine the interpersonal skills needed by teachers to work effectively with parents. The framework includes two aspects, one focusing on meeting parents' needs, the other on utilizing parents' potential contributions. Different skills are needed by teachers for each component of these two aspects.

Skills related to parents' needs

Communication

All parents of children with SEN need to have effective channels of communication with the teachers who work with their children. They need information about the services available and they need to understand their rights and responsibilities. Parents also look to teachers for feedback on how their children are doing at school. Parents need to feel that they can contact teachers directly when they have a concern about their child. They typically regard teachers as a major source of information and support and therefore need to have a working partnership with them. Teachers can facilitate this by establishing a variety of forms of contact with parents such as through telephone calls and home visits in addition to meeting with parents at school. Teachers therefore need to develop effective communication skills, including those involved in written and oral communication with parents. Teachers also need the organizational skills necessary for maintaining contact with parents through meetings, home visits, letters and telephone calls (see Hornby, 2000).

Education

Most parents of children with SEN are keen to obtain guidance from teachers that is aimed at promoting their children's progress or managing their behavior. Some parents would rather receive such guidance on an individual basis while others are interested in participating in group parent education workshops. The most effective format of workshops for parents seems to be one that combines educational input with opportunities for parents to share concerns and ideas. Similar workshop formats have been found useful for use with siblings, fathers and grandparents of children with SEN. In order to effectively provide guidance to families, teachers need to have good listening and assertion skills, and also need to develop the skills of group facilitation. In addition, teachers need the skills required for involving parents in their children's education such as in home–school reading schemes or home–school behavior programs. Good group leadership skills will enable them to organize various group experiences for parents, such as parent education workshops (see Hornby, 2000).

Support

Many parents of children with SEN will, at one time or another, be in need of supportive counselling. Although some parents cope extremely well with the demands of raising children with SEN without ever needing such counseling, others definitely benefit greatly from it. Typically, parents will approach teachers who work with their children, rather than professional counsellors, in search of help for the problems that concern them. Teachers in training should, therefore, have a level of basic counselling skills sufficient to be good listeners and to help parents solve everyday problems. They should also have the skills and knowledge to be able to refer parents on to qualified counsellors when problems raised are beyond their level of competence (see Hornby *et al.*, 2003).

Skills related to parents' potential contributions

Information

All parents can contribute valuable information about their children with SEN. Information concerning children's likes and dislikes, strengths and weaknesses, along with any relevant medical details can be gathered by teachers at face-to-face meetings or by telephone. Many parents feel more comfortable on their own territory and generally appreciate it when teachers offer to visit them there. A home visit can also be useful for meeting other members of the family and for gaining an understanding of the strengths and limitations of the home environment. Gaining an impression of home circumstances and making full use of parents' knowledge of their children leads to more effective practice. In addition, it makes parents feel that they have been listened to and that an active interest has been taken in their children. In order to fulfil these functions teachers need to develop good listening skills including paraphrasing, passive listening and active listening (see Hornby, 1994).

Collaboration

Most parents are able to collaborate with teachers by following up intervention programs at home. This could be something as simple as supervising homework or carrying out behavior management programs. Some parents, though, are not able to do this. It may be that their resources are already fully committed in coping with their children at home, so they are not able to do anything extra. This is one situation for which making home visits can be useful in allowing teachers to see exactly what parents with children with SEN have to cope with. Often resentment at parents' apparent lack of cooperation can turn into admiration for their ability to cope with seemingly impossible conditions. At a later time family circumstances may change and parents may then be able to become more involved in intervention programs with their children. Therefore, teachers must respect parents' rights to make this decision on behalf of their children and be prepared to accept that, although they must offer all parents the opportunity to collaborate with them, some parents will not take this up until some time in the future.

Since most parents usually do wish to collaborate, teachers should make a point of attempting to involve all parents in their children's education. For parents who are reluctant to participate, teachers need to be able to assertively put the case for them being involved without pressuring parents into taking on extra work for which they don't have the time or the energy. For those parents who agree to participate but then don't follow through, teachers need to sensitively check the reasons for this and then attempt to problem solve any difficulties and work with parents on finding solutions.

Altruism

Many parents, after having come to terms with their child's SEN, and having established some stability in their family lives, begin to feel altruistic, particularly towards other parents of children with SEN. Many of these parents have the time and the ability to help others in various ways. Some may wish to act as voluntary aides, either helping other students in the classroom, or in the preparation of materials. Some parents are able to contribute their expertise through membership of parent or professional organizations. Others may wish to get involved in setting up or helping with a parent support or advocacy group. Still others may be able to provide emotional and practical support to other parents of children with SEN, for example through parent-to-parent schemes. Some parents will have the confidence and ability to provide inservice training for teachers by speaking at conferences or workshops, or by writing about their experiences. Teachers should continually be on the look-out for parents who can contribute in this way, so that their assets can be used to the full. In order to do this they need the listening and assertion skills noted above, plus the skills of enabling such as mentoring and empowering skills (Hornby, 1994).

Model for developing the attitudes, knowledge and skills needed by teachers

The content of initial teacher education (ITE) programs in countries such as the USA, New Zealand and the UK has in recent years been largely set by government education policies. Communicating and working with parents is now part of the professional standards for qualified teacher status in such countries, for example in the UK (TDA, 2007) and in the USA (NCATE, 2002). Also, several countries, such as the UK, now have specific government policies promoting parental involvement (see DfES, 2007). Yet, despite these policies there are still no specific requirements in most countries to include comprehensive courses on working with parents and families. The importance of comprehensive courses for providing teachers with the skills to work effectively with parents has been widely acknowledged (Epstein, 2001). Because government policies in many countries do not specify the content of such courses, they are typically not included in ITE programs.

Typically in countries where ITE is not standardized, limited time is devoted to working with parents in ITE programs and the input is variable depending on the emphasis in their course. This is in contrast with the situation in the USA where accreditation standards (NCATE, 2002) require the topic of parent involvement to be a compulsory course in ITE programs. Although this is an improvement on what typically happens in the UK and New Zealand, a recent survey conducted in the USA of the staff who teach these courses has concluded that they do not include sufficient practical experiences of parental involvement to ensure that teachers are adequately prepared to work effectively with parents (Flanigan, 2007). Preparing pre-service teachers to work with parents requires content knowledge and the practical experiences which need to be provided by schools.

Content of courses on working with parents

Ideally, a minimum of 20 contact hours is required to teach the attitudes, knowledge and skills identified above and elaborated in various sources (Hornby, 1994, 2000). Another 20 hours needs to be set aside for reading relevant literature, and a further 20 hours for completion of an assignment. The assignment should involve interviewing parents or other family members of a child with SEN and writing a report which relates findings from the interview to the literature on families of children with SEN.

Practical experiences of working with parents

Teaching practices in schools provide opportunities for pre-service teachers to gain experience of working with parents generally and those who have children with SEN in particular. Schools must involve pre-service teachers in the full range of aspects of working with parents including: parent–teacher meetings; home–school diaries; home visits; telephone contact; and preparation of newsletters for parents. Pre-service teachers should be fully involved in the IEP process with parents of students with SEN that they teach. They should also be involved in any parent education activities such as parent workshops that the school offers. Involvement in such workshops has been found to be a particularly effective way of providing pre-service teachers with practical experience of working with parents and an opportunity for using the skills, knowledge and attitudes they have learned (Hornby and Murray, 1983).

Once qualified, teachers will need ongoing support from schools in order to continually improve their practice of parental involvement. This will involve attending relevant professional development courses, for example, on working with parents from diverse backgrounds.

Conclusion

In order for students with SEN in inclusive schools to achieve their full potential, teachers need to capitalize on the involvement of their parents. In order to do this, pre-service teachers need to learn how to work effectively with parents. The model outlined in this chapter provides a framework for organizing this learning in order to optimize parental involvement, thereby enabling students with SEN in inclusive schools to achieve their full potential.

References

DfES (2007) *Every Parent Matters*, London: Department for Education and Skills.
Desforges, C. and Abouchaar, A. (2003) *The Impact of Parental Involvement, Parental Support and Family Education on Pupil Achievement and Adjustment: Research Report 433*, London: Department for Education and Skills.

Epstein, J. L. (2001) *School, Family and Community Partnerships,* Boulder, CO: Westview Press.

Fan, X. and Chen, M. (2001) "Parent involvement and students' academic achievement: A meta-analysis", *Educational Psychology Review, 13*(1): 1–22.

Flanigan, C. B. (2007) "Preparing preservice teachers to partner with parents and communities: An analysis of college of education faculty focus groups", *School Community Journal, 17*(2): 89–109.

Henderson, A. and Berla, N. (eds) (1994) *A New Generation of Evidence: The Family is Critical to Student Achievement,* Washington DC: Centre for Law and Education.

Hornby, G. (1994) *Counselling in Child Disability,* London: Chapman and Hall.

Hornby, G. (2000) *Improving Parental Involvement,* London: Cassell.

Hornby, G. and Murray, R. (1983) "Group programmes for parents of children with various handicaps", *Child: Care, Health and Development, 9*(3): 185–98.

Hornby, G., Hall, E. and Hall, C. (eds) (2003) *Counselling Pupils in Schools: Skills and Strategies for Teachers,* London: RoutledgeFalmer.

Jeynes, W. H. (2005) "A meta-analysis of the relation of parental involvement to urban elementary school student academic achievement", *Urban Education, 40*(3): 237–69.

Jeynes, W. H. (2007) "The relation between parental involvement and urban secondary school student academic achievement: A meta-analysis", *Urban Education, 42*(1): 82–110.

NCATE (2002) *Professional Standards for the Accreditation of Schools, Colleges and Departments of Education,* Washington, DC: National Council for Accreditation of Teacher Education.

Pomerantz, E. M., Moorman, E. A. and Litwack, S. D. (2007) "The how, whom and why of parents' involvement in children's academic lives: More is not always better", *Review of Educational Research, 77*(3): 373–410.

Scorgie, K. (2010) "Fostering empathy and understanding: A longitudinal case study", in C. Forlin (ed.), *Teacher Education for Inclusion,* London: Routledge, pp. 84–92.

TDA (2007) *Professional Standards for Qualified Teacher Status and Requirements for Initial Teacher Training,* London: Training and Development Agency for Schools.

Chapter 11

Using reflective practices for the preparation of pre-service teachers for inclusive classrooms

Umesh Sharma

Learning outcomes

- Understand reflective teaching.
- Develop a theoretical framework in support of using reflective practices to prepare pre-service teachers for inclusive classrooms.
- Identify various tools that academics can use to promote reflective practices in initial teacher education (ITE).

Introduction

The philosophy of including students who are frequently excluded (e.g. students with disabilities) into regular schools is widely accepted around the world. Several countries now either have legislation (e.g. USA, UK, Canada) or policies (e.g. Hong Kong, Singapore and India) that emphasize the need to educate students with disabilities in mainstream classrooms alongside their non-disabled peers. There are several barriers, though, that have hindered the progress of implementing inclusion policies at classroom level. Lack of appropriate training of teachers is one such major barrier. Often pre-service teachers do not receive sufficient training in teaching students with diverse abilities in their classrooms (Larrivee, 2000). They also complain about their inadequate preparation to meet the needs of students with disabilities who would be enrolled in their classrooms (Sharma *et al.*, 2007). There is a need to identify innovative ways of training pre-service teachers so that they not only feel positive about including students with disabilities into their classrooms but also demonstrate practices consistent with their beliefs.

Reflective teaching is one such approach that has the potential to prepare teachers with the necessary attributes to successfully implement inclusive practices not only for children with disabilities but also for all other children who are frequently excluded from mainstream education. This chapter briefly describes reflective teaching followed by a theoretical framework. How to teach reflective practices in ITE programs is the focus of the next section. The chapter concludes with some of the challenges that teacher educators need to be aware of if they decide to adopt this approach to train pre-service teachers.

What is reflective teaching?

Dewey (1933) defined reflection as "active, persistent, and careful consideration of any belief or supposed form of knowledge in the light of the grounds that support it and the further conclusions to which it tends" (p. 9). This definition suggests that reflective teachers constantly question their beliefs and practices. When they come across new education theories relevant to their teaching, they first closely examine the theory, then undertake a pilot test in their classroom before fully incorporating such ideas into their teaching. Reflective teachers also "look back on events, make judgments about them and alter their teaching behavior in light of craft, research, and ethical knowledge" (Valli, 1997, p. 70). Reflection is based on the premise that what one believes may be wrong (Larrivee, 2000).

According to Dewey (1933), three characteristics that most affect how teachers think and act like reflective teachers are open-mindedness, responsibility and wholeheartedness. Dewey (1933) defined open-mindedness as an active means to examine the many facets of one issue. Such teachers are receptive to new information, others' viewpoints and to different types of diversity (Garmon, 2005). Teachers who lack open-mindedness will either reject new information or they will interpret it in ways that will be consistent with their current views (Garmon, 2005). The second characteristic is responsibility. These teachers are deliberate in taking responsibility for their actions and consequences. The last characteristic, wholeheartedness, is a fusion of the first two characteristics. According to Dewey (1933), this characteristic binds teacher's commitment to open-mindedness and responsibility.

Theoretical framework: why reflective teaching?

The chapter is based on the premise that preparing teachers for inclusive classrooms requires that their beliefs and practices are shifted from a special education paradigm to an inclusive education paradigm (Kinsella and Senior, 2008) and that using reflective practices can facilitate the transition. The predominant belief behind the special education paradigm is that if a child does not learn then something is wrong with the child and such a child should be separated and taught in a special environment. The roots of this paradigm are firmly based in the medical model of disability (Finkelstein, 2001). Within this paradigm, disability is viewed as a form of illness or physical condition which is intrinsic to the individual and believed to cause significant disadvantage (Finkelstein, 2001). As a result the treatment revolves around finding the cause of the problem within the individual and solutions are mainly to control the impact of disability. Teachers who believe in this paradigm are more likely to refer students with disabilities for special education placements.

On the other hand, the inclusive education paradigm is based on the premise that if a student does not learn then the problem is not with the student but in the way he or she is educated. In other words, if the educational needs of a student are not met then the problem is with the system rather than with the student. The key principles of this paradigm are based on the sociological model of disability (Finkelstein, 2001). This model is based on the premise that barriers posed by society are the ultimate factors in defining who is disabled and who is not. The model recognizes that some people may function differently from other people because of their physical or mental impairments but they will not be disabled if society is ready to accommodate and include them in similar ways as would those who are not 'disabled' (Kinsella and Senior, 2008). Shifting pre-service teachers' views from special education to inclusive education can be a significant challenge.

Christensen (2004) reports that pre-service teachers' previously held views about teacher behaviors and the act of teaching influenced their learning as they enter into teacher training programs. Pre-service teachers make judgments about pedagogy based on what they experienced during their 16 years of schooling. It is possible that during these schooling years they never came across a student with disability in their classroom. When asked to include students with disabilities in their classroom, these teachers resist inclusion and find evidence from their schooling years in support of segregating such students. Using reflective practices during teacher training may allow pre-service teachers to rethink past experiences of teaching and learning and reconceptualize their notions of effective teaching and membership of regular classrooms (Christensen, 2004). This approach may allow these teachers to view inclusive schooling as a better option for all those students who are traditionally excluded from participating in mainstream schools.

Argyris (1990) proposed that our beliefs are self-generating, and rarely tested, based on conclusions drawn from our selected observations. She further commented that we tend to choose data that matches our views and understanding of the world and we ignore data that does not fit into our schema of the way things should work. We use such selective observations to draw conclusions, adopt beliefs and act according to these beliefs. Pre-service teachers who believe in a special education paradigm will continue to look for evidence (often anecdotal) suggesting that special schools are better for children with special needs. They will tend to refuse or refute research that supports inclusive schooling as a better option for students with disabilities.

Teacher educators can train pre-service teachers with the necessary technical skills such as managing student bahavior, creating engaging classrooms and keeping students on task (Larrivee, 2000). However, if this does not tie personal beliefs of pre-service teachers with micro teaching skills, it is less likely that skills learnt during their training will be sustained.

According to Larrivee:

> [When] teachers become reflective practitioners, they move beyond a knowledge base of discrete skills to a stage where they integrate and modify skills to fit specific contexts, and eventually, to a point where the skills are internalized enabling them to invent new strategies.
>
> (Larrivee, 2000, p. 294)

It is proposed that reflection on their teaching practices allows pre-service teachers to change their apprehensive attitude to include all students. The change in attitude then promotes practices that sustain inclusive culture in classrooms. Once a pre-service teacher has reached this stage then teaching micro teaching skills becomes much easier.

Teaching reflective practices to pre-service teachers

Larrivee (2000) states that the process of becoming a reflective practitioner cannot be prescribed. Dewey further suggests that:

> Reflective practice is not a series of steps or procedures, it is a holistic way of meeting and responding to problems, a way of being a teacher. Reflection involves intuition, emotion, and passion and is not something that can be neatly packaged as a set of techniques for teachers to use.
>
> (Dewey, in Zeichner and Liston, 1996, p. 9)

Becoming a reflective practitioner is challenging and often highly emotional for the person who engages in reflective practices. More importantly, pre-service teachers tend to value and learn skills of a reflective practitioner when they are taught by academics who also value reflective practices (Christensen, 2004). A number of components have been found to promote reflective practices in pre-service teachers. Some of these components enhance the use of reflective practices within an inclusive framework:

1. Evaluating personal teaching philosophy

Often teachers are asked to state their teaching beliefs and philosophy when they apply for job interviews. Unfortunately, not much attention is paid to this aspect during teacher training. Teaching beliefs and philosophy are written as idealistic statements but rarely does any relationship exist between what a teacher writes in his or her philosophy and what he or she actually practices in the classroom. One question that needs to be asked of each pre-service teacher early in an ITE program is: "What are your beliefs about teaching students who are frequently excluded from mainstream schooling?"

University academics can use different tools to gather this information. Asking pre-service teachers to write a paragraph about their teaching beliefs may be useful. Pre-service teachers "must be made aware of their own attitudes, beliefs and life experiences as they relate to issues of diversity before they will be able to critically examine and change them" (Garmon, 2005, p. 278). Teachers who lack self-awareness and are also not willing to self-reflect will not demonstrate much growth in accepting diversity in their classroom (Garmon, 2005). Teachers are more likely to embrace ideas and information that is consistent with the beliefs held by them and they will reject ideas that are inconsistent with these. Discussion of personal beliefs allows pre-service teachers to think how these may act to resist inclusion of students with diverse abilities in their classrooms. Research suggests that when pre-service teachers are challenged about their beliefs in a safe and encouraging environment, they are less likely to become defensive and resistant and more likely to share, reflect and change their beliefs (Garmon, 2005).

2. Effective questioning

Asking appropriate questions is fundamental to the art of reflective teaching. If a teacher never questions the goals and the values that guide their work, the context in which they teach, or never examines their assumptions then they cannot be said to be engaged in any form of reflection (Zeichner and Liston, 1996). Reflective teachers ask questions that allow them to grow and become better teachers. They critically examine their practices to determine how it will lead to a change, a commitment to quality and respect for difference (Jay and Johnson, 2002). According to Sparks-Langer *et al.* (1990) *why* questions are most crucial for teachers. *Why* questions allow teachers to look for strategies that enhance success of students in the classroom as well as explaining why some students are not learning adequately.

It is important for teacher educators to scaffold the kind of questions pre-service teachers should ask about their teaching. Questions that identify barriers in learning within the environment provoke teachers to look for strategies that will work with students with diverse abilities. In this regard, Tripp (1993) has provided an excellent framework that teacher educators will find useful to introduce to their pre-service teachers. His framework consists of four sequential steps: what happened, why did it happen, what might it mean, and what are the implications for my practice.

Step 1: What happened?

At this stage the teacher writes down a description of a critical incident that happened in the classroom. It is important that at this stage that no attempt is made to understand *why* aspects of the incident. It is best to describe the incident in as much detail as possible.

Step 2: Why did it happen?

This is the most crucial step in understanding the incident (Tripp, 1993). A pre-service teacher spends time to evaluate the context to explain the critical incident. Jay and Johnson (2002) stress the need to discern salient details about the incident as oversimplification can lead to a misinterpretation of the scenario. They add that "carefully and persistently describing significant details can help avoid the mistake of jumping to conclusions or seeing only what one wants to see"(p. 78). Reflection should not stop at this stage. The teacher needs to remain engaged in the reflection process and look for the meaning in the subsequent step.

Step 3. What might it mean?

At this stage the teacher analyses information from the previous stage to understand the meaning of the incident. Does the incident say something about the teaching practice? Jay and Johnson (2002) recommend that a classroom incident should be seen from the perspective of another teacher, a student, a counselor, a parent and so on. When we look at an incident from different perspectives, it allows us to discover meanings that we might otherwise miss (Jay and Johnson, 2002). It is important to note that it is through reflection at this stage that the teacher recognizes that he or she has choices available to do things differently. The last phase of the process relates to action-oriented behaviors.

Step 4: What are the implications for my practice?

This is perhaps the most crucial step in the reflective process. By gaining an improved understanding of a critical incident (or many critical incidents) in the classroom, the teacher decides on actions and implements them in his or her classroom. This change should result in substantial change in the teaching practices of a reflective teacher.

Asking relevant questions should allow pre-service teachers to gain a better understanding of the learners and the context. It should also provide them with some understandings of using existing resources to creatively and collaboratively solve any problems to facilitate inclusion of all students.

3. Collaborative problem solving

Reflection may seem to be a solitary activity, however, true reflection necessitates that teachers work closely with other teachers and professionals and seek feedback from their colleagues about their practices. There are many instances when a teacher faces a problem related to their teaching and they do not know how to deal with it. This may be particularly true with new teachers when they come across a student with a disability (e.g. social emotional disorder) in which they have had limited experience during their teaching practicum. At this moment teachers need to be aware that they are not, and need not be, experts in dealing with *all* students. They must, though, be willing to work alongside their professional colleagues (e.g. education psychologists) to enhance the inclusion of such students in their classrooms.

Teacher educators, therefore, must emphasize that collaboration with other professionals is a necessary requirement for effective, reflective and inclusive teaching. Based on an extensive review of conceptual and empirical literature, Hobbs and Westling (2002) conclude that inclusive education is characterized by a problem solving process; and consultation, collaboration and problem solving are necessary attributes of effective inclusive teachers. Collaboration between teachers and other professionals is necessary to improve the performance of students with special needs (Glatthorn, 1990) as teachers can rely on expertise of professionals to deal with specific problems in relation to their students (Pugach and Johnson, 1989). It is also a helpful tool to effectively manage the increasing responsibilities associated with the inclusion of students with disabilities (Hobbs and Westling, 2002). Considering that collaborative problem solving is an important skill, attention must be paid by teacher educators in ensuring that pre-service teachers acquire this skill. It may be useful to devise teaching activities that require pre-service teachers to work in small cooperative groups during their ITE. One example of such activity is asking students to work in small groups and take on different roles (e.g. parent, special education teacher and psychologist) to identify the best way to include a student who frequently has problems in class.

4. Identify, evaluate and use evidence-based practices

Another fundamental skill that inclusive pre-service teachers need to acquire is an ability to identify, evaluate and use best practices in the field. They will need to question why they use a particular strategy and what research base supports its use. It is possible that when they ask such questions they will find out that the teaching strategies they are employing in their classes are inappropriate. This immediately creates a need to look for alternative strategies that are likely to be more successful in their teaching context.

Pre-service teachers, therefore, need to be exposed to the best teaching practices relevant to the inclusion context. Teacher educators may need to scaffold how a research article should be interpreted and when findings from it should be considered powerful enough to be tried in classrooms. The US Department of Education (2003) provides a user-friendly guideline to read, evaluate, and reflect upon education research. Asking pre-service teachers to reflect upon articles based on literature reviews or a meta-analysis and apply some of the principles during their practicum could be a useful strategy. One way these practices could be promoted during ITE is by presenting different educational problems for them to find evidence-based strategies that can be employed to address such problems. Working in small groups, pre-service teachers can present the information in a way that could be implemented in a classroom. This exercise will require them to first identify articles based on a criteria that they can use to evaluate research studies (see US Department of Education, 2003) and to reflect upon the research and decide how the information can be translated into classroom practice.

Challenges for using reflective practices

There are at least three challenges that teacher educators need to be aware of if they plan to use reflective practice in training pre-service teachers. First and foremost challenge relates to their style of teaching. Use of this approach requires academics to practice what they preach. They should be ready to share their personal stories that might have caused cognitive conflicts during their school or university teaching and allowed them to change the way they teach now. Such stories convey an important symbolic message to pre-service teachers that their professor is indeed a reflective practitioner. This is by no means easy but without this attribute practicing reflective teaching will be difficult if not impossible.

Secondly, reflective teaching by its definition requires pre-service teachers to challenge the existing literature and the ideas conveyed by university academics. This could be particularly challenging in many Asian countries where arguing against an academic could be considered a sign of disrespect. Both the academics and the pre-service teachers need to adopt new roles which are likely to create heightened tension in the classroom. This point is well noted by Wormnaes (2008), when she states, "as a consequence of the obedience to authority in education, knowledge that is presented from a respected lecturer, and that is based in respected Western textbooks, will not easily be questioned or be subjected to critical analysis by students" (p. 220). How such change can happen is an important question for further research.

The last challenge relates to the philosophy of reflective teaching. In the field of special education, we have always believed that pre-service teachers need to have necessary technical skills. When reflective teaching approaches are used to train pre-service teachers there is a danger that we may end up paying too much attention to these skills and very little attention to the necessary technical skills needed to work with students with a range of special needs. A balance between reflective practitioner skills and technical skills is necessary.

Conclusion

Use of reflective practices to prepare pre-service teachers for inclusive classrooms is a fairly recent trend. There is no doubt that this approach has the potential to prepare teachers who are positively disposed to include students with disabilities in their classrooms. A number of questions remain unanswered and need to be investigated further: Do teachers trained using reflective pedagogy use better teaching strategies compared with teachers trained in a traditional format? What factors promote the use of reflective practices in pre-service teachers during ITE programs? What characteristics of pre-service teachers are most conducive to introduce reflective practices? In other words, is this approach equally effective for all pre-service teachers or are there some teachers who are more likely to benefit from this approach compared with other teachers?

References

Argyris, C. (1990) *Overcoming Organisational Defenses*, Boston, MA: Allyn and Bacon.

Christensen, L. (2004) "Through the looking glass: Reflection or refraction? Do you see what I see", *Journal of Social Studies Research*, 28(1): 33–46.

Dewey, J. (1933) *How We Think: A Restatement of the Relation of Reflective Thinking to Education Process*, Boston: Heath.

Finkelstein, V. (2001) *The Social Model of Disability Repossessed*. Leeds University Disability Studies Archive. Online. Available at: http://www.leeds.ac.uk/disability-studies/archiveuk/finkelstein/soc%20mod%20repossessed.pdf (accessed 18 February 2009).

Garmon, M. A. (2005) "Six key factors changing pre-service teachers' attitudes/beliefs about diversity", *Educational Studies*, 38(3): 275–86.

Glatthorn, A. (1990) "Cooperative professional development: Facilitating the growth of the special education teacher and the classroom teacher", *Remedial and Special Education*, 11: 2–34.

Hobbs, T. and Westling, D. L. (2002) "Mentoring for inclusion: A model class for special and general educators", *The Teacher Educator*, 37(3): 186–201.

Jay, J. K. and Johnson, K. L. (2002) "Capturing complexity: A typology of reflective practice for teacher education", *Teaching and Teacher Education*, 18: 73–85.

Kinsella, W. and Senior, J. (2008) "Developing inclusive schools: A systematic approach", *International Journal of Inclusive Education*, 12(5): 651–65.

Larrivee, B. (2000) "Transforming training practice: Becoming the critically reflective teacher", *Reflective Practice*, 1(3): 293–307.

Pugach, M. and Johnson, L. (1989) "The challenge of implementing collaboration between general and special education", *Focus on Exceptional Children*, 21: 1–8.

Sharma, U., Loreman, T. and Forlin, C. (2007) "What concerns preservice teachers about inclusive education: An international viewpoint", *KEDI Journal of Education Policy*, 4(2): 95–114.

Sparks-Langer, G. M., Simmons, J. M., Pasch, M., Colton, A. and Starko, A. (1990) "Reflective pedagogical thinking: How can we promote it and measure it", *Journal of Teacher Education*, 41(4): 23–32.

Tripp, D. (1993) *Critical Incidents in Teaching: Developing Professional Judgment*, New York: Routledge.

US Department of Education (2003) *Identifying and Implementing Educational Practices Supported by Rigorous Evidence: A User Friendly Guide*, Institute of Educational Sciences: Washington, DC. Online. Available at: http://www.ed.gov/rschstat/research/pubs/rigorousevid/index.html

Valli, L. (1997) "Listening to other voices: A description of teacher reflection in the United States", *Peabody Journal of Education*, 72(1): 67–88.

Wormnaes, S. (2008) "Cross-cultural collaboration in special teacher education: An arena for facilitating reflection", *International Journal of Disability, Development and Education*, 55(3): 205–25.

Zeichner, K. M. and Liston, D. P. (1996) *Reflective Teaching: An Introduction*, Mahwah, NJ: Lawrence Erlbaum Associates.

Chapter 12

Preparing pre-service teachers for effective co-teaching in inclusive classrooms

Mian Wang and Paul Fitch

Learning outcomes

- Definition of co-teaching as a model of inclusion.
- Understand the features and key elements of a successful co-teaching program.
- Discuss the implications of a successful co-teaching program for initial teacher education (ITE) in the era of inclusive education.

Introduction

Inclusion of students with disabilities has become a common practice in today's schools supported by legislation or government policies in many western countries (Forlin, 2008). As many schools try to respond to the call for inclusion, co-teaching has emerged as one of the answers to effective inclusive practices.

Despite an emerging consensus in the field that acknowledges co-teaching as an exemplary model for inclusive education, researchers are still puzzling about the barriers of co-teaching practices (Reinhiller, 1996) and various issues of adopting co-teaching in ITE programs (Walther-Thomas, 1997). Teacher educators are particularly concerned that in conventional ITE programs necessary skills, dispositions and organizational support mechanisms are not emphasized and well developed, for pre-service teachers to become successful teachers in the inclusive classroom. In this chapter, we introduce an ITE program that centers on co-teaching through emphasizing collaboration as a coherent and pervasive philosophy of pedagogy. We also discuss some important lessons learned from this program and implications for teacher preparation in an era of inclusive education.

Conceptual framework of co-teaching

Kloo and Zigmond (2008) characterized co-teaching as having become "the most frequently used special education service-delivery model for inclusive classrooms" (p. 12), a model "... in which two certified teachers – one general educator and one special educator – share responsibility for planning, delivering, and evaluating instruction for a diverse group of students, some of whom are students with disabilities" (p. 13). Furthermore, they noted that most of the published literature about co-teaching has focused on logistics of co-teaching practices involving issues of co-planning, relationship of co-teachers (e.g. personal compatibility and mutual trust), instructional arrangements, and administrative support.

Several co-teaching variations have been employed, all of which involve the collaboration of two teachers, usually one general education teacher and one special education teacher. Collaboration may also occur between teachers and therapists and teachers and aides. The main variations of co-teaching include: team teaching, station teaching, parallel teaching, alternative teaching, and one teaching, one assisting. In team teaching, both teachers share planning, instructional and management responsibilities equally. In station teaching, co-teachers facilitate learning stations through the cycling of subgroups of students. In parallel teaching, each teacher instructs subgroups of students in the same or different content in the same classroom. In alternative teaching, one teacher instructs a small group of students for specialized instruction often in a different setting, while the other teacher instructs the remainder of the class. In the one teaching, one assisting model, the general education teacher provides content area instruction, while the special education teacher provides support for students who require it.

Any of these variations may be mixed and matched with each other or with the more traditional one teacher in the room model. The belief is that the presence of two teachers in the classroom will foster the participation, acceptance, and success of all students in an integrated general education setting. Myriads of anecdotal information from teachers, principals, and supervisors and empirical evidence of research suggest that co-teaching is a thing of beauty when it works well, and that co-teaching can be a chaotic catastrophe when it does not. In a recent metasynthesis of co-teaching practices, Scruggs *et al.* (2007) found that the one teaching, one assisting model is the most commonly used model of co-teaching in 24 of the 32 studies synthesized. The troubling fact of the predominant use of this model is that the special education teacher is seen as subservient to the content area teacher and, therefore, is treated as an aide rather than a fully equal co-teacher.

Although both inclusion and collaboration models have been in practice for two decades, few currently employed teachers have received specific training in this area. Some teachers have attended a single workshop and hardly any have taken a for-credit course. Seldom is there follow-up discussion or opportunities for discussion of these models. In traditional ITE programs, some coursework and fieldwork may be devoted to co-teaching only for teachers of students with disabilities. Collaboration is perceived as one of many models of instruction which may be encountered by special education teachers.

Benefits of co-teaching

Both general and special education teachers can benefit from building a solid relationship. Teachers generally report that they have benefited professionally from co-teaching experiences on numerous fronts: learning from the partner and becoming a better teacher (e.g. increase of content knowledge for special education co-teachers and skill improvement for general education co-teachers on classroom management and curriculum adaptations) and a better collaborator (Scruggs *et al.*, 2007).

Co-teaching also benefits students with and without disabilities in the inclusive classroom. Morocco and Aguilar (2002) pointed out that co-teaching is "one of the most promising and intricate forms of collaboration in support of diverse learners ..." (p. 316). Teachers have observed increased cooperation among students in co-taught and inclusive classes. Apart from the benefit of extra teacher attention (Scruggs *et al.*, 2007), students can benefit simultaneously from general education teachers' expertise in the specific content area and special education teachers' expertise in individualized instruction methods. There are also social benefits for all students upon including students with disabilities in co-taught and inclusive classrooms.

Influencing factors of co-teaching

Co-teaching practice is time consuming and demands great commitment from both teachers who have completely different training backgrounds to plan and work together collaboratively (Reinhiller, 1996). Lack of planning time, scheduling conflict, special education teachers' caseload concerns, lack of administrative support, and too few opportunities for staff development are commonly identified barriers to co-teaching (Walther-Thomas, 1997).

It is important that co-teachers can give their input on the assignment of co-teaching. Factors such as compatibility of style, knowledge of content area, and teaching skills should be considered upon assignment. Common training opportunities should also be available for both teachers before assignment and during their partnership. Common planning time, in addition to traditional contracted preparation time, is a must for partnerships to thrive (Scruggs *et al.*, 2007). In addition, a subtle, yet crucial, factor regarding the success of partnership is the respect of each teacher for the other partner and the value each teacher places on the other's knowledge and skills.

Historically, ITE programs are separated into regular and special education courses in the USA and have not provided pre-service teachers with the intensive training and experience they need to be effective collaborators in planning, teaching, and evaluating instruction (Cramer *et al.*, 2006). Cramer *et al.* (2006) noted that the majority of co-teachers who participated in their studies reported no pre-service preparation for the work demands of their current teaching positions. In discussing the lack of staff development for co-teaching as a common barrier, Walther-Thomas (1997) concluded that most teachers involved in co-teaching have never been formally trained to co-teach. Such barriers are more likely to exist for new teachers who feel forced to co-teach and who do not get along with the partner in co-taught classrooms.

A five-year collaborative teacher education program

A Collaborative Teacher Education (CTE) program was instituted in response to the push for inclusion in the late 1990s in New Jersey. The CTE program has graduated three classes of pre-service teachers who are currently working in a variety of education settings. In this program, a small (30–35) cohort of pre-service teachers is admitted annually into this five-year, dual degree (BA/ MST) and dual certification (elementary and special education) program. All members of each cohort are carefully selected for this restricted major.

The pre-service teachers in the CTE program see themselves as either general education teachers who will be better trained to educate all children or special education teachers who will be better prepared to work in inclusive classrooms. Indeed, the intent of this program was to prepare these pre-service teachers to work in inclusive classrooms at elementary schools. The pre-service teachers are cohorted for taking all of their common pedagogy courses, education subject courses and many other optional courses. The program emphasizes and facilitates the pre-service teachers' collaboration on assignments and activities in almost all classes and field placements throughout their five-year program. Inclusive classrooms, with both elementary and special education teachers present, are sought as the first choice of field placements. As compared with graduates of other ITE programs who seldom receive specific training in collaboration, the CTE program graduates enjoy five years of intensive training in collaboration.

Besides cohorting the pre-service teachers, the interdepartmental faculty drawn from teacher education, special education and reading departments are associated with this program and often see the pre-service teachers in multiple courses and field placements throughout the five years. While cohorting is sometimes offered in other ITE programs, it is usually restricted to two years and is not as pervasive as in the CTE program, a model of togetherness. In fact, the very close and involved relationship between the cohort members and faculty/staff prevents or reduces much of the anxiety and stress regularly encountered by most pre-service teachers in dealing with the typical college experience. The unparalleled support of the cohort and faculty/staff was demonstrated on numerous occasions involving medical and personal issues, accidents, deaths of family members, issues with bureaucracy, self-imposed roadblocks, and academic issues. The continued connection between the cohort graduates and faculty in both professional and personal activities has reinforced the perceptions of the value and strength of the CTE program.

The cohort is together for five full years, as full-time students. They room together, join the same social and service organizations, and generally socialize together. Many have leadership roles in organizations and graduate with multiple honors. They participate in joint presentations with faculty.

An equally important component of this program is the abundance and quality of the field experiences provided from the first semester through student teaching. After four years of increasingly more involved field placements, the pre-service teachers spend their entire fifth year in clinical practices of four days per week for one semester and five days per week for another semester. This is an unusually extensive amount of time spent in the field before beginning student teaching in the last semester clinical practice. The successful experiences provided by these multiple field placements result in exceptionally high-level confidence among the CTE program graduates. The pre-service teachers have identified coursework activities that emphasize collaboration in the field placements (e.g. unit plan, classroom management plan, assessment plan, and behavior support plan) as the most valuable assignments for developing their teaching skills as pre-service teachers.

Some preliminary evaluative studies have been carried out to understand the CTE program graduates' opinion about the co-teaching. Anecdotal evidence has supported our assumption of program graduates as experts in collaboration. In an initial study (Fitch, 2006) of the perceptions of the graduates of this program, the respondents indicated that the strength of the cohort and the abundance and quality of the field placements were the strongest components of the program. The pre-service teachers also commented positively on the genuine involvement and interest of the faculty members in the program. Nearly all the participants indicated that the support they received from their peers throughout this five-year program was the most significant factor in their success as pre-service teachers and they expected this cohesiveness to continue beyond graduation. Most rated the solidarity and cohesiveness of the cohort highly. They praised the support of the cohort during the job-search process and believed that they would maintain contact with cohort members over time.

As for concerns and problems of the CTE program, some graduates complained about the heavy workload of the program. Another problematic issue related to the pre-service teachers who cannot follow the strict sequence of courses because all program courses are single section offered once a year. So they are forced to "drop down" to another cohort, thus turning a five-year program into a six-year program. Additionally, opportunity for greater exposure to parent interactions during field placements was identified as an area of need. Typically, the opportunities for parent interactions are limited in the university classroom and early field experiences. Usually, pre-service teachers do not participate in parent–teacher conferences, IEP meetings and general parent communications until their student teaching.

A survey of the principals of the teachers who graduated from the CTE program found a high level of satisfaction when these principals were asked to compare the co-teaching program graduates with those from other more traditional ITE programs (Fitch and Wang, 2007). The co-teaching program graduates were evaluated on the areas of lesson planning and implementation, assessment, behavior management, organization, parent interaction, knowledge of both general and special education practices, peer collaboration, and direction/supervision of teaching assistants. Comments received from the responding principals elaborated on the survey findings and provided input. The principals indicated that the CTE program graduates were well prepared, possessed the maturity of well-seasoned teachers, worked exceptionally well with colleagues, and were well versed in diverse instructional techniques to meet the needs of all learners. In one of the most glowing statements, one principal said, "Not only does xxx do an excellent job instructionally, she has also added so much to our school community. She has run special programs for the children and provides excellent support to other teachers."

Overall, the CTE program graduates were recognized as highly competent teachers who contributed strongly to their learning community. These survey findings corroborate the anecdotal information received from the various teacher educators who have worked with this group as field supervisors.

Implications for teacher education in the era of inclusive education

Several implications are derived from the summary of literature and analysis of this co-teaching program. We focus on several key factors regarding the success of co-teaching practices based upon the lessons that we have learned from our experience with the CTE program.

First, collaboration elements must be incorporated into courses and field work in all ITE programs. Previous research suggests that the effort in adding an introductory special education course and adding a field placement in inclusive settings has not given rise to adequate preparation of pre-service teachers for teaching in inclusive settings (Stayton and McCollum, 2002). Coursework and fieldwork must become more collaborative systematically and consistently in general education and special education ITE programs. We do not suggest that an ITE program with five full years of training in collaboration is necessary, but more attention to and emphasis in collaborative teaching should be ensured.

Second, the value of placing students in cohorts should be considered in all ITE programs for the strength it brings, both professionally and personally. Previous research has identified both positive and negative aspects of cohorting ITE programs. Positive aspects included: small class sizes which facilitate friendship-making; immediate social support, an ethic of generalized good will, and mutual friendliness beyond the casual; common group identity, characteristics of a strong community, such as respect, caring, encouragement, and cooperation, and a student-unexpected mutual development of professionalism. Negative aspects usually refer to the exclusion of some cohort members because of cliques within the cohort, inequitable contributions on cooperative assignments, and petty jealousies. Based upon our experience, the negative impact of cohorting is incomparable to the benefits received by the cohort members.

Third, opportunity for placement in multiple collaborative field placements where there are guided observations by coaches fluent in inclusive practices is essential because pre-service teachers can see best practices in action. In addition to training in collaborative teaching strategies, training in administrative/organizational aspects to enhance the success of collaboration should be undertaken.

Fourth, multiple opportunities to work with program faculty in classes, seminars, and field placements should be arranged so that the faculty is invested in the cohort at a similar level. Everington et al. (1996) pointed out that there is a need to establish a team teaching model in the ITE program where special education and general education faculty can collaborate and model co-planning and co-teaching for the pre-service teachers. They noted that one of the barriers to faculty team delivery of coursework is the current university reward system in which resource allocation is based on course delivery for individual faculty. Another barrier is that current faculty schedules and workload can be a deterrent to allocation of the time needed to co-plan and co-teach. In addition, training for administrators and faculty who support and are willing to engage in collaboration needs to be discussed in future education leadership programs.

Finally, the benefits of selecting a co-teaching partner, common planning time, training in collaboration and conflict resolution, proactively seeking opportunities for partner involvement in lessons, and issues of scheduling and grading should be incorporated and emphasized in ITE programs, teacher professional learning and school leadership training.

Conclusion

In conclusion, we found that the pre-service teachers trained through this program that centers on collaboration have perceived more successful and positive experiences than those trained through different traditional ITE programs regarding co-teaching practices. The benefits of co-teaching identified through studying this program can be utilized in a variety of ITE programs rather than limited to a five-year model. Emphasis should be placed on key elements of successful co-teaching, such as common planning time, teacher input on collaborative partnerships, long-term assignment of partners, opportunities for joint training of partners, and the use of in-house collaborative partners to share their success strategies with other potential collaborative partners. All ITE programs should embrace the key elements of successful co-teaching to train better collaborative teachers for 21st-century inclusive education.

References

Cramer, I., Nevin, A., Thousand, J. and Liston, A. (2006) "Co-teaching in urban school districts to meet the needs of all teachers and learners: Implication for teacher education reform", proceedings of annual conference of the American Association for Colleges of Teacher Education, San Diego, CA, January.

Everington, C., Hamill, L. B. and Lubic, B. (1996) "Restructuring teacher preparation programs for inclusion: The change process for one university", *Contemporary Education,* 68(1): 52–6.

Fitch, P. J. (2006) "A pilot survey of teacher-candidate perceptions of selected components of the Rowan University Collaborative Education Program", unpublished evaluation report, Rowan University.

Fitch, P. J. and Wang, M. (2007) "Teacher beliefs about collaboration by graduates of three teacher preparation programs", paper presented at the Annual CEC Convention, Louisville, KY, April.

Forlin, C. (2008) *Catering for Learners with Diverse Needs: An Asia-Pacific Focus.* Hong Kong: Hong Kong Institute of Education.

Kloo, A. and Zigmond, N. (2008) "Co-teaching revisited: Redrawing the blueprint", *Preventing School Failure,* 52: 12–20.

Morocco, C. and Aguilar, C. (2002) "Co-teaching for content understanding: A schoolwide model", *Journal of Educational and Psychological Consultation,* 13: 315–47.

Reinhiller, N. (1996) "Co-teaching: New variations on a not-do-new practice", *Teacher Education and Special Education,* 19: 34–48.

Scruggs, T. E., Mastropieri, M. A. and McDuffie, K. A. (2007) "Co-teaching in inclusive classrooms: A metasynthesis of qualitative research", *Exceptional Children,* 73(4): 392–416.

Stayton, V. D. and McCollum, J. (2002) "Unifying general and special education: What does the research tell us?" *Teacher Education and Special Education,* 25(3): 211–18.

Walther-Thomas, C. (1997) "Co-teaching experiences: The benefits and problems that teachers and principals report over time", *Journal of Learning Disabilities,* 30: 395–407.

Chapter 13

Teacher education online

Towards inclusive virtual learning communities

Paul Bartolo

Learning outcomes

- Understand the building of learning communities as a basis for Initial teacher education (ITE) for inclusive education.
- Recognize the innovative potential for building inclusive virtual learning communities (VLCs) through technology-enhanced learning as exemplified in an e-learning module undertaken by a group of pre-service teachers.
- Understand the possible challenges in building and sustaining inclusive VLCs.

Introduction

Inclusive education has long been associated with the idea of learning communities. Inclusion is first of all a social phenomenon that enables all students to belong fully to their classrooms and schools by being called upon and supported to participate in collaborative learning. Such a process entails a responsive and constructivist approach to teaching and learning (Bartolo *et al.*, 2007). Psychological constructivism calls for learner-centred teaching that encourages and enables meaningful learning by giving each learner an opportunity to link new knowledge to prior experience; and social constructivism calls for collaborative social interaction as an indispensable tool for learning. These inclusive and constructivist approaches need to be reflected also in pre-service teacher education (Bartolo and Smyth, 2009).

Collaborative learning has taken a new meaning through the use of social networking tools that are enabling the creation of VLCs, i.e. virtual communities of learners who share a common interest, idea, or goal and enter into an electronic communication network of interactions "through which the process of knowledge acquisition is collaboratively created" (Palloff and Pratt, 2007, p. 5).

This chapter describes how an e-learning module on responding to student diversity, undertaken by a group of pre-service teachers in Malta, enabled their collaborative preparation for inclusion. The account highlights four major requirements in the building of VLCs, namely: using structures and processes for active learner engagement; widening access to collaborative learning; stimulating and sustaining online communication; and using appropriate technical support. The description is based on evaluation data on the module, including participants' reflective journals, a brief final account of their professional development, online forums, and responses to a post-module questionnaire, supplemented by an external expert evaluation (Mackintosh, 2007).

An innovative module on responding to diversity

The e-learning module was developed through a European Union funded project, *DTMp: Differentiated Teaching Module–primary: Preparing trainee teachers to respond to pupil diversity* (Bartolo *et al.*, 2007). The project partners were from seven higher education institutions from Malta (coordinator), Czech Republic, Germany, Lithuania, Netherlands, Sweden, and the UK. The module was prepared through transnational meetings and online interaction among the partners over three years, supported also by the Avicenna Virtual Campus, a UNESCO–Eumedis project with one of its Knowledge Centres in Malta (Eumedis, 2008).

The module content was itself an innovative product of the multiculturalism and multi-expertise of the partners (see Figure 13.1). Two of its six Parts (1 and 6) highlighted action research and inclusive teaching practice as main tools for professional development. The other four Parts (2–5) explored major issues in responding to student diversity, namely: (2) discrimination against minorities and developing more inclusive attitudes; (3) the holistic approach to education and the importance of collaborative relationships for building supportive learning communities; (4) the constructive learning process and the diversity of cultural and personal baggage children bring with them to school; and (5) learning to diversify curriculum content, process and product to meet student strengths and needs.

The module was equivalent to a 28-hour face-to-face credit unit. It was undertaken around a teaching practice placement of six weeks, with initial content sessions as preparation, followed by supervised teaching practice, and concluded with an evaluation of the inclusiveness of the teaching experience.

This chapter focuses on how the e-learning process empowered the participants for collaborative and inclusive learning. An account is first given of four major online community features implemented, followed by a description of some challenges that arose in the process.

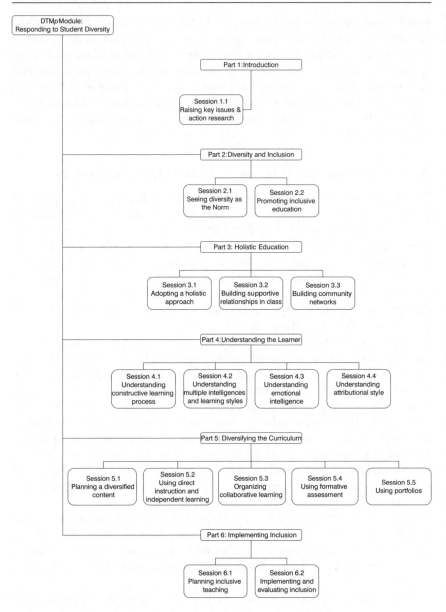

Figure 13.1 Structure of the module into six main parts and 17 sessions

Table 13.1 Example of advance organizer for the first learning outcome of Session 2.1.

Outcome	Activity	Evidence
Recognize diversity in the European context	Reflect on the diversity of your students	Write reflective notes in your journal on student diversity

Enabling active learner engagement

The first important principle for effective e-learning is that participants must be enabled to engage in self-directed and collaborative learning. The DTM*p* module addressed this through pedagogically well-structured materials as noted by the external evaluator (Mackintosh, 2007). Figure 13.1 shows how the module was divided into 17 independent learning sessions that participants could access and work on as separate topics. Participants were guided through advance organizers at the start of each session setting out the *Learning outcomes*, and *Activities* to be undertaken, and *Evidence* to be produced for the completion of each outcome (see Table 13.1).

The module also had a set of online resources consisting of readings, videos, and exercises. Participant reflective writing per session could be logged on a web Reflective Journal that was private to participants individually, while collaborative reflections could be logged to online forums. Participants were also offered a choice of topics, readings, and exercises.

Interaction was based on an asynchronous system so that participants worked collaboratively but at their own pace and time. The materials required frequent responses from the learner in the form of (a) reflections on classroom experience, readings, videos, or practical exercises and (b) sharing of ideas with others in an online forum. These logs constituted the evidence for the module assessment, and included reflections on teaching practice.

These procedures gave participants an experience of more autonomy as they themselves reported: "The best part was the fact to have learned everything by myself through my readings. It was very fulfilling not to rely on the tutor to learn."

Widening of access to learning

The DTM*p* was offered as an alternative to face-to-face delivery in a compulsory credit for BEd third-year full-time students in Malta. Half the cohort (26 of 53) opted for the online version (though only 20 were accepted, 10 for each of two tutors), seeing the choice as offering more accessibility, such as the possibility of working from home at comfortable hours for the mother of a young child, or as an innovation for the more adventurous.

The online mode offered new opportunities for some participants to engage in group discussion. One participant was amazed that the distance did not inhibit interaction but rather increased it: "People who rarely talk in a lecture at university, were constantly giving their opinions in this course." Another explained it: "In some cases the forum provided a space for colleagues who are normally shy in giving a verbal opinion during a regular lecture." On the other hand, half the group had opted for face-to-face delivery.

Building and sustaining dynamic interaction

The major principle for effective e-learning that also matches the aims of inclusive education is the creation of collaborative learning communities. The module aimed to achieve this by providing a structure for interaction: (a) a news forum gave participants space for requesting technical support or any information about the course, or to make their own suggestions; (b) a discussion forum on each topic gave students space to engage in discussion, share ideas or their own reflections on the issues related to the course aims; and (c) a time-frame for the completion of each topic enabled students to engage with similar material and discussion on the forum within the same week, though asynchronously. Participants made use of this opportunity: "I enjoyed the forum area of the module because I found myself sharing experiences, learning more from my colleagues as well as feeling a sense of communication and understanding of particular concerns or issues."

This interaction, though, needs to be stimulated and monitored (Coomey and Stephenson, 2001). The very engaging debates that occurred among the Maltese students were first stimulated by the tutors. Participants were immediately asked to start writing to each other during an introductory, hands-on session in the computer lab where the structure of the course including the need for dialogue was introduced. The tutor himself started off the news forum by asking for feedback from students about the course material. Participants' queries on technical or learning management of the course in the news forum were answered without delay.

Participants' engagement was further ensured through obliging each one to participate in each topic forum; encouraging comment on particular videos or readings; responding to participant feedback regarding the need for adjustment of time-frames for completion of sessions; giving responses to participants' ideas if necessary; and sometimes challenging lines of thinking or interaction.

This led to the students themselves raising issues with such titles as: 'Challenges in teaching a child with an impairment'; 'Removing barriers to learning'; and 'Much theory and little practice'. Participants also began to share resources from the internet that peers could easily access.

The sense of community peaked when there was an emotional issue that touched everyone. One participant wrote how she was 'panicking' at the amount of work she had to do in addition to preparations for teaching practice. This reaction spread very quickly (31 inputs in two days) and needed to be managed empathically, flexibly, and effectively by the tutor.

One can argue that this is not much different from what happens in effective face-to-face learning when students are given a voice. As already observed, though, the web format allows for much more peer-to-peer interaction over time: computer mediated communication allows for more diverse views to be expressed and considered as well as allowing for wider interaction among peers.

Having appropriate technical support

This pedagogical structure and process were developed along the lines of self-directed learning materials. The services of a teacher trained in ICT pedagogy were, however, necessary for putting them on a web platform that provided user-friendly advance organizers, sequential but flexible organization of information, and organization of the resources and web journal and forums, and dealing effectively with hitches inherent in a new venture.

There was also a decision to take regarding the web platform. *Moodle*, an open source learning management system (http://moodle.org), was chosen as the platform that was later adopted for all the university's online courses. *Moodle* provides a digital space for delivering instruction with facilities for registering on a course, accessing online instruction and learning resources, engaging in asynchronous group discussions, submitting and re-editing of work and its assessment, as well as interpersonal interaction. Other Web 2.0 functions such as Wikis can also be added to widen collaborative learning (Ghislandi *et al.*, 2008, p. 2).

The tutor needs to have sufficient knowledge of the platform in order to use their editing potential in making any small changes or additions to the materials, pacing of course work, and to operate the communication system generally. Similarly, it is useful if participants can be introduced to the navigation system and facilities offered by the platform. Technical support is also required throughout the module, particularly when students have problems accessing materials or for creating any new facility, such as regrouping of enrolled students.

Challenges

The implementation of the DTM*p* module also raised the following three challenges.

More accessibility or a digital divide?

One size, even in online learning, does not fit all. As in face-to-face delivery, one has to plan for a diversity of learners by exploiting the full potential flexibility of online learning environments. This can be achieved at the design stage by asking, "What are the learning objectives I want my learners to meet?", and then, "What are the many ways or the many learning activities that can be used to meet these learning objectives?" (Treviranus and Roberts, 2006, p. 491).

It must be kept in mind that, despite the high hopes that e-learning would be "a catalyst for fundamental change and a tool for achieving European policies on social inclusion, language learning, addressing the skills gap and intercultural dialogue ..." (European Commission, 2003, p. 4), empirical evidence continues to point to a 'digital divide' that tends to recreate the social divisions in society and among nations (OECD, 2008). There are economic divides (physical accessibility to computers and internet), usability divides (level of digital literacy skills), and empowerment divides (participation inequality) (Nielson, 2006) that need to be considered in the courses that are offered.

Transformation of tutors' and learners' roles

Successful online tutoring requires preparation. E-learning requires a new "collaborative relationship between learner and instructor, with learners themselves as key players in the education experience as they bring in diverse work, location, family, and cultural experiences into online discussion" (Heythornthwaite, 2006, p. 15). Innovative online tutoring is, therefore, "probably the most important critical success factor in learner acceptance of e-learning," and requires academic retraining as familiar face-to-face teaching solutions may not work in VLCs (McPherson and Nunes, 2004, p. 2).

Tutors need great skills also in stimulating peer-to-peer interaction. They have to create opportunities for learners not only to acquire skills and concepts but also to contribute to the learning community. Indeed, it has been suggested that the whole way of organizing web interaction in VLCs should not be around courses but around interests, allowing for people to be in the community of a course as only one of many unifying interests among a university community, who will all be regarded as 'co-learners' rather than e-learners (Colazzo et al., 2008).

New learner roles from "passive 'consumers' of didactical presented knowledge to self responsible initiators and organizers of learning" (Hamburg et al., 2003, p. 13) may also require preparation of participants. They need not only training in low-level skills such as web navigation and online social skills, but also higher metacognitive skills on creative use of web tools (McPherson and Nunes, 2004).

Need for a practice component

Another important issue for e-learning as a self-directed process is its insufficiency when used for professional development courses, such as for inclusive education which is primarily a human rights and attitudinal issue (Bartolo and Smyth, 2009). For instance, Kim and Morningstar (2007, p. 125) found that the impact of an online training program for secondary special education teachers that relied only on self-directed learning "was not powerful enough to change perceptions of competence or enhance already positive attitudes." They concluded that "[p]rofessional development providers must address not only teachers' knowledge but also their beliefs if they wish to affect how these teachers will plan, enact, monitor, and evaluate new interventions" (Kim and Morningstar, 2007, p. 126).

Thus, e-learning for professional development needs to be linked to challenges in practice. Even in face-to-face learning, significant impact on pre-service teachers was found only when supervisors engaged the teachers in critical reflection on their practice, such as asking how far an otherwise quality lesson was relevant and appropriate in terms of subject matter and instructional strategies for students from various cultural backgrounds.

The DTM*p* team addressed this challenge by linking the module to implementation of inclusion during participants' teaching practice. Several commented on this aspect:

> The credit gave a lot of insights of what really happens in class, as there were even quotes from teachers. Still, there were times when I found it difficult to understand what I was reading because I could not envisage the setting. Then I stepped into class and I encountered these situations myself and I fully understood the concepts.

Trying out inclusive practice was essential for learning:

> Previously, I was not really sure if I can really carry out differentiated teaching and learning because I never saw it actually happening. This was a great challenge for me to try it out myself, but ... I learned from trial and error as well as learning from my colleagues' experiences.

It had originally been planned to provide another multicultural challenge to students by having them discuss issues with student teachers in other European countries doing the same module. But the need for the same time frames for topic coverage across countries was not met.

The potential of intercultural dialogue was, however, experienced among the project tutors, themselves a group of collaborative learners in the development of the module through a blended procedure of face-to-face meetings and electronic interaction. One partner, on seeing earlier scripts of the module, had queried the relevance of the materials for non-English speaking students in her country. This led the team to search for local texts to supplement the English materials and the production of hard copies of the handbook in the seven different languages of the partners (Bartolo *et al.*, 2007). The team's openness to multicultural behaviors, values and concepts, including the idea of inclusion itself, was much improved through this dynamic interaction.

Virtual multicultural and international communities might perhaps offer the possibility for individuals to be challenged by the actual dynamics of a multicultural group. Having participants in a VLC challenged respectfully and being guided to react similarly to this challenge within the community can be a form of practice of intercultural and inclusive skills.

Conclusion

This chapter has set out the potential of the use of web-based VLCs for promoting inclusion as well as the preparation of teachers for inclusive education. It has suggested that e-learning is a very appropriate tool because of its potential to provide an additional alternative access strategy for ITE, to focus on learner-directed learning, and to enable the development of VLCs that can support the contribution of all members to the learning experience. At the same time, it has been noted that such an endeavor is not an easy option, particularly because it requires a rethinking of teaching and learning situations, including: (a) very skilled preparation of the learning environment to ensure a process-oriented organization that enables more autonomous learning and wider and multiple access and modes of engagement and contribution by the participants; (b) very skilled moderation of the participants' experience by tutors that are able to ensure the creation and development of a dynamic VLC; and (c) technical support to ensure the exploitation of constantly developing web social networking tools.

References

Bartolo, P. A., Ale, P., Calleja, C., Hofsäss, T., Humphrey, N., Janikova, V., *et al.* (2007) *Responding To Student Diversity: Teacher's Handbook,* Malta: University of Malta. Online. Available at: www.dtmp.org (accessed 18 February 2009).

Bartolo, P. A. and Smyth, G. (2009) "Teacher Education for Diversity", in A. Swennen and M. van der Klink (eds), *Becoming a Teacher Educator,* Netherlands: Springer, pp. 117–32.

Colazzo, L., Molinari, A. and Villa, N. (2008) "Learning to live in the knowledge society", in M. Kendall and B. Samways (eds), *IFIP International Federation for Information Processing,* 281, Boston: Springer, pp. 329–38.

Coomey, M. and Stephenson, J. (2001) "Online learning: It is all about dialogue, involvement, support and control – according to research", in J. Stephenson (ed.),

Teaching and Learning Online: Pedagogies for New Technologies, London: Kogan Page, pp. 37–52.

Eumedis (2008) *Avicenna.* Online. Available at: http://www.eumedis.net/en/projects/results/achieved_results/387.html (accessed 18 February 2009).

European Commission (2003) *Commission Staff Working Paper [SEC (2003) 905]: eLearning: Designing Tomorrow's Education – A Mid-Term Report,* Brussels. Online. Available at: http://ec.europa.eu/education/archive/elearning/doc_en.html (accessed 18 February 2009).

Ghislandi, P., Mattei, A., Paolino, D., Pellegrini, A. and Pisanu, F. (2008) "Designing online learning communities for higher education: Possibilities and limits of moodle", paper presented at ED-MEDIA 2008, World Conference on Multimedia, Hypermedia and Telecommunications, Vienna. Online. Available at: http://www.editlib.org/ (accessed 5 November 2008).

Hamburg, I., Lindecke, C. and Ten Thij, H. (2003) "Social aspects of e-learning and blending learning methods", *4th European Conference E-Comm-Line 2003,* Bucharest, 25–6 September.

Haythornthwaite, C. (2006) "The social informatics of e-learning", paper presented at the Information, Communication and Society (ICS) 10th Anniversary International Symposium, York, England, September. Online. Available at: https://www.ideals.uiuc.edu/ (accessed 30 October 2008).

Kim, K.-H. and Morningstar, M. E. (2007) "Enhancing secondary special education teachers' knowledge and competencies in working with culturally and linguistically diverse families through online training", *Career Development for Exceptional Individuals,* 30(2): 116–28.

Mackintosh, W. (2007) "Evaluation review: Differentiated teaching (FTZ515)", report submitted to the Malta Avicenna Knowledge Centre. Online. Available at: www.dtmp.org (accessed 18 February 2009).

McPherson, M. A. and Nunes, M. B. (2004) "The role of tutors as an integral part of online learning support", *European Journal of Open, Distance and E-Learning – Electronic Journal,* 2004(1): 1–10. Online. Available at: http://www.eurodl.org/materials/contrib/2004/Maggie_MsP.html (accessed 18 February 2009).

Nielson, A. (2006) *Alertbox: Digital Divide: The Three Stages.* Online. Available at: http://www.useit.com/alertbox/digital-divide.html (accessed 18 February 2009).

OECD, Centre for Educational Research and Innovation (2008) "Trends shaping education – 2008 edition", *OECD Education and Skills,* 4: 1–90.

Palloff, R. M. and Pratt, K. (2007) *Building Online Learning Communities: Effective Strategies for the Virtual Classroom,* 2nd edn, San Francisco: Jossey Bass.

Treviranus, J. and Roberts, V. (2006) "Inclusive e-learning", in J. Weiss, J. Hunsinger, J. Nolan and P. Trifonas (eds), *The International Handbook of Virtual Learning Environments,* Netherlands: Springer, pp. 469–96.

Chapter 14

Evaluating inclusive teacher education programs

A flexible framework

Spencer J. Salend

Learning outcomes

- Understand the importance of evaluating inclusive teacher education programs.
- Tailor the framework presented in this chapter to evaluate your inclusive initial teacher education (ITE) program.

Introduction

Global transformations and concerns about the efficacy of segregated special educational programs have resulted in educators throughout the world seeking to implement inclusive education. Although the concept and implementation of inclusion varies greatly by country (Mitchell, 2005), one critical variable in the successful implementation of inclusive education is the quality of the preparation that educators receive (Forlin and Lian, 2008; Salend, 2008). As a result, ITE programs throughout the world have been utilizing innovative pedagogies and approaches to help develop the knowledge, skills, and dispositions to implement inclusive education effectively. Since it is important for these innovative programs to be effectively evaluated this chapter presents a flexible framework that can be tailored for use by faculty also involved in inclusive professional learning (PL) efforts.

Identifying evaluation dimensions and questions

Program evaluation focuses on important evaluative dimensions related to the critical aspects of inclusive ITE programs. Critical aspects of these programs often address the program's (a) core beliefs, (b) curriculum and competencies, (c) pedagogical practices and learning activities, (d) field-based experiences, (e) recruitment and graduation of a diverse pool of pre-service teachers, (f) faculty diversity, and (g) impact on the field (Salend *et al.*, 2006). An overview of these critical programmatic aspects, evaluation dimensions, related evaluation questions, and potential data sources are presented in the following sections.

Table 14.1 Sample evaluation questions and data sources: Core beliefs related to inclusive education.

Evaluation questions	Data sources
1. Are the program's core beliefs identified, communicated to others, and related to current research and innovation in the field and relevant social, philosophical, political, cultural and economic factors within the country?	• Surveys • Interviews • Observations • Instructional and program artifacts
2. What actions can be taken to maintain and enhance the extent to which core beliefs related to inclusive education are consistently and fully integrated into the program?	• Pre-service teachers' portfolios • Program portfolios • Reflective journals

Core beliefs related to inclusive education

Inclusive ITE programs reflect the faculty's core beliefs related to inclusive education, which should be consistent with current research and innovation in the field. The core beliefs underpinning inclusive ITE programs vary based on each country's educational philosophy and history as well as a range of social, political, cultural and economic factors (Mitchell, 2005). Thus, in many countries social justice and multicultural education are viewed as being inextricably linked to inclusive education, which has broadened the focus of inclusive education beyond disability to include issues of race, linguistic ability, economic status, gender, learning style, ethnicity, cultural and religious background, family structure, and sexual orientation (Salend, 2008). Sample evaluation questions and potential data sources related to an inclusive ITE program's core beliefs are presented in Table 14.1.

Curriculum, courses, and competencies

The program's core beliefs inform the inclusive ITE program's curriculum, which in turn shapes the development, delivery, and sequence of the courses that make up the program. The curriculum delineates the essential competencies needed to be effective inclusive education practitioners. As a central aspect of an ITE program, the validity of the curriculum, the courses that make up the program and their sequence, and the extent to which program competencies relate to the knowledge, skills, and disposition teachers use to work effectively in inclusive education, serve as the source of major evaluation questions (see Table 14.2).

Inclusive pedagogical practices and learning activities

Faculty in effective inclusive ITE programs employ inclusive pedagogical practices and learning activities within courses to foster mastery of the

Table 14.2 Sample evaluation questions and data sources: Curriculum, courses, and competencies.

Evaluation questions	Data sources
1. Is the program's curriculum complete, valid, and linked to professional standards? 2. To what extent are the courses within the program related to the program's curriculum and sequenced appropriately? 3. To what extent do the program's competencies relate to the program's courses and address the knowledge, skills, and disposition that teachers need to work effectively in inclusive education settings? 4. What types of problems are pre-service teachers having with the courses? 5. What aspects of the program's curriculum, courses, and competencies work well? Need revision? 6. What actions need to be taken to maintain and enhance the validity of the curriculum, the content and sequence of the courses, and the relevance of the program's competencies?	• Surveys • Interviews • Observations • Instructional artifacts • Program artifacts • Pre-service teachers' portfolios • Program portfolios • Reflective journals • Rubrics • Examinations

program's curriculum and competencies. These innovative pedagogical practices include providing pre-service teachers with numerous opportunities to reflect on their learning and to interact with individuals with special educational needs and their families (McHatton, 2007). Through various learning activities, pre-service teachers produce authentic assignments that allow them to demonstrate their success at applying program competencies and translating research into practice. The use of a range of pedagogical practices and learning activities also allows faculty to model effective and reflective inclusive teaching and assessment practices. Given the importance of these pedagogical practices and learning activities, it is essential that evaluation questions and data sources examine whether they are effective in achieving their intended outcomes (see Table 14.3).

Field-based experiences

The field-based experiences that pre-service teachers complete throughout their inclusive ITE program are integral parts of the program's pedagogical practices and learning activities. Through a variety of field-based experiences reflecting wide contextual and student diversity, pre-service teachers are provided with authentic experiences in inclusive educational settings designed to help them: (a) link theory and practice; (b) view exemplary professionals implementing inclusive education; (c) apply the program's competencies in inclusive educational settings; and (d) think critically about their values and beliefs and practices. In light of the essential role these varied field-based

Table 14.3 Sample evaluation questions and data sources: Inclusive pedagogical practices and learning activities.

Evaluation questions	Data sources
1. Are the program's pedagogical practices and learning activities aligned to the program's curriculum, courses, and competencies? 2. Are faculty using pedagogical practices that are inclusive, and effective in helping pre-service teachers master the program's competencies? 3. Are learning activities completed by pre-service teachers authentic, reflective, and effective in helping them develop and demonstrate mastery of the program's competencies? 4. What pedagogical practices and learning activities work well? Need revision? 5. What actions need to be taken to enhance the inclusiveness, authenticity, effectiveness and variety of the faculty's pedagogical practices and the learning activities completed by pre-service teachers?	• Surveys • Interviews • Observations • Instructional artifacts • Program artifacts • Pre-service teachers' portfolios • Program portfolios • Reflective journals • Rubrics • Examinations

Table 14.4 Sample evaluation questions and data sources: Field-based experiences.

Evaluation questions	Data sources
1. Do the program's field work and practicum sites serve as exemplary models of inclusive education and enhance pre-service teachers' knowledge of the lives of diverse students and families, and broaden their views and understanding of diversity? 2. What roles and activities do pre-service teachers perform in their field-based placements? 3. Do field work and practicum sites provide pre-service teachers with opportunities to develop and demonstrate their mastery of the program's competencies, and reflect on their values, beliefs, and professional practices? 4. How do pre-service teachers rate the quality of their field work and practicum experiences and the supervision and feedback they received? 5. What aspects of the program's field work and practicum experiences work well? Need revision? 6. What actions need to be taken to enhance the inclusiveness, diversity, authenticity, variety, and effectiveness of the program's practicum and field work experiences?	• Surveys • Interviews • Observations • Instructional artifacts • Program artifacts • Pre-service teachers' portfolios • Program portfolios • Reflective journals • Rubrics

Table 14.5 Sample evaluation questions and data sources: Recruitment and graduation of a diverse pool of pre-service teachers.

Evaluation questions	Data sources
1. What are the demographic characteristics of the program's pre-service teachers? 2. What efforts have been implemented by faculty to recruit and graduate a diverse pool of pre-service teachers and how successful have they been? 3. What factors are affecting the program's success at recruiting and graduating a diverse pool of pre-service teachers? 4. What actions need to be taken to recruit and graduate a diverse group of pre-service teachers?	• Surveys • Interviews • Program artifacts • Program portfolios • Pre-service teachers' portfolios • Reflective journals

experiences play in inclusive ITE programs, their effectiveness needs to be the focus of evaluation questions (Maheady *et al.*, 2007) (see Table 14.4).

Recruitment and graduation of a diverse pool of pre-service teachers

The recruitment and graduation of pre-service teachers who represent the diversity of the communities served by inclusive ITE programs is a critical challenge (Salend *et al.*, 2006). The issues of participation and completion are interrelated and impact the extent to which inclusive ITE programs model inclusive practices and infuse diversity into all aspects of their programs. Therefore, the research questions examining the success of these in responding to the challenge of enrolling and graduating a diverse pool of pre-service teachers is an often overlooked but crucial component of program evaluation (see Table 14.5).

Faculty diversity

In addition to a diverse group of pre-service teachers, inclusive ITE programs are strengthened by having a diverse faculty (Salend *et al.*, 2006). A diverse faculty allows pre-service teachers and faculty to learn from and interact with individuals who have different areas of expertise, experiential and cultural backgrounds, pedagogical practices and teaching styles. Therefore, the evaluation questions related to the diversity of the faculty including their varied roles, expertise, backgrounds, and teaching practices are an integral part of program evaluation (see Table 14.6).

Impact on the field

The impact on the field is the ultimate measure of the efficacy of inclusive ITE programs (Ainscow *et al.*, 2006). The primary factor in assessing the

Table 14.6 Sample evaluation questions and data sources: Faculty diversity.

Evaluation questions	Data sources
1. What efforts have been implemented to encourage and support faculty diversity and how successful have these efforts been? 2. What factors are affecting the program's success at having a diverse faculty? 3. What actions need to be taken to enhance the diversity of the faculty?	• Surveys • Interviews • Program artifacts • Program portfolios

Table 14.7 Sample evaluation questions and data sources: Impact on the field.

Evaluation questions	Data sources
1. In what ways do pre-service teachers and graduates promote student learning and aid schools in implementing effective inclusive education practices? 2. To what extent do graduates employ the knowledge, skills, and disposition they gained in the program in their inclusive education classrooms? 3. What outreach activities do faculty and pre-service teachers perform and how do these activities impact schools, teachers, students and families? 4. In what ways do faculty disseminate their research on inclusive education and support professional learning of teachers? 5. To what extent are graduates finding employment in inclusive educational settings? 6. How do graduates and their employers rate their job performance? 7. What actions need to be taken to enhance the program's impact on the field?	• Surveys • Interviews • Observations • Instructional artifacts • Program artifacts • Pre-service teachers' portfolios • Program portfolios • Reflective journals • Rubrics

program's impact on the field is the extent to which the program's graduates teach effectively in inclusive educational settings, which can be established by demonstrating the connection between their participation in an inclusive ITE program and their use of effective teaching practices that foster positive academic, affective, social, behavioral, and attitudinal outcomes for their students (Goe *et al.*, 2008). These educational changes in students can be documented via use of standardized assessments, curriculum-based measurements, and analysis of student work samples over time. These data can be supplemented by an examination of other indicators of student progress such as graduation rates, attendance patterns, participation in extracurricular activities, behavioral referrals, and course failures as well as student success in making the transition from school to adulthood (Salend, 2008) (see Table 14.7).

The program's impact on the field also can be documented by the outcomes associated with the outreach activities that faculty and pre-service teachers perform, and the faculty's success at disseminating their research on inclusive education practices and delivering professional development to inservice teachers. Other program impact factors include the success that program graduates have in finding employment and fostering inclusion in their work settings, and the extent to which employers are satisfied with their job performance. Sample evaluation questions related to a program's impact on the field are presented in the tables.

Selecting evaluation data collection methods

A range of methods can be used to collect qualitative and quantitative data to address the program's identified evaluation dimensions and questions. In developing and selecting these data collection tools and strategies, program faculty should consider such factors as validity, reliability, comprehensiveness, generalization, utility, practicality, acceptability, and credibility (Goe *et al.*, 2008).

Surveys and interviews

Important evaluation information can be obtained by surveying and interviewing pre-service teachers, faculty, professionals who work with pre-service teachers in their field-based placements, and employers of program graduates (Morningstar *et al.*, 2008). Surveys and interviews can be employed at appropriate times within the program's cycle to elicit reactions to specific aspects of inclusive ITE programs. For pre-service teachers and faculty, surveys and interviews can solicit information about their feelings and suggestions about the program's core beliefs, curriculum, competencies, courses, learning activities, faculty pedagogical practices, and field-based experiences. Follow-up surveys and interviews with program graduates also can provide data regarding the validity and need for revision of program assumptions, competencies, and learning activities; their preparedness and use of effective practices in their inclusive classrooms; and the extent to which these practices have promoted student learning. Professionals who work with pre-service teachers in their field-based placements or employ program graduates also can complete surveys and interviews directed at identifying their perceptions of the quality, preparedness, and effectiveness of the program's pre-service teachers and graduates.

Observations

Real-time or digitally recorded observations of pre-service teachers in their field-based experiences can provide valuable information to document their mastery of the program's competencies and their impact on student learning. These observations can be used to record the impact of the program on teachers' progress in demonstrating subject matter knowledge, differentiating their instructional and assessment practices, interacting positively with students and other professionals, and fostering a positive learning environment (Goe *et al.*, 2008). Observations of program graduates' teaching effectiveness in inclusive classrooms by their employers also can be a valuable source of evaluation data related to the program's impact on the field.

Peer observations of pre-service teachers and program faculty also can be used to support program evaluation. For faculty, peer observations can be periodically conducted to focus on providing data regarding the faculty's use of innovative pedagogies. Faculty also can complete a field-based site observation form when visiting schools to validate that inclusive practices are being implemented successfully and that pre-service teachers are being provided with opportunities to work with a range of students.

Instructional and program artifacts

An analysis of the instructional artifacts that pre-service teachers produce as part of their course work and field work experiences, and program graduates develop in their inclusive work settings, can provide evidence related to their mastery of the program's curriculum and competencies and use of effective inclusive education practices, and the program's impact on the field (Maheady *et al.*, 2007).

One instructional artifact that holds promise for promoting and documenting changes in pre-service teachers is the use of case methods (Goeke, 2008). An analysis of pre-service teachers' responses to a range of case studies over time can be examined to show changes in their disposition, knowledge base, problem solving skills, and practices related to inclusive education.

As part of the evaluation, program artifacts developed by faculty also can be examined. These program artifacts can include course outlines, descriptions of and protocols associated with innovative pedagogical practices, listings of recruitment activities, and copies of publications.

Reflective journals

A reflective journal maintained by pre-service teachers can be a valuable artifact containing evaluation data related to their experiences in the program and changes in their knowledge, practices, perspectives, disposition, attitudes, beliefs, intentions, and ability to engage in self-reflection (Goe *et al.*, 2008). Thus, as part of their courses and field-based experiences, pre-service teachers can write reflective journal entries regarding their experiences, thoughts, observations, accomplishments, frustrations and conflicts, and their interactions with faculty and other professionals as well as students and their families.

Portfolios

Various instructional and program artifacts can be collected in portfolios maintained by pre-service teachers and faculty (Morningstar *et al.*, 2008). Portfolios maintained by pre-service teachers can document their learning, goals, disposition, attitudes, pedagogical practices, achievements, and mastery of program competencies and professional standards established by accreditation groups, and the effect of their activities on their students. Project faculty and practicing professionals can review these portfolios to identify what they show about pre-service teachers' mastery of the program's competencies, to assess the effectiveness of individual courses and assignments, to examine the coherence of the course sequence, to document the program's impact on student learning, and to offer feedback to improve various aspects of the program.

A program portfolio maintained by faculty can provide a comprehensive, historical record of the program's activities and accomplishments and foster and enhance program evaluation. As such, a program portfolio can serve as an evaluation tool to prompt faculty to engage in continuous self-examination of the program's goals, efforts, successes, and challenges for improvement that need to be addressed.

Rubrics

Program faculty, in collaboration with pre-service and practicing teachers and other stakeholders, can develop rubrics linked to the program's competencies and core beliefs and the standards established by external program evaluation groups. These rubrics can then be used to quantitatively and qualitatively evaluate various instructional artifacts produced by pre-service teachers and program graduates in terms of their quality, authenticity, usefulness, reflection, impact on student learning, and alignment to effective practices and professional standards.

Examinations

Pre-service teachers' mastery of subject matter and knowledge of the field of education can be assessed by examinations. In addition to examining and reporting quantitative data on the overall performance of pre-service teachers on these examinations, an item analysis of performance on specific sections can provide data to assess the extent to which programs are successful in fostering pre-service teachers' knowledge of the content areas they will teach and the fields of general and special education.

Analyzing evaluation data

The quantitative and qualitative data collected should be analyzed on an ongoing basis by an evaluation team comprised of faculty and stakeholders to provide formative and summative assessment data related to the program's effectiveness and the identified evaluation dimensions and questions. Formative assessment data are analyzed to provide ongoing program feedback that is used to make decisions to foster continuous program improvements, and summative assessment data are examined to determine the program's impact and achievements at specific points in time. Formative and summative evaluation data should also be analyzed by the evaluation team to:

- document the program's effectiveness, strengths, and accomplishments;
- verify that the project's activities were implemented as designed and identify those aspects of the program that were not conducted as intended;
- validate and compare effective programmatic models, approaches, policies, and practices and identify the factors that contributed to their efficacy;
- identify program challenges that need to be improved as well as strategies for enhancing their effectiveness.

The analyzed evaluation data can then be employed to assess the overall efficacy of the program, validate effective practices, and develop an action plan to improve the program's effectiveness. Analyzed data should be disseminated to inform the field, to help others develop and implement effective inclusive ITE programs, and to obtain accreditation from professional groups and external bodies.

Cautions

In implementing this evaluation framework, faculty should be aware of several possible limitations. Faculty need to make sure that their core beliefs reflect more than the dominant culture and include historically marginalized groups. Failure to do so can result in a continuation of exclusive practices. Faculty also will need to be provided with sufficient time and resources to implement the systematic and ongoing program evaluation efforts described in this chapter.

Conclusion

Given the critical role that the preparation of teachers plays in the implementation of inclusive education, this chapter offers a framework for evaluating inclusive teacher education programs that can be used by faculty involved in both ITE and PL programs. Recognizing that the definition and implementation of inclusive education varies globally, the framework presented can be used by teacher educators in flexible ways that reflect their varied contexts so that they can examine and improve the effectiveness of their programs, approaches, and practices.

References

Ainscow, M., Booth, T. and Dyson, A. (2006) *Improving Schools Developing Inclusion*, London: Routledge

Forlin, C. and Lian, M. J. (2008). *Reform, Inclusion and Teacher Education: Towards a New Era of Special Education in the Asia-Pacific Region*, New York: Routledge.

Goe, L., Bell, C. and Little, O. (2008) *Approaches to Evaluating Teacher Effectiveness: A Research Synthesis*, Washington, DC: National Comprehensive Center for Teacher Quality.

Goeke, J. L. (2008) "A preliminary investigation of prospective teachers' reasoning about case studies with expert commentary", *Teacher Education and Special Education*, 31(1): 21–35.

Maheady, L., Jabot, M., Rey, J. and Michielli-Pendl, J. (2007) "An early field-based experience and its impact on pre-service candidates' teaching practice and their pupils' outcomes", *Teacher Education and Special Education*, 30(1): 24–33.

McHatton, P. A. (2007) "Listening and learning from Mexican and Puerto Rican single mothers of children with disabilities", *Teacher Education and Special Education*, 30(4): 237–48.

Mitchell, D. (ed.) (2005) *Contextualizing Inclusive Education: Evaluating Old and New International Paradigms*, London: Routledge.

Morningstar, M. E., Kim, K. and Clark, G. M. (2008) "Evaluating a transition personnel preparation program: Identifying transition competences of practitioners", *Teacher Education and Special Education*, 31(1): 47–58.

Salend, S. J. (2008) *Creating Inclusive Classrooms: Effective and Reflective Practices*, 6th edn, Columbus, OH: Merrill/Prentice Hall.

Salend, S. J., Whittaker, C. R. and Garrick Duhaney, L. M. (2006) "Preparing special educators to work with migrant students with disabilities and their families", *Multiple Voices*, 9(1): 185–95.

Part III

Professional learning for practising teachers

Chapter 15

Modelling and guiding inclusive practices

A challenge for postgraduate educators

Adrian Ashman

Learning outcomes

- Ways of providing professional learning (PL) to education postgraduate students via a course offered in external/distance mode.
- Ways of providing postgraduate students with flexible ways of satisfying course assessment requirements.
- The importance of regular dialogue with postgraduate students to ensure that their learning objectives are met.

Introduction

Inclusive education has emerged over almost five decades as a response to the recognition of the social injustices that kept students with special learning needs separated from their peers who were progressing according to age norms and expectations. While there have been significant developments in legislation and policy in many countries, we are still some distance from the reality of fully inclusive schools and classrooms. While one might be seduced by policies and the associated rhetoric to believe that inclusive education is not only common, but universal, the reality is that it is not, despite enthusiastic and forward-thinking government and bureaucratic initiatives and sensible advocacy (e.g., Ashman, 2007).

There is no simple way in which this situation can be redressed. One might start by looking at ways in which societies and communities deal with difference and variation. One could also begin by dealing with the historical resistances and opposition to educational mainstreaming, integration, and inclusion from parents and teachers. Many writers have addressed the issue by focusing on teachers' PL. Their goal has been to improve teachers' knowledge about disability and pedagogy that promote positive attitudes toward inclusion and student diversity. In this contribution, I focus on teachers' PL undertaken in postgraduate education programs at university.

Several characteristics differentiate involvement in system/school PL and what occurs at a tertiary institution. For example, teachers who enroll at university are often seeking credentials that will lead to career advancement (i.e., higher salary, promotion). They are generally extrinsically motivated because they are paying for their postgraduate education and may also be intrinsically motivated because they expect to apply new knowledge and skills directly to their own classrooms.

If we intend to promote inclusion, education courses and programs must be informed not only by the literature relating to effective PL but also by the vast body of research on inclusive education. While a full discussion of these topics is beyond the scope of this chapter, it is important to draw the reader's attention to at least a few key ideas.

In courses I have taught over the past half decade, I have lectured about the importance of Universal Design for Learning (UDL), curriculum differentiation, and PL as key elements that guide and promote inclusive practices that lead to positive student outcomes. I have paid attention to these notions when developing course content and preparing resources but I have infrequently taken the next step, to integrate these ideas into university course delivery, content, and assessment.

There is scant space to deal expansively with each of these concepts here. Readers can readily locate references to each through library databases or the worldwide web. For UDL, readers might look at Center for Universal Design (2008) and Scott *et al.* (2003) where the guiding principles are explained and discussed. Curriculum differentiation is hardly a new notion and an interesting starting place for readings on this topic would be Maker (1982), then perhaps Tomlinson (2003) in which differentiation seems to be conceptualized as an alternative way of framing UDL. There has also been considerable literature on PL. Duffy (1993) reported a landmark study in which he taught teachers how to incorporate cognitive strategies into their reading programs. While the focus of his four-year study was not inclusive education per se, it has significant implications if its generalization is considered. A good follow-up volume is Guskey (2000).

The project

I have been teaching postgraduate courses on special needs and inclusive education for many years. The overwhelming majority of students enrolling in these courses have been teachers working in the widest range of contexts from early childhood through to tertiary education. A much smaller number of my students have been school counselors and other education or health professionals.

In 2008, I was assigned two compulsory courses within the Inclusive and Special Needs specialization in the coursework graduate certificate, graduate diploma, and Master of Education programs. Historically, both have attracted enrollments less than 15 in each. They are entitled Issues in Special Needs Education, and Learning and Diversity: Assessment, Planning and Instruction.

Issues in Special Needs Education was introduced in the late 1990s to explore the breadth of issues that relate to the education of students with special learning needs including cultural influences, legislation and policy, internationalization in education, information, and communication technologies, peer-mediated learning, and school environments. Learning and Diversity has a shorter history and has a practical orientation. It includes topics on assessment, working with families, UDL, reading, mathematics, instructional support, and affective components of learning.

In an ideal world, students would take the Issues course in one semester and the Learning and Diversity course in the next and both would be offered internally and externally with the majority of students attending classes each week. Practically, up to half of those enrolled at any time take the courses simultaneously and nearly all have a preference for external mode due to their residential location away from the university, family commitments that limit attending classes on campus, timetable conflict, and the desire to self-initiate and self-regulate their learning. In 2008, both courses were offered in external mode only and in the same semester.

As I adopted the same general principles to instruction, I have taken this group as a collective to report the implementation and the outcomes of the courses.

The students

Issues in Special Needs Education attracted 13 students with 11 continuing beyond the second week of semester; Learning and Diversity attracted 14, with 13 continuing through the semester. Three students were enrolled in both courses, making a cohort of 20 students.

The students were enrolled in four programs: a Graduate Certificate in Education, Graduate Certificate or Diploma in Educational Studies, with the majority in the Master of Education Studies. Not surprisingly, females overwhelmingly outnumbered males and the average age of the group was just over 30 years with a range from 20 to just under 60 years. Half of the students lived within the local metropolitan area, with the largest minority living in regional cities. One lived in a rural community, and another overseas.

The professional background of the students was teaching with one exception, a health professional. Of the 19 teachers, four specialized in early childhood, five in primary education, seven in secondary education, and three had teaching experiences from early childhood through the secondary years. Nine teachers held specialist roles in schools (e.g., special education teacher, learning support, counselling), eight indicated that they had ongoing experience with students with special needs within their own classes. Only two reported no direct professional contact with such students.

Course structure

The approach I took in both courses was based upon the belief that if I am urging my students (i.e., practicing teachers) to adopt inclusive education principles, I should teach by example. In other words, I should adopt the principles and practices of UDL. I should differentiate the curriculum to the greatest extent possible, and apply adult learning procedures in line with effective PL characteristics.

The UDL provided some challenges because of the imperative to integrate content and resources, to provide multi-sensory teaching, tap multiple intelligences, differentiate instruction, use a range of information and communication technologies, and employ performance-based assessment. Such principles seem eminently reasonable in a school or early childhood setting but are a challenge at the tertiary level. I decided to focus on applying the principles of equitable and flexible use, simple and intuitive application, and the development of a positive instructional climate to the greatest extent possible. Added to these were recommendations (again coming from a school context) from Algozzine and Anderson (2007) and Rock *et al.* (2008) that promoted (among other ideas) choice and flexibility in delivery of a curriculum, a responsiveness to individual student needs, the integration of assessment with instruction, and ongoing adjustments to instruction to meet student needs.

Below is a list of the key course delivery issues that guided my practice.

1 Model high quality engagement: interest in student progress; quick turn around on queries and assessment feedback; positive and critical feedback.
2 Focus on school- and site-based PL: practical application of new knowledge by encouraging students to focus their assignments on practical procedures that will change their classroom practices, perhaps by collaborating with a colleague in their own school.
3 Demonstrate improvements in school/classroom outcomes: the aim is to make a difference to children's and teenagers' learning outcomes.
4 Take into consideration the needs and characteristics of the participants: paying attention to the teachers' backgrounds and by providing as much guidance and resource support as possible.
5 Flexible delivery options: employing the foundations of UDL by providing individualized learning approaches and assessment alternatives aiming at developing expert learners, that is, learners who are strategic and goal-directed, resourceful, purposeful, and motivated.

At my university, lecturing staff provide a mandatory digital course profile on the university's courses website. The site for each course includes a description of course aims and objectives, learning resources, the graduate attributes sought, assessment details and their contribution to the final grade, available course files (generally details about assignment marking criteria), and University policies and guidelines. Many lecturing staff provide additional material via a course web-based Blackboard site. This includes announcements, course information such as style guides and assignment/ assessment submission requirements, a discussion board, and external links.

Dialogue

In practical terms, I attempted to operationalize the five key delivery issues by entering into a dialogue with individual students. I provided access to predetermined resources, responded to spontaneous requests for information, and allowed assessment items that satisfied the needs and interests of individual students.

Perhaps the most fundamental issue for me was engagement with the students. Having taken external courses many years ago during my pre-university study years, I still recall the isolation resulting from the lack of personal contact with the lecturer and other students.

I began a dialogue with the students via the e-learning Blackboard site before the beginning of the semester – once enrollments had been finalized – to give each person an idea of my background, interests, and idiosyncrasies. I also invited them to give me a word picture of themselves. Students responded in kind, writing about their personal and professional lives. Several wrote lengthy emails indicating that the prospect of studying via external mode was new and scary and that it presented a significant challenge. Others wrote short comments expressing their optimism about the forthcoming semester.

Two weeks into the course, I sent a short email to the students asking about their reactions to the course structure and inviting them to identify specific interests so that I could pass on useful resources that might assist in their assignment preparation or professional life generally. I asked about their purpose for enrolling in the course, expectations about the development of their teaching skills, and the suitability of the resources already provided. This email again generated short and long responses. Several students commented on the fresh, interactive approach I had taken to the course. All wrote about specific issues and topics that appealed to them. These included ASD, Asperger's syndrome, gifted and talented students, social skills, and challenging behavior, to name just a few. Several asked if I had resources that I could forward to them or to which I could refer them to initiate their own explorations.

One student who lived outside the metropolitan area wrote that he was interested in the *Index for Inclusion* and expressed some exasperation about not being able to locate journal articles or other references about its use. This student wrote to me a number of times about his wish to use the *Index* as the vehicle for a project he wanted to undertake in his school, which would be the focus of his second assignment. His continuing frustration about finding a copy led me to locate one among my colleagues, which I sent to him.

The overwhelming majority of interactions with students were unsolicited. They wrote spontaneously in the first few weeks of the course about difficulties they were encountering but the content of their emails soon changed to comments about their successes and the supportive nature of the resources that were available to them and my responses to them.

Learning guide and course readings

The two courses used different resource sets due to their different foci. The learning guide for Issues in Special Needs Education contained an introductory component for each of the twelve topics, each of which provided a broad background to a topic. This was followed by two recommended readings and an abstract of each. The readings were available digitally as full text via the university library website specifically created for the course. These introductions were intended to provide breadth to the topic so that students with a wide range of personal and professional experiences might explore diverse interests rather than being constrained by a narrowly focused reading list.

I adopted a slightly different approach in Learning and Diversity based upon the knowledge that there were several students enrolled in both courses. Each topic in that Learning Guide was also prefaced by an extended introductory piece. The course-specific website contained a collection of 126 papers across the twelve topics. I selected two from the list as recommended readings for each topic and drew students' attention to the diversity of full-text papers held in the library database. There were no resource overlaps across the two courses.

These Learning Guides were not especially innovative and seem to be typical of the many provided to external students that I have seen over several decades. Notwithstanding this, the Guides appeared to hit the target with most students. One, for example, wrote that the Guide was very helpful once it had been located on the Blackboard site. She said that some of the readings were interesting and challenging. Another thought that my introductory notes to several of the topics were highly amusing.

Generally, the readings were well accepted. While I leaned toward including papers that had a practical orientation, there were also others that were theoretical, included because they provided substance that I thought would assist students when they were formulating their approaches to their chosen assignment topics. Again, I seem to have hit the target with the majority of students, although some found several of the academic papers demanding.

Assessments

I was keen to allow students great flexibility to select their study activities and assignments so that it would be relevant to their individual work environment and consistent with the reason for their enrolment in the course. I anticipated that students would have an education background and this was an issue for one student who was not a teacher although he worked in a special education context. This complication led to an extended dialogue with the student about both assignments and discussion about how the assessment could meet his professional needs.

Most students found the opportunity to pursue personal interests of considerable value even though the open-endedness of the task was initially challenging. Several commented that they found it difficult to get started but were pleased that they had the opportunity to explore areas and topics that had not been an option in previous courses that they had completed.

Student reception

Over the course of the semester, I communicated with students via email on a daily basis. Some were more discursive than others; one student had only one interaction with me over the course of the semester, other than via notes on her assignments. Two students reported that the freedom to direct their learning was very challenging but both completed the course with very satisfactory grades. Many volunteered comments about the value of my interactions and my apparent interest in them and their progress, in two cases comparing my communication and feedback with those provided by lecturers in courses taken previously.

Throughout the semester, I was mindful of one point raised by Guskey (2003) about PL, that is, the flow-through from such programs to classroom practices to student outcomes. This was my reason for providing students with the opportunity to work on topics that were of professional importance to them. Several students wrote about the way in which they hoped to apply the knowledge gained during the semester to their classrooms (or schools) and followed these with positive reports of student outcomes. Several wrote at length about self-reflections that had encouraged interactions with teacher colleagues, parents, school administrators, and their own students. One wrote generously about the classroom project she had undertaken for her second assignment and the extremely positive outcomes that were acknowledged by the students' parents. In a very animated email, she described the changes that had occurred in the school and the sense of belonging that students with learning problems had developed as a result of her project.

Some concluding remarks

At my university, one third of all courses offered are evaluated each year via a mandatory course evaluation that asks students to reflect upon the structure and quality of the course they attended. Neither of my courses was chosen for review this semester, but at the end of the semester I invited students to make final comments that might help me to develop the course further.

You will note that I have not included verbatim comments from any of my students, as I had no intention to use the experiences in these courses as a data-gathering exercise, a research activity, or a publishing opportunity. I sought feedback from students simply to provide them with the support I had contracted to provide. To report their comments directly would have required university ethics approval and students' consent to do this prior to the commencement of the courses.

Notwithstanding the lack of data presented in this contribution, I can confirm that my students overwhelmingly reported positive outcomes. Many expressed the view that the experience had led them to make significant changes to their teaching practices and the way in which they interact with their own students, and with their colleagues. Several noted that they are now strong advocates of school reform.

For me, the experience of the semester has been both enlightening and rewarding and one that has implications in educational settings well beyond my own context, nationally and internationally. I thoroughly enjoyed the interactions that I had with my students, albeit in a somewhat remote way via emails. I was surprised when I began receiving positive comments after my first set of interactions with them and I admit that these encouraged me to work even harder to help them achieve their goals (positive reinforcement, anyone?). Throughout the semester I returned to the literature on UDL and curriculum differentiation several times, looking for ways in which I could apply the principles to external postgraduate teaching. There are some principles that I never addressed, for example, I don't believe that I achieved a true community of learners where students could interact with others via a bulletin board although there are certainly some student comments that indicated connection with the course and with me.

Notwithstanding this, I believe that I addressed and achieved the fundamentals of UDL:

- Student to control the method of accessing information.
- Encouragement of students' self-sufficiency.
- Knowledge and the facilitation of learning.
- Removal of barriers to access rather than removal of challenges.
- Alternative means of gaining knowledge and essential concepts.
- Work units that accommodated levels of skill, preferences, and interests.
- Alternative ways of expressing mastery.

There are some suggestions that students have offered that will be incorporated in future. For example, I intend to introduce podcasts or mini-lectures on selected topics to augment written material, and to work on developing a community of learners through a bulletin board on the course Blackboard site (many of my colleagues already do this).

There is much more I could report about students' and my reactions to the course. I would like the final words to come from one student whose comments reflect the achievement of the goals I established for the course and myself at the beginning of this project. She commented that the flexible structure, my prompt responses to emails, and the feedback that I provided had made the course very rewarding. The most pleasing outcome, however, was the impact that she had on her own students as a result of the assessable project that she designed and implemented.

References

Algozzine, B. and Anderson, K. M. (2007) "Differentiating instruction to include all students", *Preventing School Failure*, 51: 49–54.

Ashman, A. F. (2007) "School and inclusive practices", in R. M. Gillies, A. F. Ashman and J. Terwel (eds), *The Teacher's Role in Implementing Cooperative Learning in the Classroom*, New York: Springer, pp. 163–83.

Center for Universal Design (2008) *Universal Design for Learning Guidelines, version 1.0*, Wakefield, MA: Center for Universal Design.

Duffy, G. G. (1993) "Teachers' progress towards becoming expert strategy teachers", *The Elementary School Journal*, 94: 109–20.

Guskey, T. R. (2000) *Evaluating Professional Development*, Thousand Oaks, CA: Corwin Press.

Guskey, T. R. (2003) "The characteristics of effective professional development: A synthesis of lists", paper presented at the 84th Annual Meeting of the American Educational Research Association, Chicago, IL.

Maker, J. (1982) *Curriculum Development for the Gifted*, Rockville, MD: Aspen.

Rock, M. L., Gregg, M., Ellis, E. and Gable, R. A. (2008) "Reach: A framework for differentiating classroom instruction", *Preventing School Failure*, 52: 31–47.

Scott, S. S., McGuire, J. M. and Shaw, S. F. (2003) "Universal design for instruction: A new paradigm for adult instruction in postsecondary education", *Remedial and Special Education*, 24: 369–79.

Tomlinson, C. A. (2003) *Fulfilling the Promise of the Differentiated Classroom: Strategies and Tools for Responsive Teaching*, Alexandria, VA: Association for Supervision and Curriculum Development.

Chapter 16

Humanizing online learning

Ways of engaging teachers in contemporary understandings and practices

Phyllis Jones

Learning outcomes

- Demonstrate the movement towards online learning for teachers of students with severe intellectual and developmental disabilities.
- Illustrate the role that technology plays in providing meaningful inservice opportunities for these teachers.
- Become aware of one approach to online learning that supports teachers to challenge current assumptions, understandings and practices and engage in discussions about inclusion.

Introduction

This chapter presents a way of working with teachers of students with severe intellectual and developmental disabilities (IDD), which explores inclusive teaching and learning practices in an online format. The work is based in the south-west of Florida where recent legislative initiatives have called for the development of courses specifically aimed at this group of teachers. *No Child Left Behind* (NCLB, 2002), mandates highly qualified status for teachers of this group of students by 2010. The status can be obtained through successful engagement in endorsement courses that cover current evidence-based practices in identification, assessment, instruction, evaluation and transitions in the light of changing policy and practices.

Online learning

A constant element of higher education learning is online learning (Walker and Fraser, 2005), which is a complex phenomenon that is demanding teacher educators grapple with new pedagogies. The online development in this chapter is blended between asynchronistic modules and virtual real-time meetings. Ludlow *et al.* (2005) identify personnel preparation programs in severe IDD as one of the first to adopt distance education technologies, particularly for those programs that serve rural communities. Online education supports access to professional learning (PL) for teachers who may live a significant distance away from the campus.

Smeaton and Keogh (1999) highlighted the challenge and complexity of online development, and how the quality across universities can be sporadic and haphazard. This chapter, though, will show how online learning can bring teachers together in a virtual learning space to promote dialogue and critical reflection of understandings and practice in the field.

The need to engage teachers in new and different perspectives

The reauthorization of the Individuals with Disabilities Education Improvement Act, IDEA 2004, demands that students with severe IDD are taught in a natural least restrictive environment (LRE) to the maximum extent possible. The LRE refers to appropriate student access to the general education curriculum in classrooms with students who are non-disabled: "While the Act and regulations recognize that IEP teams must make individualized decisions about the special education ... IDEA's strong preference is that, to the maximum extent appropriate, children with disabilities be educated in regular classes with their non disabled peers with appropriate supplementary aids and services" (Wright and Wright, 2008, p. 209). For many teachers of students with severe IDD this calls for a paradigm shift in not only what students are taught but also where they are learning. It also calls for high-quality professional learning (PL), which encourages teachers to consider different perspectives and reflect upon current beliefs and practices about this group of students. In an earlier international project, teachers of students with severe IDD from Washington State, USA and the north-east of England, UK, shared their moments of best PL (Jones *et al.*, 2006). From this, elements of effective learning affirmed in the literature were highlighted (Wilson and Floden, 2003). These include:

- an explicit relationship between theory and the practice being established;
- teacher learning that is mediated by someone who has experience teaching;
- the opportunity to learn from other teachers on the course;
- the opportunity to participate in sustained reflection in action.

Online professional learning

The challenge to teacher educators is to design online environments, which reflect these elements, where teachers are supported to question current practices and beliefs about this group of students. Such online learning should give teachers the opportunity to develop the skills necessary for informed professional decision making in inclusive LRE and to create learning that allows a balance between individual student strengths, needs and preferences, and core academics. Research demonstrates that when this happens in inclusive environments, education outcomes for students with severe IDD are more likely to improve (Ryndak *et al.*, 1999).

Theory of transactional distance

To improve online learning experiences, a teacher educator may need to consider issues beyond the usual pedagogy of adult learning. Moore (1993) offers a conceptual framework of transactional distance theory (TDT) as a lens to better understand the learner experience in online learning. This theory is potentially helpful in online course development and evaluation for teachers of students with severe IDD as it focuses upon improving the learner engagement in the learning.

In TDT, distance is a pedagogical phenomenon that needs to be reduced; the "sense of distance" a learner encounters between themselves and the product and process of learning is an important marker of successful course design and delivery. For example, a teacher in an online environment who is able to engage in learning that links theory to practice, is supported by a respected mediator, allows for interaction between teachers and encourages reflection in action, is more likely to connect to their learning. Instructors are instrumental in being able to reduce feelings of distance through careful design, implementation and evaluation.

Moore (1993) discusses three elements of TDT as dialogue, structure and learner autonomy. Dialogue is defined as two-way communication and interaction. Structure refers to course organization and student engagement. Learner autonomy represents the learners' perception of their participation in the course and is directly related to levels of self-directed learning.

An example of one course design

The course, Curriculum and Instruction for Students with Severe IDD, is part of a three-course teacher state endorsement program of study. The course is designed to extend teachers' knowledge related to current best practices in curriculum models, data-driven instruction and evidence-based instructional strategies for students with severe IDD. This includes inclusion in general education settings. The course is designed to engage teachers in learning which embraces the effective elements identified by teachers in international research (Jones *et al.*, 2006; West and Jones, 2007) and is influenced by the tenets of TDT (Moore, 1993). During the course, five web-based asynchronistic modules are integrated with five virtual real-time sessions.

- Module One: This video presentation demonstrates instructor experience in the field and offers an introduction to each of the modules. Teachers are introduced to the experiences they will have through each module. This module serves as training for the online engagement and aims to reassure teachers.

- Module Two: Understandings of historical and legal perspectives of curriculum models for students with severe IDD emphasize the current developments towards a blended academic and functional curriculum.
- Module Three: Curriculum access points support teachers to make meaningful connections between academic curriculum standards and individual learning needs, preferences and strengths.
- Module Four: Instructional practices for students with severe IDD explore the design of instruction to support successful student learning. Evidence-based practices are examined.
- Module Five: Data-driven instruction is explored that supports teachers' informed professional decision making.

Each module is designed in a similar way so that teachers can familiarize themselves with the structure and expectations of the online learning quickly. This is intended to help teachers build a comfort level with the process of online learning.

Organization of modules

In each module the participating teachers move through seven stages of activity. These are developmental in nature, beginning with an introduction to module content and progressing to more sophisticated teacher engagement of knowledge, skills and practice. Table 16.1 demonstrates the stages of the modules with an illustration of teacher engagement and expectations.

Everything the teacher needs to complete the module is packaged together. The Blackboard learning platform is used to host course material. (See www. Blackboard.com for more information.) Teachers move through the modules flexibly. They submit completed modules at set times during the semester in order to engage in written dialogue with the instructor. Ongoing written dialogue occurs five times in each module excluding course assignment feedback.

A closer look at Module Two

Module Two is the first substantive content modules in the course containing seven stages and illustrates the pedagogy of all the modules. At Stage One, teachers watch a 20-minute video introduction to pertinent historical and legal issues of curriculum. Teachers are offered a frame of reference to engage with the materials that embraces multiple ways of thinking about what 'curriculum' means for this group of students. Stage Two asks teachers to spend time reflecting upon their current understandings and practices

Table 16.1 Module stages with teacher expectation.

Stage of engagement	Expectation of teacher
One	To watch the introductory video presentation or read PowerPoint to engage with key issues of module.
Two	To take a few moments to consider the professional experience and expertise brought to the course content.
Three	To complete assigned reading activity (text book/article or literature review).
Four	To complete video analysis using tool(s) provided to enable application of new learning in unfamiliar practical context.
Five	To complete a school-based activity outlined in module to enable application of new learning in familiar classroom/school context.
Six	To complete assigned writing activity.
Seven	To share work with a colleague in the course and complete a peer review following the format given.

around curriculum and analyze what expertise and experience they bring to the module. At Stage Three, they are introduced to eight articles that represent a historical timeline as well as changing practices in curriculum models and implementation. Teachers choose four to analyze that are relevant to their interest and professional context. A format to process their reading is provided, which helps to analyze key ideas, and to apply the ideas to teachers' own practice. In addition, they are asked to consider how this impacts their understandings about curriculum entitlement for their students.

At Stage Four, the teachers view and reflect upon two videos. One video is a historical photographic timeline of students in class from the 1970s to the present day. This is a multimedia presentation, which demonstrates a movement away from self-contained functional curricula of the 1970s to more inclusive blended curricula of today. Teachers reflect upon the similarities and differences in student engagement and complete prompts that help to focus upon curriculum activities and LRE. In the second video, teachers are introduced to Amanda Baggs (2008) through a link to a video. Amanda Baggs is a woman with severe disabilities who would not be out of place in any of the teachers' classrooms. Amanda found her voice through technology and has become an eloquent and informed video maker. In the video, *About being considered retarded*, Amanda provokes the viewer to challenge their preconceptions of disability. Teachers reflect upon their role as teachers in the light of Amanda's video.

They then move to the School Activity Stage (Five) where they choose someone to interview about understandings of the role curriculum plays in the education of students with severe IDD, how these have changed over time and how this impacts professional/personal lives. Finally, they ask about the social and political influences that appear to shape the curriculum for this group of learners.

The Writing Stage (Six) is where they construct a 3–4 page referenced reflection paper about issues of curriculum developments for students with severe IDD. In the final stage (Seven), teachers share their work with each other on a peer buddy schedule. Following a given format they make comments about the pertinence and relevance of each other's module engagement. The teachers collate and submit their module engagement to the instructor. Feedback is detailed, positive and constructive and may include teachers being asked to delve deeper into their reflections and thinking. Feedback is given to teachers within five days of receipt. There may be issues that emerge across multiple students' work. For example, confusion/concern around how applicable LRE is for students with severe IDD. Emerging issues can become a focus of a virtual real-time session, where teachers are given additional processing and discussion time.

Real-time virtual sessions

Real-time virtual sessions occur through Elluminate. Elluminate is an interactive synchronistic learning platform that allows virtual meetings to occur via the computer. In this virtual space, teachers can listen and talk to each other (verbally or through instant messaging), share documents, present PowerPoints, surf the web and watch videos together (See www. Elluminate.com.) For Elluminate, teachers need to have some minimum computer requirements, a headset and microphone. During Elluminate sessions, teachers are given the opportunity to process and discuss issues in small and larger groups and also make presentations to the class. There are five real-time sessions.

Elluminate real-time meetings

Session One, at the beginning of the course, connects teachers with each other and resolves technical issues. It introduces a course survey where teachers record their experience and expertise in relation to course content, and develop personal targets for the course, identifying in the syllabus where they can engage with these targets.

Session Two, three weeks into the course, focuses upon instructional strategies relating to the Access points. Session Three, eight weeks into the course, is where students introduce PowerPoint presentations to each other about connecting academic subject standards with individual student needs, preferences and strengths. Session Four, at week twelve, is an open-agenda meeting where teachers submit questions for group discussion. The final session, at the end of the course, returns to the completed survey. Teachers review what they have gained from the course and where they would like to go next in their PL. Course evaluations also occur in this session.

The log-in link to the virtual classroom is placed on Blackboard on the day of the session and teachers enter the virtual classroom with a simple click. During the first hour, an Elluminate trained technician is available to help resolve technical issues.

Reflections on course design

Table 16.2 illustrates where the current course design reflects the characteristics of effective learning previously discussed and elements of TDT.

Teachers' experiences are an essential component of any course evaluation and teacher data will be analyzed in a subsequent publication. A simple indication of course success, however, is gleaned through the University Course Evaluation Process where the course received the highest grade by 100 per cent of the teachers.

Engaging in new learning that may question current practices can be very challenging for teachers and it is essential for instructors to mediate a positive interaction with the course content. In this course, notions of LRE and access to general education curriculum may present as a very different approach to some of the teachers. Facilitating connections between the teacher and the subject matter can support teacher engagement with

Table 16.2 Course design matched to characteristics of effective learning and elements of TDT.

Characteristic of effective learning	Course design
Establishment of relationship between theory and practice	Introductory module Stages four and five of module Elluminate small group work
Teacher learning mediated by experienced teacher	Introductory module Ongoing instructor feedback Each Elluminate session
Opportunity to learn from others	Stage seven of module Elluminate small group work
Opportunity to reflect on practice	Stages two, four, five and six of module
Elements of TDT	
Dialogue	Each Elluminate session Peer sharing process Ongoing instructor feedback
Structure	Module design and organization Module One
Learner autonomy	Course survey Elluminate sessions three and four Reading choice

challenging content. The video by Amanda Baggs is a successful example of this. It is known that many teachers of students with severe IDD often feel isolated from their colleagues and might indeed be the sole teacher of this group of students in their schools (Jones, 2005). This is not a healthy environment to challenge current understandings and practices. Creating different modes of interaction across an online course helps teachers to connect with each other and course material.

Reflections about online learning

Four key lessons can be learned from this course design initiative, including time for planning, teacher group size, training, and support for planning and course construction through collaboration with technical experts.

Firstly, this type and level of online development can take a great deal of time to design, develop, implement, maintain, support and evaluate, and it is important that this is considered from an organizational perspective in higher education.

Secondly, there is a tendency for online courses to equate with very large numbers of students as the limiting of physical space of a classroom is eliminated. This may be appropriate for some subjects, but when designing courses to engage teachers in personalized meaningful learning experiences that are then applied to practice, large teacher numbers do not help. What this course attempts to do is to humanize online learning, to retain the human connection characterized in face-to-face teaching. Through this, teachers are able to take risks with their learning and are held accountable for their responses. This cannot be done in a large teacher group.

Thirdly, this type of online design and development requires technical prowess. Training for instructors is an important element of developing effective online education. Such training needs to be meaningful, showing the potential role of technology in PL.

Fourthly, the need for collaboration between instructors and technical experts is essential. Collaboration of this nature is also important to translate effective pedagogy to the online environment without the instructor having to have a degree in computer technology. Clearly, this also has organizational and funding implications for higher education.

Conclusion

By 2010, it is anticipated that a large portion of special education courses will be delivered in an online format (Walker and Fraser, 2005). Online learning can offer the potential of reaching many teachers who enjoy the access and flexibility of distance-learning mediums (Todd, 2006). This initiative has shown that online learning can offer positive ways to engage teachers in current developments about meaningful inclusive practice for students with severe IDD. Quality online learning also requires evaluation and research. Meyen *et al.* (2002) identified need for "a systematic approach to research the pedagogy of online instruction, interface designs, the application of technologies to e-learning, and the framing of constructs to guide needed research" (p. 4). In order to develop effective online teacher education for inclusion it is important to evaluate the process of effective online developments as well as researching teacher experiences. In this way, online learning can play an important role in PL to support the provision of meaningful inclusive contexts for students with severe IDD.

References

Baggs, A. (2008) *About Being Considered Retarded*. Online. Available at: http://www. youtube.com/watch?v=qn70gPukdt (accessed 1 November 2008).

Jones, P. (2005) "Teachers' views of their pupils with profound and multiple learning difficulties", *European Journal of Special Needs Education,* 20(4): 375–85.

Jones, P., West, E. and Stevens, B. (2006) "I realized I knew nothing, that I had an awful lot to learn, and that I would have to help others see teachers in a different light: An international perspective on effective moments of teacher learning", *British Journal of Special Education,* 33(2): 83–9.

Ludlow, B., Conner, D. and Schechter, J. (2005) "Low incidence disabilities and personnel preparation for rural areas: Current status and future trends", *Rural Special Education Quarterly,* 24(3): 15–24.

Meyen, E., Aust, R., Gauch, J., Hinton, H. and Isaacson, R. (2002) "E-learning: A programmatic research construct for the future", *Journal of Special Education Technology*. Online. Available at: http://jset.unlv.edu/17.3/smith/smith.pdf (accessed 26 October 2008).

Moore, M. (1993) "Theory of transactional distance", in D. Keegan (ed.), *Theoretical Principles of Distance Education,* New York: Routledge.

NCLB (2002) *No Child Left Behind Act. Reauthorization of the Elementary and Secondary Act.* Public Law No. 107–110, 2102(4).

Ryndak, D., Morrison, A. and Sommerstein, L. (1999) "Literacy before and after inclusion for students in general education settings: A case study", *Journal of the Association for Persons with Severe Handicaps,* 24: 5–22.

Smeaton, A. and Keogh, G. (1999) "An analysis of the use of virtual delivery of undergraduate lectures", *Computers & Education,* 32: 83–94.

Todd, B. (2006) "Social software in academia, educause quaterly". Online. Available at: http://www.e-learningcentre.co.uk/eclipse/Resources/academic.htm (accessed 13 January 2009).

Walker, S. and Fraser, B. (2005) "Development and validation of an instrument for assessing distance education learning environments in higher education: The distance education learning environments survey (DELES)", *Learning Environments Research,* 8: 289–308.

West, E. and Jones, P. (2007) "A framework for planning in technology: Considerations for low incidence disability teacher preparation programs", *Rural Special Education Quarterly,* 26(4): 3–15.

Wilson, S. and Floden, R. (2003) *Creating Effective Teachers: Concise Answers for Hard Questions*. An addendum to the report, "Teacher preparation research: Current knowledge, gaps and recommendations" (2001) University of Washington. R-01-3.

Wright, P. and Wright, P. (2008) *Wrightslaw: Special Education Law*, 2nd edn, Hartfield: Harbor House Law Press.

Chapter 17

Attending to diversity

A professional learning program in Mexico

Ismael García Cedillo and Todd Fletcher

Learning outcomes

- Understand the context and manner in which inclusive education has been implemented in Mexico and other Central American countries.
- Know the salient features of a professional learning (PL) program for special and general education personnel.
- Some lessons learned that could be useful for the international community as they begin to prepare professionals for inclusion.

The context at the beginning of inclusive education in Mexico

Mexico has approximately 105 million inhabitants. Almost 75 per cent of the school-age population is enrolled in elementary school, 11 per cent in middle and high school, and 7 per cent in post-secondary settings (0.5 per cent in Normal Schools, 6 per cent in undergraduate programs and less than 0.5 per cent in graduate programs).

The challenges faced by the Mexican educational system are daunting: 50 per cent of the schools are multi-grade, there are over 68 ethnic languages (INALI, 2007), and most small towns are rather isolated. Approximately one third of the population lives in extreme poverty. Many school buildings are inhospitable with few instructional materials and little or no technology. There is a unique core curriculum for basic education. Teachers tend to be poorly prepared. The teacher's union is very powerful and frequently identified as one of the greatest barriers to educational reform and change. Many of these challenges are shared by other countries in the region, particularly those related to a lack of material resources, endemic family poverty and inadequate teacher preparation.

Background information

Inclusive education was mandated in a reform to the General Law of Education in 1993. The term originally used in Mexico was educational integration. As the reform was mandated and poorly implemented in a top-down bureaucratic manner, the idea of inclusion caused confusion, fear, and rejection in the educational community. Based upon this growing concern, the educational authorities decided to fund a research project during the 1995–6 school year to determine the status of inclusion throughout the country (García et al., 2003).

This research showed that inclusion was far from becoming a reality since most schools were not receiving students with special needs education (SEN). In general, teachers and parents supported inclusion, however, they demanded more information, resources and support. In particular, special education staff demanded more information and training to comply with their new role in the reform. This was similar to what was being reported by other countries throughout Latin America and the Caribbean (García, 2009).

Based on this research, the National Ministry Public of Education (SEP), with the support of the Mexico–Spain Mixed Fund for Technical and Scientific Cooperation, conducted a National Research and Innovation Project on Inclusive Education (PNIE). The main goals of this project were:

- To design, implement and assess a PL program for general and special educators.
- To select and assess a series of teaching materials that would support students with SEN to access the regular curriculum.
- To design, implement and evaluate a series of educational experiences following reform guidelines to identify the best conditions and factors under which inclusion could be successful.
- To design and evaluate a tracking system to monitor and follow up on students with SEN into general education environments.

The PNIE was designed during 1996 and 1997. This first version was implemented for three consecutive school years. During the first school year (1997–8) three states and over 1000 teachers participated. During 1998–9 another three states became part of the project and the total number of participating teachers increased to 2257. By the third year (1999–2000), another five states enrolled in the program, with eleven states participating in the program in total, and almost 3000 teachers. The PL program was delivered to a total of 6263 Mexican teachers during these three school years. Afterwards, the program was revised and implemented in all but seven Mexican states for three more years. The PL program trained a total of over 20,000 teachers between 1997 and 2002. Then the PNIE became PNFEEIE, the national program for the strengthening of special education and educational integration (SEP, 2002).

The professional learning program

The program includes five modules. Teaching contents were drawn from the Mexican core curriculum for general education and the free national textbooks in use by all the students at the time. The conceptual framework was inspired by UNESCO proposals for school integration (1993). The program was delivered in the form of seminars. The fundamental idea was to facilitate informed discussion so that participants' concerns, doubts and interests were addressed and the participants arrived at significant conclusions about the specific problems and themes discussed.

The activities were designed first and foremost to respond to the theoretical questions and practical problems expressed by professionals in the research conducted to determine the status of inclusion in Mexico, reported earlier (García *et al.*, 2003). We used a modular system to organize the program thematically. The modules are described below.

- *Module One. Introduction.* In this module the evolution of theoretical and practical constructs of special and inclusive education were contrasted and confronted with teachers' beliefs and practices.
- *Module Two. Inclusive education* (IE). In this module the main concepts of inclusion were analyzed and discussed in terms of their implications. These concepts were: disability, SEN and inclusion.
- *Module Three. Curriculum, pedagogy and curricular adaptations.* This module included the principle problems associated with teaching and learning, curriculum development and curriculum adaptation. Emphasis was placed on the reorganization of the school to respond to inclusion.
- *Module Four. Evaluation.* Various evaluation tasks were used to provide opportunities for participating teachers to reflect on their teaching practices. Evaluation tasks included individual and group experiences where the development of processes rather than the achievement of products or outcomes were analyzed.
- *Module Five. Parental involvement.* This module questioned the traditional roles of parents and their relationship to schools and teachers. Alternative views of more inclusive schools and collaborative school communities were discussed.

Each module included the following elements:

- *Instructor's guide.* This guide describes the conceptual underpinnings and the practical dimension of the content.
- *Introduction.* This provided an overview of the content and suggestions to conduct the seminars. It also provided the rationale for topic inclusion and their relationship to the project as a whole.

- *Content units.* Each module was divided into content units which included a detailed description of the topic, case studies and various learning activities to promote teacher participation and involvement.

Besides the modules, other support materials were developed:

- Twenty-two videos with conferences, case studies and other relevant information
- A collection of three books written by Mexican experts on topics of central interest for general and special education teachers:
  - *IE in the general education classroom: Principles, objectives and strategies* (García *et al.*, 2000).
  - *Communication and Language: Theoretical and practical aspects for teachers* (Romero, 1999).
  - *Elements for detection and IE for students with hearing loss* (Romero and Nasielsker, 1999).

Strategy

In order to conduct this project a four-layer participation strategy was implemented. The first layer was formed by the core research team which coordinated the project, made the initial proposals, made adjustments based on the input of the other participants and provided training and action guidelines to the local teams. The other three layers were: a group of consultants formed by three experts from Spain; groups of local researchers at each participating Mexican state; and the principals, teachers, families, and students at the participating schools.

The primary operating principle of the project was to provide ongoing training, support and supervision to all educational personnel involved. From the very beginning and at all stages, the project incorporated the suggestions and recommendations provided by participating teachers. Overwhelmingly, teachers felt the need to understand the conceptual and methodological principles of inclusion in order to effectively implement it in their schools.

Designing the professional learning program

The focus of the intervention was the process of teaching and learning within the context of diversity. Therefore, the program promoted: (a) a reflection on the principle questions tied to inclusion, (b) an analysis of the underlying concepts, and (c) the resolution of practical problems.

The program was designed taking into account the needs, expectations and suggestions of all participants. The notion of ongoing PL was central in the design, in addition to developing the content. In order for teachers to be able to teach diverse students, they needed to have a pool of materials to draw from as required. The system of modules gave us the opportunity to offer plenty of activities from which we could choose the most appropriate, taking into account the needs of the group being trained.

The PL program was designed to facilitate the active participation of teachers in the analysis and discussion of the concepts, of the problems encountered in their schools and communities, as well as in finding ways to carry out collaborative work to redefine and clarify the relationships and roles of general and special education teachers in the provision of services for all students.

Core concepts

Even though the program was collaboratively designed, some core concepts were present throughout.

1 The school as an intervention unit.

In order for inclusion to be successful, the school has to participate in the process as a whole. In fact, the principle of inclusion guided the selection of participating schools, and only those which demonstrated reasonable consensus among their staff were allowed to participate. Unlike other PL programs delivered by the Minister of Education, in this program teachers and the rest of the academic personnel of the participating schools did not receive any incentive other than improving their teaching practices as a result of the training. Throughout the process, this principle was emphasized mainly by defining the role of the school and the general education teacher as primarily responsible for the academic progress and success of all their students. Whereas the school and the teacher can count on the special education personnel to conduct certain activities, they should bear in mind that students' academic progress is primarily the responsibility of general education. The special education personnel can collaborate by identifying students' SEN; designing curricular adaptations, materials, pedagogical activities, and providing parent counseling, etc. This vision represents a dramatic change in the conditions and characteristics of the role of the special education personnel. It implies that the work of the specialist and of special education in general responds to the principles, goals and outcomes of general education.

2 The general curriculum as point of departure.

In the program the general curriculum was the point of departure for all teaching actions, to make the process of integrating students more meaningful and coherent. This meant that students with SEN would in principle be taught the same contents as their peers. Students' needs had to be taken into consideration, however, and curricular adaptations were to be made for students whenever necessary. This focus called for a creative approach to teaching and learning, and required overcoming some traditional special education practices based on students' disabilities with no reference to the school curriculum.

3 Collaborative work.

The process of integrating students constituted a novel situation for most schools which could not be dealt with successfully unless teachers worked collaboratively. One of the principle procedures in the analysis of educational experiences and the differing attitudes of individuals confronted with diversity, disability and inclusion, is the art and practice of collaborative reflection. Thus, the program promoted the active participation of all involved through respectful discussions of ideas and experiences. The program also included a self-evaluation component to support teachers' reflection on their educational practices and the implications for students' learning and socialization.

The program was aligned with the suggestions and recommendations as outlined by Moriña and Parrilla (2006). Their conceptualization of preparing teachers for inclusion is based on seventeen core principles, many of which were incorporated in the Mexican PL program.

Results of the evaluation of the professional learning program

This section will report only on the results of the implementation of the program conducted between 1997 and 2000. During this time the PL program was closely monitored and results were systematically documented. While this experience took place almost ten years ago, we believe that it is still relevant as the opportunity to do research and training on this scale only comes along once in a while in Latin America. A project of this size is important and can be a guidepost for future work.

The implementation of the PL program was completed in two phases. The first one was called the intensive phase. Core and local team researchers met for approximately five days with the teachers to work intensively for a total of 20 hours, as the school day is four hours long, in order to cover the main contents of the program. The second one, called the permanent phase, was conducted during the school year through monthly meetings and was led by the local group of researchers. During this phase, local researchers also conducted site visits to observe and support teachers, to discuss cases and to review materials.

The results of the evaluations over three years included both the intensive and permanent phases and suggested that the primary goals of the project were met.

Intensive phase

The intensive phase was assessed through questionnaires and interviews. The main topics in these instruments were: (1) quality and relevance of content and activities and (2) organization in terms of: timing, resources, coordination, etc.

1 Quality and relevance of content and activities.

- Teachers considered that the content and its organization in modules and activities facilitated the work of the participants, as they could revisit them at any time, according to their needs.
- Overall, participants agreed that the activities were useful tools for teachers to learn how to design lesson plans and make the necessary accommodations for individual students based on their educational needs.
- Most participants had positive comments regarding the content and quality of the seminars. Teachers considered that the program: (i) provided a strong conceptual and theoretical basis for IE, (ii) included content that would benefit their students, (iii) had a good balance between theory and practice, and (iv) gave them the opportunity to learn about their attitudes towards disability, IE and students with SEN.
- Participants considered that the content of the program provided them with the necessary information and skills to address the needs of the students they were working with.

2 General organization of the intensive phase: timing, resources, coordination, climate, etc.

- The organization of each intensive seminar was, in the teachers' opinion, conducted in a flexible manner, as it responded to the interests and needs of the participants.
- Participants considered that group coordinators and facilitators (all part of the core and local teams) were well prepared to deliver the content and to conduct group activities.
- Participants considered that the resources and settings were appropriate. Timing was the only factor that teachers rated negatively, as in most cases, they would have wanted to spend more time on some topics or activities.

- Participants valued the climate of trust and respect prevalent in the seminars as it allowed for open and sincere dialogue among participants.

Even though, on average, the program was highly rated, teachers did provide some suggestions on how to improve various aspects of the program, all of which were taken into consideration to make the materials and contents more appropriate.

Permanent phase

The permanent phase was critical to the consolidation of the project for both general and special education personnel because it provided the opportunity to engage in collaborative work. This phase was evaluated through interviews and site visits conducted by the local teams. These evaluations showed that the permanent phase of the professional learning program addressed the purpose for which it was designed. The main results of this evaluation were:

- The commentaries in the evaluations emphasized the strategic importance of the monthly meetings as an effective learning tool to improve teacher practices, support ongoing professional development and improve school management and academic leadership in general.
- The individual evaluations conducted at the end of each school year showed that the great majority (> 95 per cent) of school principals, general and special education teachers reported that the learning opportunities provided by the PL program and particularly the permanent phase influenced their teaching practices, making them more inclusive.
- According to the participants, the permanent phase provided opportunities to (a) revisit questions brought up during the intensive seminars, (b) analyze conceptual and practical problems with greater depth and breadth than in the intensive seminars, (c) analyze real case studies of integrated students, and (d) make informed decisions according to individual and contextual needs.
- All negative evaluative comments focused on time limitations and inappropriate school facilities used to conduct the meetings. Teachers considered that they always needed more time to elaborate on the topics related to IE. In most schools, the only available area to hold the meetings was a small room designated for Advisory Board meetings.

The PL program was the most visible, important and effective strategy of the PNIE. This research project became a National Program (PNFEEIE) in 2002, which is being implemented in all Mexican states with a total of 19,000 regular schools participating, integrating over 233,000 students (Martínez and Santos, 2008). In the PNFEEIE, the states assumed the responsibility for training the personnel and no evaluation data is available. Unfortunately, the PL program is no longer delivered as designed and in many states was substituted by a self-study course with no collaborative work component, thus eliminating one of its most valuable attributes.

Lessons learned

This experience taught us many lessons, some of which can be useful to others as they embark on the difficult but gratifying task of promoting effective IE.

1   In order for a PL program to be successful, educational planners must take into account teachers' needs and the reality they deal with on a daily basis. Creating programs based on best practices or coherent and up-to-date theoretical principles is not enough. The Mexican experience showed that teacher involvement was a key element to the successful adaptation of a coherent set of principles and methods to effectively respond to the needs of teachers, students and parents.

2   Professional development programs in Latin America are often implemented using the "cascade model" where a small group of professionals are trained to become trainers of other professionals who in turn train other professionals, and so on. One of the benefits of this model is its low cost. However, it does not guarantee that trainees at the middle and lower levels understand and implement the principles being taught. In the long run, it is more cost-effective to invest in a direct training model to preserve the quality of the program being delivered.

3   One of the greatest challenges facing IE nowadays is the transformation of professional roles. Traditionally, special education professionals have been trained to be responsible for the academic and social success of students with special needs. Within the framework of IE, special education professionals' role is to support general teachers and families so that they can effectively support the students with SEN. A professional development program for IE needs to effectively communicate this new role and its rationale to all participants.

4   All professional development programs need to consider sustainability strategies. One such strategy can be to take advantage of already existing academic leadership structures within schools by strengthening all modes of collaborative work so that professionals can continue learning together without depending on external support.

References

García, I. (2009) "Educación inclusiva en Latinoamérica y el Caribe. El caso mexicano [Inclusive education in Latin America and the Caribbean. The Mexican case]", *Banco Mundial-Universidad Autónoma de San Luis Potosí*, México.

García, I., Escalante, I., Escandón, M. C., Fernández, G., Mustri, A. and Puga, I. (2000) *La integración educativa en el aula regular. Principios, finalidades y estrategias*. [Educational integration in the regular classroom. Beginnings, endings, and strategies] Secretaría de Educación Pública-Fondo Mixto México–España.

García, I., Escalante, I., Escandón, M. C., Fernández, L. G., Mustri, A. and Toulet, I. (2003) "Proyecto de investigación: Integración educativa, Perspectiva internacional y nacional. Informe final de investigación (Ciclos escolares 1995–1996) [Research Project: Educational integration, international and national perspective. Final Research Report (School cycles 1995–1996)]". En Integración educativa, 1996–2002 Informe final, Secretaría de Educación Pública, Compact Disc.

INALI (2007) "Catálogo de las lenguas indígenas nacionales: Variantes lingüísticas de México con sus autodenominaciones y referencias geoestadísticas [Catalog of national indigenous languages: Mexican linguistic variants with its self-denominations and geo-statistical references]". Online. Available at: http://209.85.173.132/search?q=cache:http://www.inali.gob.mx/catalogo2007/ (accessed 3 January 2009).

Martínez, F. and Santos, A. (2008). "¿Avanza o retrocede la calidad educativa? Tendencias y perspectivas de la educación básica en México. Informe Anual. [Educational quality: Forwards or backwards? Tendencies and perspectives of basic education in México. Annual Report]" México, Instituto Nacional de Evaluación Educativa.

Moriña, A. and Parrilla, A. (2006) "Criterios para la formación docente del profesorado en el marco de la educación inclusiva [Criteria for professional development of teachers in the framework of inclusive education]", *Revista de Educación*, 339: 517–39.

Romero, S. (1999) "La comunicación y el lenguaje: aspectos teórico-prácticos para los profesores de educación básica [Communication and language: Theoretical and practical views for teachers of basic education]", *Fondo Mixto de Cooperación Técnica y Científica México–España*, México: Secretaría de Educación Pública.

Romero, S. and Nasielsker, J. (1999) "Elementos para la detección e integración educativa de los alumnos con pérdida auditiva [Elements for detection and educational integration of students with hearing loss]", *Fondo Mixto de Cooperación Técnica y Científica México–España*, México: Secretaría de Educación Pública.

SEP, Secretaría de Educación Pública (2002) *Programa Nacional de Fortalecimiento a la Educación Especial y la Integración Educativa* [National Program towards the Strengthening of Special Education and Educational Integration], México: Subsecretaría de Educación Básica y Normal.

UNESCO (1993) "Necesidades especiales en el aula. Conjunto de materiales para la formación de profesores [Special needs in the classroom. Compilation of materials for professional development of teachers]". Online. Available at: http://www.unesco.org/education/inclusive (accessed 14 November 2007).

Chapter 18

Engaging teachers in supporting positive student behavior change

Robert Conway

Learning outcomes

- Understand how to support teachers in helping students with difficult behaviors in classrooms and other school settings.
- Employ a consultancy model based on training specialist teachers through direct professional learning (PL).

Introduction

Students whose behaviors annoy or disrupt classroom learning and teaching are one of the greatest concerns of both beginning and experienced classroom teachers. Pre-service teachers have also expressed concern at their ability to cope with classroom behavior of students when they graduate, and often feel far better prepared to teach curriculum content than support student engagement, a key to successful learning (Darling-Hammond and Bransford, 2007). Data suggest that one of the key reasons that beginning teachers leave the profession in their initial years is student behavior (Australian Education Union, 2008). This report showed that management of student behavior in classroom was the highest concern for beginning secondary teachers and the second highest for primary teachers.

In order to address these concerns, education systems have sought to assist classroom teachers. This has occurred through a range of strategies, management documents and support staff models. In the USA, there has been a movement towards a consistent approach to management of student behavior through models such as Positive Behavior Intervention Support (PBIS), funded as a national project and implemented over a majority of states (see www.pbis.org – the national website for the project). In other jurisdictions national approaches have been adopted through a combination of multimedia resources, advice, and teaching materials. An excellent example is the Behavior4Learning approach in the UK (see www.behavoiur4learning. ac.uk for the website and access to the array of advice and materials for PL). This model has recently added a video dimension through YouTube to provide additional resource formats.

Little and Houston (2003) sought to formalize PL across the state of Florida. In their model, scientifically based practices were to be identified, staff trained and the implementation evaluated. The weakness of such a model is that it imposes the PL content in order to achieve state outcomes rather than developing PL with, and for, teachers. Other studies of PL which are set and implemented across schools have also demonstrated the difficulty of gaining uniformity (see for example Crone *et al.*, 2007). Crone *et al.* (2007) implemented a training program for the use of Functional Behavior Assessment (FBA) across ten schools but found the idiosyncrasies of the schools made the process difficult. Programs that have tried to provide a set model of PL have then failed to meet the needs of individual teachers and schools, and hence there is a need to conceive a type of PL that has general parameters but that allows each staff member and school to access the skills and content that can be adapted to their individual personal and school's needs. The two models discussed in this chapter have been implemented by the author to meet these needs in differing ways. A basis for the models is provided in Conway (2009) with an emphasis on the ecology of the situation in the classroom and the school as a foundation for PL relating to student behavior in mainstream settings. Learning and teaching in a classroom is seen as the constant interaction of four key factors: students, the teacher, the curriculum and teaching resources, and the physical setting. The cause of behavior disturbances lies in the influences of all four factors and not simply the student(s) identified as having a behavior problem. Addressing classroom misbehavior requires attention to all four factors and not just "disciplining" the student seen as having the behavior problem.

Model 1 – Supporting teachers and schools through trained specialist behavior teachers

This model is based on employer-sponsored training of a selected group of teachers to provide consultancy and support to classroom teachers on management of student behavior, as well as to schools on integrated school-wide management approaches. The training model had two main components: six months of full-time training as specialist teachers in the area of behavior problems, followed by six months full-time specialist training in special education including inclusion of students with special needs in mainstream education.

Each section of the training provides a formal university qualification. The first provides a Graduate Certificate in Educational Studies (Emotional and Behavioral Disorders) and the second a Master of Special Education, built on the first award. At the completion of the training, participants graduate with both qualifications and are eligible to be appointed as specialist behavior teachers within the state education system which sponsored the training. The reason for the two parts of the training is to provide the employing authority with the flexibility to place the graduating teachers in either a specialist behavior or special education role.

All graduates over the five years of the model were placed in specialist behavior roles. These ranged from working as specialist behavior support to regular schools [termed Support Teachers–Behavior or ST(B)], or in one of a wide range of specialist behavior settings from suspension centres to schools within juvenile justice centres or psychiatric hospitals. In total, over 300 graduates were placed into specialist roles.

Training was based on full-time release on full salary by the teachers' employing education authority over the year of the training. Training was provided at a central location and university staff and teachers commuted or moved to that location for the training.

The training program within both components was provided through three days of lectures and seminars and two days of in-school placement each week for six months with an extended placement at the end of each semester. The lecture component within the specialist behavior training consisted of four postgraduate courses: *Foundation studies in behavior problems*; *Assessment and planning in behavior problems*; *Interventions in behavior problems*; and *Using resources in behavior problems*. The content of the courses was designed by specialist academic staff in conjunction with the sponsoring employer. The course was implemented by the university staff and qualified specialist behavior staff from the sponsoring employer who acted as seconded academic staff. In this way, the model provided an integrated blend of academic, practical and on-site training each week. The content of the training is shown in Table 18.1.

In addition to the ongoing weekly placements in schools where assessment tasks were undertaken, a series of visits to a range of specialist behavior settings was provided. In mainstream schools the focus was on maintaining the student's enrolment by supporting the student, teachers and administration. In the second half of the training year with the focus on students with special needs, the training incorporated working with students with special needs who required additional behavior support in both inclusion and special settings.

The outcomes of the training were to provide to the employing authority a group of up to 30 additional specialist behavior teachers who were able to support the expanding support needs of classroom teachers in the area of management of students with behavior problems. The model has subsequently been taken up by a number of government education authorities across the country and by a number of non-government education authorities. The model has also been used with existing specialist behavior staff who do not have a formal behavior qualification. In this case, practicum placements have been in the teacher's own setting but with release for short-term visits to alternate setting. Training is provided in intensives with the main tuition provided through distance learning.

Table 18.1 Preparing specialist behavior teachers to act as teacher support for student behavior change.

Content	Assessment
Foundation Studies in Behavior Problems	
• Conceptual models of behavior problems • Home, school and community factors • Role of mental ill-health in behavior problems • Specific behavior problems in schools (internalizing and externalizing)	• An understanding of the roles of different conceptual models in working with students, teachers and other professionals • An understanding of the roles of school, home and community in addressing behavior needs • An understanding of the relationship between mental ill-health and behavior problems • An awareness of the literature on identifying and supporting students with specific behavior problems
Assessment and Planning in Behavior Problems	
• The role of the cycle of assessment, planning, implementation and evaluation (APIE) in supporting behavior change • Functional Behavior Assessment (FBA) as a methodology for data collection and program implementation • Behavior problems and students with special needs	• The role of the APIE cycle • Conduct of an FBA
Interventions in Behavior Problems	
• Alternate settings for students with behavior problems from least restrictive (mainstream settings) to most restrictive (juvenile justice, psychiatric wards) • Planning and implementing programs for students with behavior problems • Teaching strategies (e.g. behavioral, cognitive–behavioral, social skills approaches)	• Structured reports of visits to behavior settings • Planning and implementing behavior improvement programs including the trialling of teaching strategies for behavior improvement
Using Resources in Behavior Problem	
• The role of action research in improving teacher practice in behavior • Interpersonal skills in working with students, teachers and parents	• Conduct of an action research project on an aspect of the professional role • Activities focused on aspects of interpersonal skills such as conflict resolution and anger management

Model 2 – Supporting mainstream teachers directly through sustained professional learning

In this model there are two foci: providing teachers across an education system with a common understanding of students with behavior problems in mainstream setting; and how behavior support can be provided to maintain student enrolment in that education system. The model was implemented in a very large non-government system that has a deliberate employment strategy of ensuring that schools have a balance of teacher experience, age and gender. In this way some of the important variables in managing students with behavior needs have been proactively addressed.

The PL was designed as an extended, integrated and supported experience for staff and badged as a Mini Certificate in Behavior, awarded by the university to all staff who successfully completed the program. Staff who had a particular interest in having a greater understanding of behavior were sponsored to complete a Graduate Certificate in Educational Studies (Behavior) through the university.

The program consisted of four sessions across a semester with the education authority providing two full days of teacher release and the staff attending two after-school twilight sessions in their own time. The sequence was full day 1, twilight 1, full-day 2, twilight 2. In total, 18 hours of formal PL took place. Staff were encouraged to attend as mini school teams so that the learning could be taken back into the school through in-school activities. Until mid-2009, over 600 teachers and school leaders have been involved in the training, which is ongoing. The plan is that over a seven-year cycle, all schools would have ongoing access to the knowledge and its application through the Mini Certificate in Behavior.

The PL was designed to incorporate the education authority's management approaches to students with behavior problems into a broader understanding of the reasons for student behavior, and the ways in which classroom teachers and school administrators could support the student within the school and the education system. The educational jurisdiction developed a manual for a four-step procedure for the management of student behavior in conjunction with the author and an Individual Positive Behavior Plan format within which to provide a systematic behavior support framework. The program was developed over a six-month period with the author and the educational jurisdiction working collaboratively on the format and content.

The program was designed so that teachers and administrators would gain and share information during the sessions and have the opportunity to trial ideas and knowledge between sessions. Extensive use was made of the resources of the educational jurisdiction during the sessions. Case studies of specific behavior problems were used so that those attending could apply their experiences and school situations in looking at possible student support approaches.

Table 18.2 Class and school approaches to supporting student behavior change.

Session	Focus
Day 1	• Introduction to when behavior becomes problem behavior • Classroom factors in developing and maintaining student behavior problems (student, teacher, curriculum and resources, physical setting) • School-wide behavior issues including all school locations and the positive behavior support model (PBIS) • Linking mental ill-health and behavior problems in schools • Disability Standards for Education Act (Parliament of Australia, 2005) and it effects on students with special needs, including students with emotional disorders • Assessment of behavior problems and the Functional Behavior Assessment (FBA) process • The school community and management of student behavior needs
Twilight 1	• Risk assessment and management and the jurisdiction's policies and procedures • Developing individual positive behavior plans for students, including the jurisdiction's policies and procedures • Supporting student behavior in the classroom – disruptive student behaviors (case studies) • Supporting students with ADHD behaviors (case studies)
Day 2	• Supporting students with withdrawn, OCD and depressed behaviors (case studies) • Violent, explosive and aggressive behaviors in schools • Supporting students with violent behaviors, ODD, and CD (case studies) • Bullying behaviors in schools (case studies)
Twilight 2	• Management of students with special needs where behavior is not the primary factor • Behavior support needs of students with ASD and AS (case studies) • Student well-being – risks and strategies • Whole school well-being strategies • Staff well-being – maintaining well-being as a teacher

The format for the PL program is set out in Table 18.2. While it has similarities to the training for specialist behavior teachers in Model 1, the focus here is on appropriate solutions for the teachers' own classes and schools based on a behavior problems knowledge base.

In each case study, the focus is on identifying the key classroom factors that may have exacerbated the behavior and those that maintain the behaviors. Participants are asked to look at how the behaviors could be supported in terms of teaching and learning in the classroom, social skills needs, whole school management issues, and risk management issues. The aim is to ensure that, while all areas need to be acknowledged, the impact on each would differ depending on the specific behavior needs. Hence minor disruptive behaviors would have an impact on teaching and learning strategies, but most likely not on whole-school management strategies and risk management. For a student with violent and oppositional behavior, there would be a significant impact on all four areas. At all times, the model was one of exploring possible options rather than there being defined approaches.

This PL approach has been in effect for three years and all schools in the jurisdictions have been included in at least one of the seven rotations a year. In addition there are semester overview sessions with all senior management and consultants in the jurisdiction and the program is highlighted at principal review sessions annually. While primary teachers and principals have been enthusiastic in their support and many principals have chosen to complete the Mini Certificate themselves, no secondary principals have attended and there is considerably more resistance to the program among secondary teachers than primary teachers. This presents a key challenge to the value of the program as a systemic approach to supporting student behavior across all schools in the jurisdiction.

Implications and challenges arising from the approaches

Model 1 was designed to prepare specialist behavior-focused teachers to work in a large state education system that has a considerable number of specialist behavior staff (over 500 staff), employed across a diverse number of specialist behavior settings and catering for a considerable number of students from that and other education providers in that state. The need to have a qualified base of staff was a key priority for the development of the training program. In addition, the system had made a commitment to provide all schools with access to specialist teacher support in managing student behavior within the mainstream school. This had placed considerable strain on the numbers of qualified staff available to fulfill this role.

Model 2 is a proactive strategy which enables staff to be provided with a sustained PL program that is designed to support activities in the schools; supports the jurisdiction's integrated approach to supporting student behavior change at classroom, school and systems level; and provides the opportunity for staff to access PL as part of an integrated approach to learning and teaching. Having a commitment to an evolving model over a series of years also allows schools to remain in contact with current practices and ideas as different staff attend each year. It also ensures that policies and practices are reinforced through the learning and activities.

The two models address differing needs. While the first develops skills of specialist teachers to provide support to mainstream teachers, the second focuses directly on improving teacher understanding and skills within their classroom and school. The value of this approach is that the PL is thus personalized, challenged and validated concurrently.

References

Australian Education Union (2008) *New Educators Survey.* Online. Available at: www.aeufederal.org.au/Publications/2009/Nesurvey08res.pdf (accessed 5 May 2008).

Conway, R. N. F. (2009) "Behavior support and management", in A. F. Ashman and J. Elkins (eds), *Education for Inclusion and Diversity,* Sydney: Prentice Hall, pp. 123–66.

Crone, D. A., Hawken, L. S. and Bergstrom, M. K. (2007) "A demonstration of training, implementing, and using functional behavioral assessment in 10 elementary and middle school settings", *Journal of Positive Behavior Interventions,* 9:15–29.

Darling-Hammond, L. and Bransford, J. (eds) (2007) *Preparing Teachers for a Changing World: What Teachers Should Learn and Be Able to Do,* New Jersey: Jossey-Bass.

Little, M. E. and Houston, D. (2003) Research into practice through professional development, *Remedial and Special Education,* 24(2): 75–87.

Parliament of Australia (2005). *Disability Standards for Education Act.* Attorney General's Department, Australian Government.

Chapter 19

Professional learning as collaborative inquiry

Working together for impact

Joanne Deppeler

Learning outcomes

- Teacher professional learning (PL) is effective when it achieves improved student learning.
- Teacher PL should be reframed from something that is done to teachers to something that teachers continue to do together.
- Learning Improves in Networking Communities (LINC) uses collaborative inquiry (CI) as a vehicle for PL, demonstrating positive outcomes for teachers and their students.

Introduction

Education systems throughout the world are being challenged by governments to be more responsive to the diversity of their learners and to monitor and evaluate the effectiveness of their services to ensure high standards are achieved by all students. Education reformers have recognized that standards alone are not sufficient to change practices that impact positively upon students' learning. There is good evidence that the quality of teaching has substantial impact on students' learning outcomes in countries such as Australia, Canada, Finland, France, Israel, New Zealand, Scotland, Sweden and the USA (Timperley and Alton-Lee, 2008). It is recognized that if we are to realize continuous improvement in the quality of schooling for all we must build the capacity of our teachers to meet this challenge. This chapter outlines LINC as a model of teacher PL aligned with values of social justice and the goal of improving outcomes for students. The research which informed the design principles of LINC is outlined along with the conditions that supported the implementation.

What conditions make teacher professional learning effective?

Teacher PL is effective when it achieves the goal of improving student learning. Concern over this issue has prompted researchers to consider the links between the design of the PL, evidence of changed teachers practices and the impact upon student learning outcomes (Penuel *et al.*, 2007). Education, directed towards improving the social and academic achievement of lower performing students and those with disabilities, has long been associated with a set of research-based practices that have arisen from education psychology.

While knowledge from research in education psychology has an important role to play in teaching practice, it often exists in tension or even competition with other forms of knowledge about classrooms and schools. Teacher PL has typically employed a training model in which experts provide the theory and the research-based methods; schools provide the setting in which that knowledge is practiced; and teachers provide the effort to apply the knowledge.

In Australia for example, teacher PL for supporting diversity in classrooms has emphasized 'best' practices for educating 'special' students who do not respond to the general teaching arrangements (Deppeler *et al.*, 2005). While there is some evidence that this form of PL can be successful in changing teachers' levels of confidence and attitudes towards inclusive schooling, it has been less effective in changing teaching practices and demonstrating traceable effects on improving student achievement. One of the reasons suggested for these findings is that experienced teachers do not approach PL as 'empty vessels' but rather as professionals with existing knowledge, experiences and developed theories of students learning and teaching (Timperley and Alton-Lee, 2008). PL that has focused exclusively on instructional practices is often perceived by teachers to be disconnected from their practices in the school (Lieberman and Pointer Mace, 2008). As the school environment influences the kind and form of knowledge that teachers can put to work, a connection to practices is essential. While this is important for teachers generally, it has had particular significance in respect of students who present with significant learning and behavioral challenges for teachers in mainstream schools.

For more than a decade, Ainscow and his colleagues have argued that for 'real' changes to occur in inclusive education practices, the school environment must support the teaching practices and students' learning (Ainscow *et al.*, 2006). As teaching is also a dynamic, evolving process teachers must have ongoing access to new knowledge as it emerges to review and modify their practices. Findings from 'best' available research can provide an invaluable frame to refine their conceptual and pedagogical understandings about teaching and learning. This 'new' knowledge, however, will need to be examined in light of local understandings and practices and with regard to how those findings might be interpreted and applied in their particular school environment (Parr *et al.*, 2007). In light of these issues, the current consensus is that teacher PL must be reframed from something that is *done to teachers* to something that *teachers continue to do together*.

To realize continuous improvement in the quality of schooling for *all* will require changes in the collective professional knowledge and practices of teachers that are connected with their school. Teachers and leaders will need to collaborate to evaluate the impact their practices have upon students' learning and make PL an integral and continuous part of their self-improving work. In this way, PL is distinguished from traditional forms of teacher inservice that have occurred in episodic or stand-alone workshops and bears a strong similarity to descriptions of organizational learning in schools (Mulford, 2008) and work in professional learning communities (Dufour *et al.*, 2008).

Working together for impact

The LINC project was framed by these conditions and was intended to be both responsive to inclusive education reform and generative of practices in differing school contexts (Deppeler, 2007). A brief overview follows. LINC Project 1 was conducted in eight primary and secondary schools in rural, regional and metropolitan Catholic schools in Victoria, Australia. LINC Project 2 was conducted in six Catholic secondary schools in metropolitan Melbourne, Australia. LINC Project 3 (2008–2011) has a specific focus on improving literacy in Catholic secondary schools. The stated aim is to build capacity for improved practices that strengthen outcomes for diverse learners. University researchers and school-system professionals work in collaboration to provide ongoing school-based PL for teachers in a network of schools. A range of both quantitative and qualitative research methods are employed to document and analyze measures of student learning, teachers' pedagogical practice, professional knowledge and capacity over time. Details of these methods have been documented previously (e.g. Deppeler, 2006, 2007; Meiers and Ingvarson, 2005).

An emphasis on *working together for impact* is embedded in every aspect of LINC. This is not conceived of as a simple linear process where knowledge from research is disseminated by experts to teachers in schools and then adopted. It involves a much more collaborative process that is interactive and distributed across participants, and where new knowledge is constructed to change practices. LINC places a strong emphasis on locating collective responsibility and accountability for *all* students at the school level through the investigations of conditions in each school.

Collaborative inquiry

Collaborative inquiry (CI) was adopted to describe the PL approach. LINC creates opportunities for teachers to collaborate and to use evidence to critically analyze practices in their school in order to generate new knowledge and transform practices. Teachers and leaders in each school volunteer to work together in PL teams to conduct inquiry. Teams vary between five and twelve members. At six-month intervals participants submit and present research reports for university credit and to inform the school community. The success of CI depends upon building teachers' capacity to collaborate and to engage in practitioner research; to understand and act on the challenges with which they are faced. While particular activities vary according to the goals, needs and actions of each school, PL teams follow a common cycle of evidence gathering, collaborative examination and discussion of evidence, followed by investigations of practices in each of the three phases of the program.

In Phase 1, PL teams begin with an auditing process, collecting and examining evidence about student achievement and the teaching and learning culture in their school and select a focus for development. In Phase 2, investigations are narrowed to understand in detail the effects of specific practices on student learning. In the final phase, teacher research and development work continues and the team attempts to align school-wide policy and practices with their findings.

Teachers document and share research findings at network conference and on the LINC website. University educators support teams throughout all phases and actively model dispositions consistent with CI including respect, open-mindedness, critical examination of evidence and collaborative engagement with others.

LINC: Change for teachers and impact on student learning

The CI practices previously described have supported teachers to understand, articulate and change their practices in a range of school contexts that in turn have had positive significant impacts on students' learning. Internal and external evaluation evidence has demonstrated that LINC has been highly successful in generating significant positive changes in teacher knowledge, practice, efficacy and student literacy outcomes across LINC schools (Deppeler, 2007; Dick, 2005; Meiers and Ingvarson, 2005).

One year after the completion of each project a representative of the Catholic Education Commission Victoria (CECV) school system conducted interviews with the leaders in these schools. In all but one school in each LINC project, leaders indicated that in-school inquiry processes continued to be systematically linked with student achievement and curriculum across classrooms. In one school these processes informed the work of a committee responsible for the identification and development of teacher PL. Taken together the findings from our research provide strong evidence of the effectiveness of the approach. Particular aspects of the program appeared to be important for supporting implementation and enhancing the eventual impact of the PL on practices. In the following sections, examples related to these aspects are described to exemplify findings of the program.

Collaboration and collective responsibility

This appeared to be enhanced by the initial audits that were conducted in each school. It was during these audits that teachers first collaborated in the examination of evidence. It was expected that as a key condition examination of evidence would be an important vehicle for developing common understandings and shared focus for change. What was not expected was the profound influence the audits had on teachers' beliefs about the value of inquiry and on determining their particular focus. The PL teams used a range of different tools to audit school-wide practices in order to identify foci for development and for further investigation. All schools used a questionnaire developed from a revised version of the British *Index for Inclusion* (Booth *et al.*, 2000) and student achievement data. Data were summarized by the university and returned to PL teams in each school for discussion. Teams were supported to examine their data and identify possible barriers and supports for lower-performing students and to make decisions about foci for further investigation.

For example, identified issues surrounding homework and non-submission of assignments resulted in an investigation of work assigned to students for assessment in the previous term, in a selected year level. Teachers collected assignments, assessment criteria and examples of work that had been assessed at high and low levels. It soon became clear that teachers were employing a range of different assessment criteria for similar assignments, had different understandings of various types of texts (e.g. 'report' or 'essay') and there was unnecessary duplication of tasks.

In other schools the audit prompted critical analysis of the congruence between the assessment tasks and goals for student learning and considered the relationship of teacher assessment to student achievement. In many instances, the audit prompted teachers to observe and document student responses to pedagogy across classrooms. Teachers frequently noted that the auditing process was critical for 'building the team' and developing a shared understanding of the culture of their school and for developing investigative skills. University educators believed that audits were critical for making visible the differences between the espoused values in a school and the practices that were enacted and for making these understandings explicit.

Access to research knowledge and professional expertise

This was another condition that teachers reported was not typically available in their daily work and had supported their PL. However, PL was not just about 'new' knowledge or pedagogy. The process of using evidence to link student learning with the quality of their teaching was fundamental to the development of pedagogical knowledge. We believe teachers' engagement with a professional with specific 'expertise' was important in this process for enhancing the depth of teachers' understandings and the rigor of their inquiry.

For example, in schools where literacy improvement was a focus, teachers worked with an educator with expertise in literacy. One particularly powerful activity engaged teachers in writing assessment moderation. Teachers were supported to interpret explicit assessment criteria and examine exemplars of students' writing. The exemplars were selected by a literacy 'expert' from student texts produced through the audit process. An agreed-upon set of assessment criteria for argumentative writing was used to support teachers to articulate and share knowledge. Prompting from the literacy professional enabled teachers to examine some of the overlooked assumptions they had made about students who experienced literacy difficulties and to view their customary practices in new ways.

The process highlighted how the differences in teacher's values, literacy understandings and prior experiences influenced student assessment outcomes. Teachers valued the shared analysis, because it developed common understandings about assessment, making it possible for them to reframe their practices in light of these understandings.

Consistent with Black and William's (1998) work, assessment practices that emphasized the learner's contribution as a source of data (questioning, feedback, shared criteria, and peer and self-assessment) became common. Teachers believed that professional discussion with others allowed them to deepen their understandings about theory as well as pedagogy because it was integrated and specifically connected to the curriculum and students in their school. As teachers read the theoretical and applied research literature relevant to their investigations they developed a common language to engage with their evidence and to design collaborative investigations focused on pedagogy. Teachers tested 'new' knowledge in classrooms and shared their findings with colleagues.

Teachers emphasized the importance of this work in changing not only what they noticed but also how they interpreted events. In particular, evidence of positive changes in the learning of the lower performing students was directly related to their teaching. This often surprised teachers and raised their expectations for these students.

It appears that teachers' understanding about pedagogy is closely connected to their understanding about student diversity and learning and that this is not easily separated from their understanding of the inquiry processes. As teachers became more competent and confident in engaging with evidence in order to understand their practices they became more confident in developing and testing pedagogy and reframing assessment practices.

Discussion

What is clear from this work is that teachers' learning in relation to these processes requires time to develop. This two-year program provided a majority of teachers with sufficient opportunities to build trust, skills and confidence in applying collaborative inquiry to complex problems. Approximately one third of the teachers continued to collaborate and use evidence to connect theory with practice and student learning. A small number of teachers in each of the teams were able to use some CI procedures but remained reliant upon colleagues and university educators to shape and guide their investigations. It may be that these teachers will need more time to engage with CI in their PL community.

Teachers agreed that submitting work for assessment and credit in a postgraduate subject provided both an obligation and an incentive to enact, document and report their research and enhanced the quality of their work. Purposefully designing PL may require some further thinking about what alternative practices might best provide incentives and support the diversity of teachers in schools.

There is a complex interplay of collaboration among schools and the university that creates a powerful learning space for inexperienced teachers to learn from and with experienced teachers and university educators. This process is highly challenging and included resistance and interactions filled with tension when teachers and teacher educators attempted to introduce teaching that went against current practices. What is also clear from this work is that leadership needs to be exercised at all levels. Consistent with previous research, the leaders in each of the LINC schools and administrators in the university and in the Catholic education system played a critical role in dealing with resistance and building structures to support teachers' work focused on improvement.

While CI by no means guarantees positive outcomes to the school community, PL that models democratic processes and builds upon the knowledge of teachers and leaders in seeking solutions is a necessary first step on the path to achieving school change for socially just ends. The next step is to better understand *how* teachers and leaders influence and support one another in the CI process and how this might be enhanced to influence the quality of teaching.

If we seriously believe that responsibility and knowledge should be shared rather than centered on an individual teacher or leader then we must encourage not only a collaborative approach to PL but also a greater understanding of the form and extent of collaboration and inquiry in a given school community. How do teachers and leaders adapt their CI practices to meet the changing needs of their school community and respond to the circumstances in which they find themselves?

These processes are complex and will not be easy to unravel but are important for the research community to address. The success of achieving the goals of equitable access to quality education is an ongoing process for all those involved – teachers, researchers, teacher educators, and policy developers and analysts. It will require structures and contexts that support the ongoing PL of all those who are engaged in this process and that connects research with the realities of shaping teaching and leading practice in schools.

Acknowledgments

The LINC project has been in existence since 2001 and is conducted in a partnership with the Catholic Education Commission Victoria (CECV), Catholic Education Office (Melbourne) (CEOM), and Monash University, Australia.

References

Ainscow, M., Booth, T. and Dyson, A. (2006) *Improving Schools, Developing Inclusion*, London: Routledge.

Black, P. and William, D. (1998) *Inside the Black Box: Raising Standards through Classroom Assessment*, London: NFER Nelson.

Booth, T., Ainscow, M., Black-Hawkins, K., Vaughan, M. and Shaw, L. (2000) *Index for Inclusion: Developing Learning and Participation in Schools*, Manchester: Centre for Studies on Inclusive Education Centre for Educational Needs, University of Manchester.

Deppeler, J. (2006) "Improving inclusive practices in Australian schools: Creating conditions for university–school collaboration in inquiry", *European Journal of Psychology of Education* 21(3): 347–60.

Deppeler, J. (2007) "Collaborative inquiry for professional learning" in A. Berry, A. Clemens and A. Kostogriz (eds), *Dimensions of Professional Learning*, Rotterdam, Netherlands: Sense Publishers, pp. 73–87.

Deppeler, J., Loreman, T. and Sharma, U. (2005) "Improving inclusive practices in secondary schools: Moving from specialist support to supporting learning communities", *Australasian Journal of Special Education*, 29(2): 117–27.

Dick, W. (2005) Chapter 2: Learning Improves in Networking Communities (LINC), in M. Meiers and L. Ingvarson (eds), *Investigating the Links Between Teacher Professional Development and Student Learning Outcomes: Volume 2*, (pp. 4–28), Commonwealth of Australia.

Dufour, R., Dufour, R. and Eaker, R. (2008) *Revisiting Professional Learning Communities at Work: New Insights for Improving Schools*, Bloomington, IN: Solution Tree.

Lieberman, A. and Pointer Mace, D. H. (2008) "Teacher learning: The key to educational reform", *Journal of Teacher Education*, 59: 226–34.

Meiers, M. and Ingvarson, L. (2005) *Australian Government Quality Teacher Programme: Investigating the Links between Teacher Professional Development and Student Learning Outcomes*, Volume 1, Commonwealth of Australia.

Mulford, B. (2008) *The Leadership Challenge: Improving Learning in Schools*, Camberwell, Australia: Australian Council for Educational Research.

Parr, G., Nuttall, J. and Doecke, B. (2007) *Victorian Parliamentary Inquiry into Effective Strategies for Teacher Professional Learning Submission.* Online. Available at: http://www.parliament.vic.gov.au/etc/Submissions/prof_learn/monashuniversityfacultyofeducation290607.pdf (accessed 11 November 2008).

Penuel, W., Barry, J., Fishman, B. J., Ryoko Yamaguchi, R. and Gallagher, L. P. (2007) "What makes professional development effective? Strategies that foster curriculum implementation", *American Educational Research Journal,* 44: 921–58.

Timperley, H. and Alton-Lee, A. (2008) "Reframing teacher professional learning: An alternative policy approach to strengthening valued outcomes for diverse learners", *Review of Research in Education,* 32: 328–69.

Chapter 20

A four-ply model of professional development for inclusive education

Elizabeth O'Gorman

Learning outcomes

- Review the findings from research on teachers' preferred professional learning (PL) opportunities.
- Outline the key features of the four-ply model of PL for teachers working in the area of special education needs (SEN).
- Consider the potential for international implementation of a similar model.

Introduction

This chapter examines a model of continuing PL for teachers within a framework of inclusive education and in relation to a research project undertaken with teachers who have specific responsibility for students with SEN in mainstream schools in Ireland [i.e. Learning Support/Resource/ Special Education teachers (LS/R/SEN)].

The rationale for the project derived from the recent policy reforms in special education provision in Ireland that resulted in an increasing number and diversity of students with SEN attending mainstream schools. Internationally, research has demonstrated that teachers are an important factor in the quality of student learning (OECD, 2005). In advancing a policy of inclusive education, the Irish Government Department of Education has increased provision for PL in special education in order to build capacity in the education system (DES, 2006). One aspect of this project was to explore preferred options for PL among teachers. The findings supported a four-stranded approach to PL that combines the teacher, the school community and institutions of higher education with the government Department of Education and Science sponsorship.

The four-ply model

The model of PL detailed in this chapter is one developed in Ireland as a funded program for teachers working in the area of special education.

This model engages four key stakeholders in realising the program. The interweaving of the strengths of these four strands presents a robust partnership for promoting PL in inclusion/SEN in Ireland.

Qualified teachers, working in the area of inclusion/SEN at primary (4–12 years) and post-primary (12–18 years) levels, receive government funding (which includes their course fee and a period of paid leave with substitute cover) to participate in a year-long postgraduate program of PL. Access is through an open competition supported by the school's recommendation. While the precise components of the programs vary with the host institution, they share common elements. During their paid leave, teachers are based in a university or college of education. There they participate in an intensive series of lectures, workshops, seminars and tutorials relating to a range of topics on inclusive education. Teachers also visit or take up placements in other education settings. As part of the coursework assessment, teachers write academic literature reviews and undertake school-based research projects in their own schools on diverse areas such as diagnostic teaching, developing and implementing education plans, collegial collaborative practices and parent–professional partnerships. These assignments are in addition to their normal teaching and special education related duties. They are supported in these endeavours by college/university staff who visit the schools, assess teaching practice and offer individual, team and whole-school–community in-service. Teachers who successfully complete all modules are awarded a university accredited Graduate Diploma in SEN and are entitled to an additional allowance from the government if they remain working as inclusion specialists. Since 2003, this four-ply model of PL has been available each year to teachers who work in this area in mainstream schools in Ireland. Following a review in 2006 of PL provision in SEN/inclusion, the Department of Education and Science increased funding to 300 places per year.

Overview of research project

The research was undertaken during the period May 2007 to June 2008 to explore aspects of inclusive special education in Ireland. A mixed-methods approach was utilised comprising a survey questionnaire, focus groups and semi-structured interviews. While the research covered a wide range of inclusion related areas, the focus of this chapter is on the PL sections. The specific areas of interest is on the preferred and the most effective context for PL as perceived by teachers, principals and other stakeholders.

In all, 1,492 questionnaires were distributed to all post-primary schools and to a sample of primary schools in Ireland, with a response rate of 55 per cent. The returned questionnaires contained details on the school community with particular emphasis on the special needs aspects, the teaching and learning environments and the teachers' professional experience and requirements. Interviews and focus groups took place with teachers, principals and stakeholders from a number of organisations involved in PL for teachers, the education department and course provider personnel (O'Gorman and Drudy, 2008).

Quantitative and qualitative data instruments

Separate surveys were given to teachers and principals. In both, two sections related to PL; ranking questions on their preferred context for PL and open questions on perceived effectiveness of PL contexts. In the interview and focus group schedules for teachers, principals and other stakeholders, topics included what type of in-service or PL programs and courses can best provide the requisite skills and knowledge for LS/R/SEN teachers and what is the best way of developing teaching skills.

Findings

Preferred context for professional learning

Teachers and principals were offered a listing of PL options that were available in Ireland at that time. These ranged from in-school support to on-line distance education, which respondents were required to rank in order of preference. The number one choice for the majority of respondents was a preference for block release from school to attend a college/university program. This was ranked more frequently than all other PL options (see Table 20.1).

The top three preferred options for PL were attending a college/university program, network meetings with other teachers and school-based support, which accounted for 57.5 per cent of all teachers' choices and 60 per cent of all principals' choices.

When the teachers' results were analysed by sector, there was very little difference in the ranking of options between the primary and secondary

Table 20.1 Preferred context for professional learning.

Rank	Professional learning context	Teachers n=608	Principals n=386
Most frequently ranked I	Block release to attend a college/university programme	34.4%	25.4%
2nd most frequently ranked I	Network meetings with other teachers	13.2%.	20.5%.
3rd most frequently ranked I	School-based support	9.9%.	19.9%

Other options accounted for the remaining responses.

teachers. The result was similar when analysed on a geographical basis. Contrary to expectations, there was a low preference for on-line learning from rural-based teachers, even among teachers who had experience of using on-line learning. The potential for using the internet to access PL is gaining acceptance, but is in the initial stages of development in Ireland. In all, 41.5 per cent of the respondents indicated that they had used the internet to access PL. This figure was higher for primary teachers (50.6 per cent) than for post-primary teachers (29.8 per cent). Despite this, on-line PL has the potential to become a significant factor in the future.

Overall, there was great similarity between the teachers' and principals' rankings of preferred options for teacher PL. An interesting difference, however, emerged from the sector analysis. While the preferred context for all principals was for block release to attend college/university courses, secondary principals were slightly more in favour of school-based support. This is interesting in light of secondary principals' subsequent indication that they perceived block release as the most effective means of improving teaching. Perhaps the difficulties at secondary level associated with providing substitute cover for teachers who are on block release may have had an impact on their rankings.

Most effective professional learning

In an open question, both teachers and school principals were asked to give their opinion on the most effective way for teachers to develop their teaching skills. The responses to this open question confirmed college/university courses as the most highly regarded option, though the pattern of responses here was more varied (see Table 20.2).

Table 20.2 Most effective professional learning contexts.

Most cited effective professional learning contexts	1st most cited	2nd most cited	3rd most cited
Teachers' responses n=679	19.6% Block release to attend a college/university programme	17.3% Network meetings with other teachers	12.5% In-service single-session
Principals' responses n=349	33.8% Block release to attend a college/university programme	18.4% In-service single-session	10% Network meetings with others/ On-the-job experience

A wide range of options accounted for the remaining responses.

Teachers cited tertiary courses as the most effective means of developing their skills but their responses were more evenly distributed across a broader range of options than were principals' responses. The areas included by teachers were attending block release courses (19.6 per cent), network meetings with other teachers (17.3 per cent), on-the-job observation (15.3 per cent) and in-service (12.5 per cent).

The principals' most frequently cited method of effectively developing teachers' skills was attending courses (33.8 per cent). (This contrasts with the lower percentage [25.4 per cent] that had ranked these courses as the number one preferred context.) There was a lesser degree of agreement among the principals groups on the identification of a second most effective method for developing teachers' skills. The next most cited method was in-service at a much lower 18.4 per cent with both networking and on-the-job experience next cited at a low 10 per cent.

Both teachers and principals gave a high priority to attending courses and meeting others in similar situations, advice from colleagues, on the job experience and in-service are also suggested as suitable means to develop professional knowledge and skills. It is interesting to note that all the elements cited as being effective in developing teachers skills are incorporated in the four-ply model.

Discussion

The results of the quantitative data analysis support the four-ply model of PL. The preferred options for PL, i.e. those given top rankings by both teachers and principals, are elements of the four-ply model. These are block release for attendance at courses in tertiary institutions, network opportunities with other teachers and in-school professional development. The perceived value of the extended duration of PL courses may be inferred from the high ranking given to block release to attend a college/university program and the low ranking given to day-release courses. These findings are further substantiated by the qualitative data and by the research literature.

The role of tertiary institutions in professional learning.

The quantitative data indicated that teachers and principals ranked tertiary-based courses in PL as their highest preferred option. This is attested to by a teacher comment on the criteria she would use to select a course. "It needs to be structured, it needs to be additional, it needs to be recognized, like university based, or, you know, accredited and be an add on to the one [the qualification] you've got already." This perception is shared by the international research community which perceives higher education institutions to have a critical role in the PL of teachers (Sugrue et al., 2001;

Darling-Hammond, 2006). Thus, the value accorded to higher institution based PL in the research findings gives support to the four-ply model.

The role of networking with colleagues

In identifying preferred options for PL, having the opportunity to share expertise was the second most highly valued PL option in the survey data. This was further corroborated by the interview data, for example one teacher suggested:

> I think there's a lot to be said for accessing this support in groups and having the opportunity to discuss things with the group that you are with, because you learn so much, you get so much from the feedback from others.

The concept of situated learning (Lave and Wenger, 1991) with teachers initially engaging peripherally and subsequently centrally in teaching, offers opportunities to witness others' practice and to provide new insights into alternative structures and pedagogies for SEN. However, there is a danger that, rather than interrogating current practice and conducting research to determine methods for improving teaching, poor practice is reproduced and teacher PL through communities of practice merely replicates the status quo (Edwards, 2007). This is the primary disadvantage of an apprenticeship model of PL. In contrast, in the four-ply model, through incorporating communities of practice as one of the four strands of teacher PL, the positive aspect of such an approach is accentuated.

In-school professional learning

The four-ply model also incorporates a strand that firmly grounds teacher PL within school-based practice. This is a recent feature for university-accredited PL in Ireland. Clinical practice is generally not regarded as an essential component of continuing PL, as a perusal of a listing of postgraduate education theses will reveal. Timperley *et al.* (2007), however, note in their research review that access to external expertise, such as that available through tertiary research, was a necessary but not sufficient condition in itself for teacher change. Indeed, the qualitative data from this research indicates that participants value the school-based element of PL. This is evident from teachers' comments: "you went back into your school, and then your tutors came out, visited you in your school, and you could discuss with them the way you were using what you were learning". Similarly, another teacher states the value of in-school support as: "you could discuss with them, you know, 'I'm not so sure about this or that' so you had the mixture of the theory, the learning, that you needed to learn, plus the practical side".

The key role that supported clinical practice has to play in the implementation of change in teaching is also emphasised by a key stakeholder:

> I have no doubt that lectures play a part in formation, and that online can play a part, and that workshops play a part, but I'm absolutely convinced that people will not change their behavior unless you are there with them and I don't think reading about something changes your behavior.

A key strand of the four-ply model is the school placement and the support visits by university staff to teachers' in schools to discuss the implementation of the research-based practice. Thus, the importance of the transfer of pedagogy to the school context is underpinned by the model.

System support

The fourth strand of the four-ply model is the systemic support provided by the Irish Government Department of Education and Science. This is a crucial element of the four-ply model as it emphasises the high priority given to special education/inclusion in Irish education. It is one of a range of the Department's measures to build system capacity for inclusion. The funding support covers several areas. In addition to the teachers' course fees paid and a substitute teacher provided to cover the teacher's absence from school, seconded posts are provided to the host university/institution to increase their capacity to provide personnel for lecturing, school visits and research. Furthermore, finance is available for materials and other course-related costs. Indeed, this evidence of supporting policy with funding emphasises the degree of Department of Education commitment to inclusion. As Slee (2006) has noted, treasury committees are "consistently more influential" in matters relating to disability issues than are "Ministerial think tanks" (p. 117). In effect, it is the budget allocated that defines the scope of system intervention in inclusion rather than the quality of the philosophical argument.

Notwithstanding this specific example of government support for PL for special education/inclusion through the four-ply model, there are other examples of systemic support in Ireland through a broad range of policies and other professional capacity building arrangements. Another measure is the Special Education Support Service (SESS), which delivers more traditional in-service in both schools and teacher education centres. Within government policy, teacher PL is considered a key area in contributing to social and economic goals. The expansion of capacity in the education system through teacher PL is seen in relation to the education system's potential to contribute to economic growth and to promote social inclusion. In this context, the support of the government for teacher PL in inclusion/SEN is particularly relevant. While the recent economic downturn has led to a review of educational support measures, government funding for programs in special education and disadvantage have retained their proportionate share. Findings from the literature suggest that systemic support is crucial for promoting inclusive schools (Ferguson, 2008). This support is in evidence in the Irish four-ply model.

Duration of professional learning

The extended course duration of the four-ply model for teacher PL is a feature which gains support from data. The finding that one-day release courses were not ranked highly was substantiated by interview comments on their short-term impact: "I find the tips are great but it's there for a week and it's gone, you know". Another teacher commented on short courses: "Sometimes in a one-day course you just scratch the surface and I know all the surface things. It's getting deeper into issues that I'd like to do. So, I find longer courses are better". Similarly, while acknowledging that short courses can have positive benefits, in their review of evidence for effective PL, Timperley *et al.* (2007) found that the best outcomes for students were afforded through opportunities for teachers to challenge problematic beliefs. Such reformulation of beliefs is more likely to take place in an extended reflection on the teaching role. This was substantiated through the interviews with course providers.

> I think it's better if people are open to explore their own prejudices as well though, and their own attitudes to people with disabilities [...] and a year long training really allows them just to unpack that a little bit.

Equally, other research points to the importance of significant periods of time spent in inclusive settings in developing positive dispositions towards inclusion. This emerged from an analysis of the impact of teacher experience in teaching students with SEN in Greece (Avramidis and Kalyva, 2007). Thus, findings from literature point towards long-term immersion, not one-off courses, as being essential for both practice change and mind change. Hence, both the literature and research findings support teachers' desire to engage in the year-long program as the preferred option for PL. The four-ply model features this extended duration.

Conclusion and potential for international application

In this chapter, the parameters of a four-stranded collaborative model of PL for teachers working in the area of inclusion/SEN were explored. The findings from this research and the literature indicate the strength of teachers' and principals' recognition of the value of higher-education institution-based programs; the value accorded to networking with colleagues; the need for PL to be embedded in actual school practice and the need for it to be sustained over a period of time. All of these facets of PL are incorporated in the four-ply model developed in Ireland.

Internationally, this model offers the potential for a balanced approach to PL in SEN that includes the key aspects of system-led, school-led and individual development needs. The expansion of this model of PL to other jurisdictions is advocated as a means of promoting inclusion for the diverse population that are our world's children.

The argument that the cost implications of the four-ply model are prohibitive can be countered by modifications that reduce costs but maintain the quality of the PL. The time out of school might be reduced and moved to a holiday or weekend period thus obviating the teacher substitution costs. Funding of PL for teachers has, however, languished for too long behind that of other professions and the four-ply model is a just proposition for a just society.

References

Avramidis, E. and Kalyva, E. (2007) "The influence of teaching experience and professional development on Greek teachers' attitudes towards inclusion", *European Journal of Special Needs Education*, 22: 367–89.

Darling-Hammond, L. (2006) "Constructing 21st-century teacher education", *Journal of Teacher Education* 57, 3: 300–14.

DES, Department of Education and Science (2006) *Annual Report 2005–2006* Dublin: The Stationery Office.

Edwards, A. (2007) *Collaborative Approaches to Preparing and Developing Effective Teachers: Implications from and for research*. Glasgow: UCET.

Ferguson, D. L. (2008) "International trends in inclusive education: The continuing challenge to teach each one and everyone", *European Journal of Special Needs Education*, 23: 109–20.

Lave, J. and Wenger, E. (1991) *Situated Learning: Legitimate Peripheral Participation*, Cambridge: Cambridge University Press.

OECD (2005) *Teachers Matter: Attracting, Developing and Retaining Effective Teachers*, Paris: OECD.

O'Gorman, E. and Drudy, S. (2008) *Professional Development for Teachers Working in the Area of Special Education/Inclusion in Mainstream Schools*. Dublin, Ireland: UCD/NCSE.

Slee, R. (2006) "Limits to and possibilities for educational reform", *International Journal of Inclusive Education*, 10: 109–19.

Sugrue, C., Morgan, M., Devine, D. and Raftery, D. (2001) *The Quality of Irish Teachers' Professional Learning: A Critical Analysis*, Dublin, Ireland: Department of Education & Science.

Timperley, H., Wilson, A., Barrar, H. and Fung, I. (2007) *Teacher Professional Learning and Development (BES)*. Wellington, New Zealand: MINED (Ministry of Education New Zealand).

Chapter 21

Including students with special education needs in professional learning for teachers

Leena Kaikkonen

Learning outcomes

- Consider how students with special education needs (SEN) can be involved in developments which impact on their life, education and career.
- Identify educational solutions in inclusive vocational/professional education for enhancing working life, occupational and community access.
- Review an in-service inclusive training initiative for vocational teachers.

Introduction

The promotion of inclusive education has been of high priority for years and many countries have been devoted to the shared goal of providing inclusive education practice. Progress for inclusion, however, varies. For example, in 2006 some 75 million children were not in school, 55 per cent of them girls and slightly less than two-thirds of the relevant school-age population worldwide were enrolled in secondary schooling. In wealthy countries over a third of children complete university compared with much of sub-Saharan Africa where a smaller proportion completes primary education and just 5 per cent attend university-level education (UNESCO, 2008). Hence, the global goals might be the same, but the local paths to reach education for all and especially for inclusive education are diverse.

As the developments of education systems take place in their own contexts, so too are the starting points for teacher skills and teacher pre- and in-service training. If an impact on teacher development in inclusive education is hoped to take place then solutions within teacher education need to acknowledge as a starting point the national/local existing policies, funding systems, education structures and practices besides the actual philosophies and pedagogies of inclusion to be adapted into each system.

This chapter draws upon some experiences which have taken place in European in-service training collaboration, especially those in the new member states and access countries of the European Union. It describes a

Nordic–Baltic project called 'A school for all' and particularly one initiative called the Transition Project in Lithuania under that umbrella project. This chapter focuses on experiences of student involvement in development undertaken to change the Lithuanian situation.

Vocational education as the developmental context

Much of the research on inclusion has focused on the compulsory level of education, or to some extent on the provision of early years education. Less emphasis has been placed on post-compulsory levels of education. Accordingly, much of the solutions provided in literature focus on the questions related to these levels. Ferguson (2008) proposes that development of inclusive education is not about 'quick fix' school reform, but is ongoing school improvement and renewal focusing on real fundamental changes in social institutions. This demands the creation of an inclusive culture as the heart of school improvement and raises several dimensions to be reviewed such as national and local policy, the organizational dimension, teacher development, human and material resources, pedagogical and curricular development, and values (Skidmore, 2004).

Värri (2002) claims this situation, however, might be perceived unbearable if not paradoxical for teachers who must be able to respond to societal fragmentation, challenges set by the market economy, and to develop the school on a local level as well as simultaneously provide support according to postmodern demands, taking into account each learner's needs in building their own identities. Moreover, teachers in developing countries might struggle with gaining many essential resources which are taken for granted in developed countries including basic infrastructure such as electricity, seats and textbooks (UNESCO, 2008).

Concerning vocational education, many of these questions discussed are definitely relevant. Besides the whole-school approach, however, an additional wider consideration for a whole-life approach is needed. The demand for vocational teachers' societal competence is much needed if they wish to meet the challenges entailed in the surrounding world and the needs of all their students whilst entering it. With the ever rapidly changing global world and working life, questions related to vocational education and vocational pedagogy cannot be emphasized within schools. Instead, teachers need to constantly interpret working life and demands not only for continuous identity-building but also for professional growth for all involved in broader life contexts. They also need to link their pedagogical decisions to these complex processes. Teachers need to construct a reflective attitude towards their work in order to be able to appropriately respond to the challenges of the present and future and to help their students to achieve skills needed in the quickly changing working life and life in general.

The in-service training initiative for vocational teachers

The principles of education equity and equality have only relatively recently been written into Lithuanian education regulation (Republic of Lithuania, 2003). According to these principles, special needs education can be provided by any school that offers compulsory or comprehensive education. At the moment of starting the Transition Project this was as yet not the case. In agreement with previous legislation, vocational schools were not open for students who during their compulsory education had been identified as having SEN. Consequently, students identified with SEN only had the choice of either applying for special vocational school or attending a limited one-year preparatory training course in ordinary vocational school. This approach had its history in previous decades when the structures of vocational education were based on a highly planned soviet economy and education arrangements of students with SEN, like in Eastern European countries in general, were organized in segregated settings following the dominant theory of defectology (Rose *et al.*, 2007).

Accordingly, the development of the Transition Project was influenced by the fact that participating teachers had not been involved in integrated or inclusive settings. In line with ongoing developments for more inclusive basic education, the Lithuanian Ministry of Education additionally wanted to open up post-compulsory possibilities for students with SEN, emphasizing that this would also demand training of vocational teachers. Ministry representatives urged for a very practically oriented teacher in-service training program to improve teachers' pedagogical skills to support students' participation in ordinary study groups and to establish successful transitions of SEN students from comprehensive school to vocational education. The Transition Project was considered as a pilot to gather experiences for further development of more inclusive vocational education.

The piloting was implemented in two counties from which 21 students were selected. Each of them had in compulsory education been defined as a student with SEN, which in most cases meant specific learning difficulties or social and behavioral difficulties. In the project, the Ministry of Education provided students with special permission to attend ordinary vocational education and to choose, ignoring the existing limitations, whatever vocation they would hope to study to achieve a formal qualification or diploma, in order to enter employment. The 21 participating teachers were selected according the occupational programs that students chose so that these teachers would be teaching the selected students. The project was developed to follow the chosen students from the last spring of their compulsory education until the end of the first year of their studies in vocational schools.

During the one-year process, seminars were organized for the teachers in order to help them support the students in their transition process and learning. The headmasters of the schools were also involved in some seminars, and the representatives of the Ministry of Education and Regional Education Offices were present at all the seminars. The participation of diverse partners was hoped to promote bottom-up and top-down approaches as well as further developments.

Training approach

Even though the project was about training teachers, the students were put at the forefront of the project. A significant innovation was to include the students in the seminars provided for teachers. This was done for two reasons: firstly, to highlight for the teachers that students with SEN are subjects of their own lives and can be involved in decisions concerning them; secondly, the solution supported the development of communicative and reciprocal relationships between the teachers and students. The importance of listening to the voices of students (Shevlin and Rose, 2003) was considered essential for further development within vocational education settings and thus teachers were practically engaged with gaining student insights. As the teachers had no previous experience regarding inclusive education, they were given a chance to learn through examining the situation of one student without having to worry about too many issues at a time. This case-based approach helped teachers experience that 'meeting needs of an individual' means actually 'meeting the individual'.

The previous educational practice in Lithuania was described to have been quite hierarchical, based on frontal and formal instruction. Many of the participating students seemed to be reasonably shy and were used neither to expressing themselves nor to being heard. Consequently, there was a presumption that without any supporting practical 'tools' students and teachers might have difficulties to proceed in their mutual interaction and cooperation. When working in the seminars, most of the time participants were all together, but sometimes they were divided into two groups whilst preparing for further activities. For example, when starting to work on IEPs, students first made, with the support of trainers and using pictures, posters about themselves in order to talk about their existing strengths, wishes and future plans. If the process was to be started with only discussions or papers and pens, it was expected that the situation would end with either one or both sides not feeling comfortable, or it would have easily been led by teachers. All in all, the approach posed a real challenge for interaction, as for example when training, the trainers' speech had to be considered to be for students and teachers at the same time.

Some of the seminar days were organized only for teachers and headmasters in order to fulfil their expectations to acquire knowledge on issues such as special needs, IEPs and transitions. Trainers emphasized, however, that knowledge itself would not solve the questions. Instead, the more crucial issue was how the knowledge was to be transferred to everyday practice of the teachers and schools, and how the training could or would change existing procedures. The learning tasks that teachers were working on between seminars were designed to be strongly connected with the real-life questions of their students. Finding solutions to guide the students supported not only students' individual process in the transition phase or in learning, but also teachers in their reflective practice and wider professional learning (PL). Activities and methods used were work-based and case-based and emphasized active, collaborative, experiential and contextual learning.

During the seminars there were organized times for sharing and discussing individual experiences and knowledge acquired for their solutions and developing ideas together further. As a consequence teachers had a chance to formulate a more general picture and to pay attention to wider school development. To promote reflective practice teachers made notes upon activities taken. It was hoped that by reflecting on their own process during the year some more general models could be found for schools to organize transitions in the future. Additionally, this in-service training had a so-called developmental orientation. As suitable previous practices and examples in the Lithuanian context did not exist, they had to be developed while learning. These concurrently improved teachers' abilities to constantly develop their own work, a competence definitely needed in the current rapidly changing world of work.

It was considered important to create a supportive, open and safe setting. The atmosphere in the workshops was experiential, positive and enthusiastic and it seemed to diminish the fears that vocational teachers had in the beginning of the project in terms of teaching students with SEN. It also seemed to promote the growth of self-esteem of the students. Evidence of this growth was that students who hardly had the courage to say anything in the beginning of the project, fluently answered questions asked by the interviewer about their vocational studies and future plans at the end of their first year in the final seminar of the project and in front of an audience of approximately 100 people.

Reviewing the project

The one-year project seemed to achieve quite well the targets set for it. All 21 students were able to accomplish their first year of studies quite satisfactorily. A wish to follow the process further, however, emerged, and so a small-scale follow-up study was started on student experiences and success.

Data were collected twice from the students involved in the project in both counties (called A and B). The first data collection on students' experiences of studying at vocational school was undertaken at the end of their second year of studies. Fourteen of the 21 students participated in this phase. The second batch of data on students' experiences, which focused on self-evaluation of their own success and their thoughts of transition from school to working life, was collected at the end of their third year of studies. Eight students attended these interviews. The data were collected with a structured questionnaire supported by interviews where students were asked in more detail the grounds upon which they based their answers. The students' oral answers were written down by one of the interviewers. Data of students' success were simultaneously collected from the teachers in the spring of the second study year. In the spring of their third study year teachers and county administrators gave information about students' situations at the point of completing their studies.

Students' experiences on studying at vocational school

In general, most of the students with SEN appeared to have enjoyed studying at the vocational school and were happy with their own educational performance. Most students were satisfied with the contents of lessons provided for them and additionally found the atmosphere of the school supportive, saying that helping others is usual in their groups. Further, students felt that they were accepted at school and especially that teachers respected their opinions. All students were pleased with the occupational field they had chosen (Kaikkonen *et al.*, 2006).

Moreover, students pointed out some critical issues. A majority of the students did not feel good after exams, expressing that the exams did not prove their real know-how, e.g. due to facing time constraints whilst writing. They were also critical in regards to the teaching not being illustrative enough, and that they were provided with insufficient feedback from teachers. What's more, they claimed that their study group was not peaceful enough to study in. The students in County A, however, appeared to have more negative opinions compared with their peers in County B (see Table 21.1). Students raised challenges for teachers to improve their skills

Table 21.1 Students' experiences on studying at vocational school after two years of studies.

	County A	County B
Not satisfied with the ways of working	43%	0%
Not satisfied with the space and opportunities to express their views	72%	20%
Attention not paid to the students' needs	43%	0%
Bullying experiences	67%	0%
School as insecure place	71%	20%
Teachers do not inspire students to learn	71%	0%
Worried about going to work	43%	0%

in facilitating learning. Ferguson (2008) calls this a shift from teaching to learning, i.e. enabling students to engage in more meaningful, personalized and differentiated learning. Students articulated this by hoping for varied means of learning assessment, as well as ways of illustrating, visualizing and using diverse methods in teaching. Ferguson claims that this demands moving from offering services to providing support; 'one size does not fit all' but instead, we need to ensure learning using a variety of strategies. Nevertheless, teachers themselves told of how they had improved their own skills and working methods with all students.

Students' experiences of their success in studies

Altogether 21 students started studies within the Transition Project. Three years later, students self-assessed and teachers' evaluated that 13 students were expected to pass the national vocational exams. Seven of them were also expected to pass maturity exams and to get an upper secondary education certificate. Additionally, one student passed only the general subject exam. When comparing these students' success with the aims set for the project, it is worth remembering that in the three-year training program students normally accomplish both the vocational qualification and the general upper secondary education certificate. The initial target set in the Transition Project for the students with SEN was to attain only the vocational qualification. Two-thirds succeeded in this, and additionally one third of them also passed, maybe a bit unexpectedly, the national upper secondary level general education exams.

Yet, by the end of the third year, schools and regional education authorities provided information that one third of the students in the end were not able to pass their studies as planned. According to the information, one of the students had applied for time off from the studies due to personal reasons, and the school expected him to return. The other six students had dropped out from the system, two girls due to getting married and having children, one boy due to going to work and another three due to moving abroad. According to the teachers, this last reason was seen as a growing tendency in Lithuania.

Transitions to working life

In the follow-up study insights into the transition from school to adult life were also gathered, in addition to how successfully this was developed for the students and how they were supported in this phase by their tutors and schools.

In the final interviews all students with SEN declared that they had developed skills to act according to the rules of working life. They considered that they had raised their self-esteem and now felt brave enough to ask for help; an issue which in the teacher-led system was not a self-evident result. Furthermore, students felt able to take responsibility for their work and cooperate with more experienced workers. Seven out of eight students fully agreed that they had learnt skills needed for working life. All agreed that their general knowledge was good, yet only two of them were fully confident with their professional-specific skills, and three students with their professional-specific knowledge. One student was not very motivated to go to work.

Students also expressed that during their vocational education they had become well acquainted with their working practice placements. As opposed to their feelings about not receiving enough feedback in the school environment, students said that they had got good feedback during their working placements and felt they also had self-evaluated and discussed their skills with their teachers in school. They received support in transition from school to work, but this was provided by their friends, parents or other close persons, not teachers. Students commented that the teachers should put more effort into building connections to working life and developing skills in career guidance and counselling. Nevertheless, most students felt that their relationship with their teachers was good; all felt that they had been able to discuss with their teachers about moving towards working life.

Even though students' opinions were mostly positive, their transition out of school cannot be said to be too promising. Of the eight students who were present at the interviews in the third spring, only three had found themselves a work placement after school. Three of them had not yet been successful in this, and two students were undergoing negotiations. It is also noteworthy to mention that of these eight students only half mentioned that they were going to work in the occupational field that they had studied. The other four mentioned some other vocational field.

Discussion

A concluding question emerges: Did this teacher training initiative involving students promote the development of more inclusive education in vocational schools in Lithuania?

Some significant changes took place. The most important of them was the amendment of education legislation, which nowadays provides more possibilities for students with special needs after completion of their basic education. The legislative change was influenced by several factors. The Transition Project, however, might take some credit for promoting this amendment through the experiences afforded in it and affecting decision making on a national level through the keen contact with local stakeholders including teachers and students, and administrators and policy makers.

The training for teachers was influenced by reflective practice where a more holistic and comprehensive approach was used to promote teacher development, aiming at pedagogical actions which take full account of both their learners' needs and the wider contexts influencing education settings and provisions. A strong focus of the training was upon the development of understanding more general questions of learning and teaching in current practice in vocational education and training, as opposed to teaching approaches specifically aimed only at young people with special needs. This experience had raised teachers' awareness of student diversity and how to cope with it among teachers and also promoted the pedagogical improvements of procedures with all students. Moreover, teachers gave opinions that attitudes, both in participating schools as well as their own, towards students with SEN had changed to be more positive, which can also be considered to be a meaningful result.

Shevlin and Rose (2003) suggest that by listening to the opinions of young people, teachers can gain insight and understanding which enables them to develop more inclusive policies and practices. This was emphasized in both the project and the follow-up which was undertaken. Based on the research data, it seems that many of the students had found this experience valuable. The most radical comment of this kind was one student saying 'this project has changed my life totally'. Other students claimed during the process that this experience had increased the growth of their life skills and self-esteem, as well as encouraged them onwards in their life.

All in all, the student achievements in the project can be said to be well in line with the targets set; students were included in vocational education and they all were able to pass the first year of their studies satisfactorily. Students wished to achieve a formal qualification or diploma in order to enter employment later on. Some drop-outs were known to have happened, due to 'ordinary' adult life changes, but the project and additional support for teachers and schools had finished after the first year. Still, the forms and continuity of guidance provided within and from schools still left challenges to be considered.

As a closing remark it is noteworthy to mention that in the beginning of the project many of the teachers doubted that students with SEN would be able to succeed in studying in ordinary vocational education. The good success of two-thirds of the students maybe surprised all involved and gave a challenging but positive lesson to reflect upon for further developments of the system.

Acknowledgements

With acknowledgements to training and research partners Ms Irmeli Maunonen-Eskelinen, JAMK University of Applied Sciences, Teacher Education College, Finland; and Ms Teresa Aidukiene, Ministry of Education and Science, Lithuania.

References

Ferguson, D. (2008) "International trends in inclusive education: the continuing challenge to teach each one and everyone", *European Journal of Special Needs Education*, 23(2): 109–20.

Kaikkonen, L., Maunonen-Eskelinen, I. and Aidukiene, T. (2006) "Supporting teachers' competencies towards development of more inclusive school – Listening to the voices of students with special educational needs in educational transitions", paper presented at ATEE Spring Conference, Riga, June.

Republic of Lithuania (2003) *Law on Education*. Lithuania Government.

Rose, R., Kaikkonen, L. and Kõiv, K. (2007) "Estonian vocational teachers' attitudes towards inclusive education for students with special educational needs", *International Journal of Special Education*, 22(3): 97–109.

Shevlin, M, and Rose, R. (eds) (2003) *Encouraging Voices; Respecting the Insights of Young People who have been Marginalised*. Dublin: National Disability Authority.

Skidmore, D. (2004) *Inclusion: The Dynamic of School Development*. Cornwall: Open University Press.

UNESCO (2008) "Overcoming inequality: why governance matters", *The 2009 EFA Global Monitoring Report*. Online. Available at: http://www.unesco.org/en/education/efareport/reports/2009-governance/ (accessed 12 March 2009).

Värri, V.-M. (2002) "Teacher's identity – from moral educator to change agent and information-flow interpreter" (in Finnish), *2002 Year Book of OKKA–Foundation*, pp. 42–64.

Chapter 22

Initial teacher training to meet the needs of students with disabilities who are culturally and linguistically diverse

Elizabeth A. West

Learning outcomes

- Describe a process for developing context-relevant professional learning (PL) using teachers' voice.
- Define the major elements of culturally responsive teaching.
- List effective practices for working with students from culturally and linguistically diverse backgrounds who have disabilities.
- Identify and consider implications for own PL context.

Introduction

The changes around the world caused by globalization and worldwide immigration have produced a diverse student base. Given the world's changing demographics a reconceptualization of effective teaching of those who are culturally and linguistically diverse (CLD) is needed. Provision of such services directly depends on teachers who are knowledgeable and skilled, but who are also able to establish trusting working relationships with children and their families.

It took the USA nearly 10 years to have all states come into compliance with its national law to support individuals with disabilities. Change is happening at a rapid pace in many countries and many teachers across the world echo a sentiment of anxiety (Bradshaw *et al.*, 2004) and concern over perceived competence (Forlin, 2005). In many countries teachers are also being asked to ensure that all their students achieve, regardless of background.

The doors have been opened but many countries are now grappling with how to prepare teachers to meet the needs of such a heterogeneous population. Understanding culture is important in that we can remove unintentional barriers to a student's success. Physical presence alone does not lead automatically to effective participation and improved achievement. The quality of education depends on the competence of teachers and competence is defined and addressed differently throughout the world. In addition, attitudes and beliefs of teachers must be examined to facilitate acceptance and growth.

This chapter will focus on providing an approach to facilitate PL for teachers who work with CLD students who have been identified as having a disability.

Professional learning

Although many resources have been committed to PL and improved teaching, studies reveal the failings and shortcomings of many of these efforts. In most parts of the world, the majority of inservice programs are "too short, too unrelated to the needs of teachers, and too ineffective to upgrade teaching knowledge" (Villegas-Reimers, 2003, p. 63). Teachers, both special and general educators, may come to the classroom with a very different initial teacher education (ITE) profile and different programs are offered in different parts of the world. Educators must not only have skills to provide modifications and accommodations but also have skills to provide instruction that is culturally and linguistically responsive.

Formal multicultural education and special education preparation for these teachers has typically been a minimal part of ITE programs, thus teachers learn on the job. Prater *et al.* (2008) identified traditional ITE preparation as being inadequate in preparing educators to teach culturally and/or linguistically diverse students. Not all ITE programs readily embrace multicultural education or culturally responsive teacher education pedagogy. Professional learning for teachers must acknowledge prior training and build upon what teachers report as being helpful to facilitate their own learning.

Teacher voice

Much of the PL currently available to teachers working with CLD children with disabilities tends to emerge out of a "top-down" process, well removed from the realities of these teachers' daily work with this population of children and their families. Topics for such PL sessions typically contain generic content and teachers are never solicited for information regarding their actual needs. Teachers must be given a voice from which PL practices can then be developed. The process of listening to the teachers themselves, as reflective co-constructors of PL programs, could serve to ensure that teachers are an explicit element of the training debate, which in turn will positively influence the way teachers respond and make meaning of their learning.

The use of data generated from interviews can lead to the identification of instructional knowledge and skills necessary for a particular setting given resources or lack of. Data can contribute to the design and implementation of model PL programs for teachers who work with CLD students with disabilities. Thus, PL goals can be developed from this data, reflecting the voice of the teachers. Key elements [based upon the National Professional

Development Center on Inclusion's (NPDCI) conceptual framework] must be examined during the PL planning stage i.e. (1) who? characteristics of the learners and contexts; (2) what? the specific content of the learning; and (3) how? the approaches.

Who: Characteristics of the learners and context

Teacher preparation programs in the 21st century for students with disabilities should focus on understanding the meaning of cultural and linguistic diversity; respecting families' home cultures; understanding the importance of family-centered practices; understanding of culturally competent practices; and being willing to confront "old" practices.

A key factor in ensuring student success is teachers' understanding and appreciation of how culture shapes academic and social development. This is particularly crucial when students come from cultures different from our own. By developing and sustaining culturally responsive practices with families, teachers can improve outcomes. In addition, knowing the "who" may help to reduce the disproportionate representation of minorities in special education programs as we generate a greater understanding of ways of learning and how to teach to meet these ways. Harry (2002) refers to the power of cultural capital and the discrepancy between schools' perceptions of such capital and the capital actually possessed by families. Further, Harry provides culturally inclusive ways to build relationships with families and suggests that a multicultural emphasis in personnel preparation programs should focus on process rather than cultural content. Knowing the characteristics of the learners and context is the first process in developing culturally responsive programs. Artiles (2002) and Gee (2001) identify that instructional methods do not work or fail as decontextualized generic practices, but work in relation to the social-cultural contexts in which they are implemented.

What: Professional learning content

How do we determine the "what" for PL within particular contexts? The "what" should reflect the themes and/or categories generated from teacher interviews.

An example

My colleagues and I describe an international research project in the USA and the UK that explores teachers' views of a recent learning experience they perceive to have been effective for them (West et al., 2006). Fourteen teachers attending graduate courses at a university in the USA (six teachers) and a university in the UK (eight teachers) formed the sample. A primary aim of this project was to identify elements of what was working well in relation to continued PL for this group of teachers, which would subsequently inform the teaching and learning opportunities developed. Individual structured interviews generated data that allowed an insight into the personal meaning making made by the teachers about their own learning experiences, and their thoughts on continued PL, for them and their colleagues in schools and across their districts.

This collaborative project illustrates that although the two groups of teachers live and work in different international contexts, similar themes relating to factors that contribute to effective learning emerged. These themes focus on relating theory to practice, mediated teacher learning, learning from others, and reflection in action. Two categories, seeing the relationship between theory and practice and learning from others, emerged as particularly important for the teachers.

A key component of this relationship seems to be how teachers are introduced to theory and how they are shown the relevance of this to their school and community context. The nature of relevance varied across the teachers with some relating to particular issues with individual students, and others relating to their classroom, school and district contexts. The important factor appears to be the personal relevance that each teacher is able to attribute through the learning experience which impacts decisions about their level of engagement in such learning. Instructors of teacher education courses need to assist pre-service teachers in making the connection between theory and practice. They must be able to understand and apply CLD theoretical orientation to particular contexts. This connection can be facilitated by designing coursework that has relevancy for a variety of CLD contexts. Results of this research reflect that teachers who were offered experiential learning opportunities, with mentor support, felt they were able to apply their new knowledge in the classrooms.

The collaborative element of sharing and learning from colleagues, parents, students and others has also been highlighted as a particularly important element in effective learning for teachers in this study. The teachers discussed this process of sharing and collaboration as being both formal and informal; formally through mentoring by instructors and engaging in collaboration during courses, and informally through sharing examples of daily experiences with each other. Partnering with CLD families who have a son/daughter with a disability is crucial as teachers seek to understand and provide responsive practices.

Teaching and learning: Culturally responsive practices

Numerous models have been developed to assist educators to be culturally responsive and to practice culturally responsive teaching. These frameworks have been minimally applied to students with disabilities who are CLD. These skills must be explicitly taught and supported to ensure teachers have the critical skills necessary to meet the needs of the child, family and community.

Gay (2002) defines culturally responsive teaching as "using the cultural characteristics, experiences, and perspectives of ethnically diverse students as conduits for teaching them more effectively" (p. 106). Gay identifies and examines five essential elements of culturally responsive teaching: developing a knowledge base about cultural diversity, including ethnic and cultural diversity content in the curriculum, demonstrating caring and building learning communities, communicating with ethnically diverse students, and responding to ethnic diversity in the delivery of instruction. Components of a variety of models in some form can be examined for PL based upon the strengths and needs of the particular context. Use of teacher interviews around such content could generate a profile for PL that ultimately builds on existing strengths.

Rather than alienate students from their home and community cultures and languages, teachers should build upon the cultures and languages of students from diverse groups in order to enhance their learning. Diversity provides rich opportunities to create learning environments in which instruction is enriched, the academic achievement of marginalized students is enhanced and the education of all students is improved. Teachers must seek to be culturally responsive and competent and realize that this is a process; it is a lifelong quest as we enter the classroom as learners.

How: Professional learning approaches

Educating students with a disability who are also CLD in inclusive environments requires collaboration by a variety of stakeholders. There are many collaborative approaches to PL, including consultation, coaching, communities of practice, lesson study, mentoring, reflective supervision and technical assistance (NPDCI, 2008). A range of PL practices exist in the context of school improvement. For example, teacher–researcher alliances have been formed (e.g. Vaughn et al., 1998) and collaborative communities developed (e.g. Englert and Zhao, 2001); professional development schools (Voltz, 2001); critical friends groups which are teacher support groups (Bambino, 2002); Friday forums where teachers support each other by relying on internal expertise (Hudson, 2002); and a variety of professional learning communities or networks.

Discussion

Teachers' response to inclusion is often associated with their perceptions of the availability of training, resources, and administrative support. This chapter has offered one example to solicit teacher voice to co-construct culturally responsive learning opportunities.

Developing a sense of community through some forum of discourse is important for educators. This appears to be a key ingredient in successful programs that prepare teachers to work with culturally and linguistically diverse students. This emerged as a key theme in our research (West *et al.*, 2006).

Mentoring is another way to allow a teacher's voice to be heard. The application of theory to practice is an essential component of learning in teacher education. The use of mentors could serve to bridge theory to practice and to provide support in an occupation that can be isolating. Mentoring is effective both in supporting new professionals as they enter the field and in retaining professionals. Teachers can be paired with mentors, and both can become part of a community-of-practice that supports each other through informal PL. Several elements of the community-of-practice framework are important. Group members share, build upon and transform what they know about effective practice. They co-construct knowledge through mutual analysis of each other's experiences and apply new knowledge. Thus, all members, regardless of professional status, contribute to the professional community's knowledge base.

To be culturally responsive, teachers must reflect upon ways to connect with the broader community and culture to align with the classroom context. Teachers can increase the academic and social achievement of students from diverse groups if they make use of, and build upon, the knowledge, skills, and languages these students acquire in the information learning environments of their homes and communities.

Conclusion

The persistent achievement gaps between various racial and ethnic groups are evidence of the challenges these students face and challenges we must address. Teacher preparation practices must be responsive to these issues and diversity as a consequence of changing demographics. Contrasting values and behaviors among participants in a given setting can lead to conflict and confusion about goals and instructional practices. Lacking sufficient understanding of the experiences of minority families, even the most dedicated teachers can hinder children's learning and progress.

An increasing body of research demonstrates that the single factor making the most difference in student learning is the quality of the teacher (NCTA, 1997). Thus, PL can serve as a catalyst for social change as it influences quality and empowers teachers. We can challenge teachers to view educational beliefs and practices through the lens of social transformation to examine which beliefs and practices foster the equality of each voice, and which beliefs and practices perpetuate oppression and marginalization of certain individuals and/or groups.

Families, teachers and administrators should be engaged in a process to provide input to facilitate the development of culturally and contextually relevant PL opportunities. To meet the needs of an increasingly heterogeneous society, it is imperative that we are prepared to respond effectively to families and children from varying cultural and linguistic backgrounds. If educators fail to understand cultural and linguistic diversity the risk of impeding the success of children from cultural orientations different from our own remains. ITE must provide activities and experiences that foster this understanding.

We must create culturally and contextually relevant professional learning experiences using teachers' voice. Improved teacher preparation programs and PL activities are necessary for realizing the goals of inclusive services for the CLD learner with an identified disability and his or her family.

References

Artiles, A. J. (2002) "Culture in learning: The next frontier in reading difficulties research", in R. Bradley, L. Danielson and D. P. Hallahan (eds), *Identification of Learning Disabilities: Research to Policy*, Hillsdale, NJ: Lawrence Erlbaum, pp. 693–701.

Bambino, D. (2002) "Critical friends", *Educational Leadership*, 59(6): 25–7.

Bradshaw, K., Tennant, L. and Lydiatt, S. (2004) "Special education in the United Arab Emirates: Anxieties, attitudes and aspirations", *International Journal of Special Education*, 19(1) 49–55.

Englert, C. S. and Zhao, Y. (2001) "The construction of knowledge in a collaborative community: Reflections on three projects", in J. Woodward and L. Cuban (eds), *Technology, Curriculum and Professional Development: Adapting Schools to Meet the Needs of Students with Disabilities*, Thousand Oaks, CA: Corwin Press, pp. 187–202.

Forlin, C. (2005) "Sustaining inclusive practices in primary school communities", in C. Newell (eds), *Disability in Education: Context Curriculum and Culture*, Australia: Australian College of Educators, pp. 13–21.

Gay, G. (2002) "Preparing for culturally responsive teaching", *Journal of Teacher Education*, 33(2): 106–16.

Gee, J. P. (2001) "A sociocultural perspective on early literacy development", in S. B. Neuman and D. K. Dickinson (eds), *Handbook for Early Literacy Research*, New York: Guilford Press, pp. 30–42.

Harry, B. (2002) "Trends and issues in serving culturally diverse families of children with disabilities", *Journal of Special Education*, 36(3): 131–8.

Hudson, J. S. (2002) "Friday forums", *Educational Leadership*, 59(6): 76–7.

NCTA (1997) *Doing What Matters Most: Investing in Quality Teaching*, National Commission on Teaching and America's Future: New York.

NPDCI (2008) *What Do We Mean by Professional Development in the Early Childhood Field*, Chapel Hill: University of North Carolina, FPG Child Development Institute, National Professional Development Center on Inclusion.

Prater, M. A., Wilder, L. K. and Dyches, T. T. (2008) "Shaping one traditional special educator preparation program toward more cultural competence", *Teaching Education*, 19(2): 137–51.

Vaughn, S., Hughes, M. T., Schumm, J. S. and Klinger, J. (1998) "A collaborative effort to enhance reading and writing instruction in inclusive classrooms", *Learning Disability Quarterly*, 21: 57–74.

Villegas-Reimers, E. (2003) *Teacher Professional Development: An International Review of the Literature*. UNESCO: International Institute for Educational Planning, Paris.

Voltz, D. L. (2001) "Preparing general education teachers for inclusive settings: The role of special education teachers in the professional development school context", *Learning Disability Quarterly*, 21: 57–74.

West, E., Jones, P. and Stevens, D. (2006) "Teachers of students with low incidence disabilities talk about their own learning: An international insight", *Research and Practice for Persons with Severe Disabilities*, 39(3): 121–42.

Chapter 23

Cooperative action research in a "Learning in Regular Classrooms" school

Huan Song

Learning outcomes

- Understand the Learning in Regular Classrooms (LRC) approach in China.
- Reflect upon how a collaborative action research program can support professional learning (PL) for a teacher engaged in LRC.

Introduction

In 1982, the newly revised Constitution of the People's Republic of China stated that "the nation is responsible for providing disabled citizens with opportunities to work, live, and be educated" (National People's Congress, 1982, Article 45). According to the Compulsory Education Law of the People's Republic of China, all children including those with disabilities who have reached the age of six shall be enrolled in school and receive compulsory education for the prescribed number of years. Due to the large number of students with disabilities and the lack of special schools, a national policy on inclusive education called "Learning in Regular Classrooms" (LRC) was delivered by the Chinese Government. Specific regulations and details of implementing the LRC program were stated in the 1994 Tentative Regulation on Implementing Learning in Regular Classrooms for Children and Adolescents with Disabilities. In 2007, the LRC program served approximately 65 per cent of students with disabilities (Ministry of Education of China, 2007).

Deng and Guo (2007) state that there exists a gap between the ideal and reality of inclusion in China. According to the results of their empirical study, the idea of full inclusion of individuals with disabilities into mainstream schools and society is supported extensively in principle. Most special education administrators, though, acknowledge that in practice it is too hard to realize this goal. A recent study on teachers in kindergarten also shows that more than 80 per cent of teachers agree with the concept of inclusion but less than 12 per cent had received special education training, and around 64 per cent do not have enough confidence to implement inclusion (Yan,

2008). Changing attitudes is not enough. Where inclusion is working, we need to ask teachers what or who is helping them to be successful, and where inclusion is not working, we need to ask what gets in the way.

Action research is a special research form which focuses on improving practice, but can also serve as an approach for teacher PL. It can lead to professional understanding, personal growth, and political empowerment. Many studies have shown that participating in action research can change teachers' concept of the teaching profession, increase teachers' self-confidence, and inspire teachers' creativity (e.g. Noffke and Zeichner, 1987). Recently, action research has been used as a powerful strategy for improving inclusive practice (Carrington and Robinson, 2004). Little attention, however, has been paid to the relationship between action research and teacher PL for inclusion. In this chapter, a case study will be described to show the effect of action research on the teacher PL for inclusion.

Action research teacher professional learning

In an attempt to investigate how teachers cope when involved in the LRC a collaborative action research project was initiated.

A school that had applied the LRC program for three years was selected. It was one of many junior middle schools located in an area between city and countryside in Chaoyang district, the most developed district of Beijing. The large number of students with disabilities and the lack of supporting conditions are problems faced by this school and teachers. There are one or two students with disabilities in most classes in this school, and most of these students have an intellectual disability.

The partner of this collaborative action research project was a 37-year-old female teacher who had taught social studies for 15 years in this school. From 2006, she engaged in the LRC program. She had one student, Xu, with intellectual disability in her class. Xu was 16 years old, and got his certificate of intellectual disability at the age of 12 when he was studying in a primary school. The teacher expressed an interest in LRC and inclusive education and Xu's parents accepted and supported this action research project. The project became possible due to the teacher being free of her routine work because social studies is not included in the senior high school entrance examination. The action research team, therefore, consisted of myself as the teacher educator, a postgraduate student majoring in special education, and the teacher.

The collaborative action research method was applied in this study. There were four phases which are summarized in Figure 23.1.

Action research is a cyclical process in which action alternates with critical reflection. The research design acknowledges that new issues may emerge and develop during the study and mirrors the complexity of classroom teaching. Data collection methods included focus group interviews,

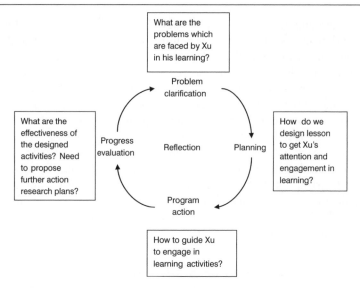

Figure 23.1 Cyclic process of the cooperative action research

individual interviews, participant observation, and reflective journals. Data analysis was both inductive and deductive in nature for the "construction of meanings of inclusion and creating the practices that said to be inclusive" (Clough and Barton, 1995, p. 12).

A story of action research and a journal of teacher learning

> It was a warm afternoon in September when I came to the school to do the first participant observation. A seat was prepared for me just beside Xu, and I spent almost the whole afternoon in the classroom to observe him. During the four lessons in the afternoon, he just sat in his seat without any textbook on his desk, looking casually around, moving his body forward and backward from time to time and dozing. He hardly caught any attention from the teachers the entire afternoon and it seemed he was in his own world.
>
> (Journal notes)

These notes are taken from the researcher's field journal. It would seem that Xu had been in a similar situation since he came into this school. Xu also complained that: "The 45 minutes of a class passed too slowly. I always feel anxious when I walk into the school gate ... I really don't know how to kill the time." The teacher once tried to connect with Xu's parents, and his parents just said: "Xu is different from others. We have no requirement for his learning performance. The only expectation is not to make trouble for teachers and family". The Chinese teacher in Xu's class tried to involve Xu in the class, but failed eventually because Xu was neither willing to participate in the studying activities nor able to understand what the teacher taught. Xu also said:

> Chinese lesson is just to repeat what is already written in the textbooks; Mathematics is always to learn pi and other things; English is to endlessly copy and recite the text ... I am not good at such rote learning for I am somewhat slow-minded.

It would seem that due to his learning difficulties and his parents' negative attitude, Xu had become accustomed to the idea of just staying in the classroom peacefully and waiting for the end of the lesson.

The first round of action research

Problem clarification

In the problem clarification of the first round of action research, the research team used reflective interviewing and analytic discourse to determine the problem. The teacher was asked to describe the problem briefly, and she stated that "Xu is so silent that he isn't concerned about teaching and learning". After the first team meeting, the teacher and the researcher began to observe Xu and complete reflective journals to clarify the problem.

In the second team meeting two weeks later, the three members of the research team shared their observation notes and reflective journals and discussed the problem with each other. From the observation notes, the research team found that sometimes Xu would exhibit some interest in the class when the teacher mentioned living examples related to the real world, especially about cars and computers. Some useful information given by Xu's parents also showed that Xu had a hobby collecting documents about cars and electronic products. The research team came to the conclusion that Xu does have an interest in learning, but does not find every lesson interesting. The problem clarified by the research team is how to call Xu's attention to learning.

Planning

Considering the former experience of Xu, the teacher suggested that the first step should be small and carefully designed. The teacher designed one or two questioning sections in each lesson. In such questioning sections, some questions were specially designed as more practical in order to arouse Xu's interest in learning and let him give the answers more easily. For example, in a lesson about the 30 years of change in China, the teacher asked students to describe some changes in their families and communities. Xu was asked to answer the same question.

Program action

This phase was to put the plan into practice. The teacher worked hard to design suitable questions and integrate them into each lesson. The design of each lesson plan and questions were discussed with other members of the research team before the class. The unit "the situation of our country" consisted of four lessons, and each question in each lesson was related to cars and computers which interested Xu. "When we talked about the change of our real life, he actively engaged in discussion ... when his answer was correct, he was so happy and called 'YEAH'" (Teacher observation notes). The teacher also wrote in her reflective journal that: "Actually he is so happy to get teacher's regards according to his performance in the lesson. He really is a simple and lovely child, and (I) should give more attention to him."

Progress evaluation

The research team met together for the third time to inspect the data collected from interview, participant observation, and reflective journals, and to evaluate the effect of the first round action plan. The teacher began to recognize that: "Xu has some abilities ... he can engage in (class), but we used to ignore him. And such neglect has been a part of our habit." She also realized that:

> Xu is stereotyped by his label. Because of his label, he found an excuse not to study and for his laziness in learning. What is expected of him is not to make trouble. And as for learning he thinks he's allowed to have poor performance due to his "abnormality".

After the first round of action research, the teacher not only knew more about Xu, but also worked out the strategies to stimulate the learning motivation of such students with disabilities like Xu. The most important was that she learned to be empathetic and to treat those students with respect and kindness. As Darling-Hammond *et al.* remind us:

> The most important differences in what happens to children at school, depend on who their teachers are: what they understand about children and about learning, what they are able to do to respond to the very different approaches and experiences children bring with them to the learning setting, what they care about and are committed to as teachers.
> (Darling-Hammond *et al.*, 2002, p. 150)

The teacher and other observers, though, gradually found that Xu would engage more in the questioning section, but often move back to the original status for the rest of class. What was the next step they should take?

The second round of action research

Problem clarification

Data from observation notes and reflective journals showed that Xu learned little of the social studies curriculum despite behaving better in the class than before. Therefore, in the fourth research meeting the teacher clarified the new problem: how to engage Xu in meaningful learning not just in talking about topics related to his interests. According to Freire and César:

> ... it is not enough to put all the children together in a regular school setting, even in a regular classroom where they share a common curriculum, if they are not provided with the means to successfully appropriate it. Therefore, school has to facilitate each child reaching his/her potential and appropriating a set of shared "tools" that will allow them to fully develop their potentialities and become fully included in the society of which they are a part.
>
> (Freire and César, 2003, p. 351)

Planning

> Sometimes our teachers feel that we should treat students equally, but the requirements fall down when we face students like Xu. In fact we shouldn't treat him in this way. Maybe he can't reach the level like others, but he can arrive at a lower level.
>
> (Xu's teacher in interview)

In the second round of action planning, inquiry learning activities were initiated into the class. Teaching social issues through inquiry allowed students to conceptualize a question and then seek possible explanations that respond to that question. Inquiry is suitable to students with intellectual disabilities for its characteristics such as authentic, collaborative, self-regulation, and intuitionist approaches (Arends, 2004). The designed inquiry learning activities were related to the topics of the curriculum of social studies. For example, students were divided into several groups to collect the information on different nations of China when the teacher taught about "China as a multinational country". Xu also joined one of the student groups to take inquiry learning.

Program action

At the beginning, the teacher asked the leader of the group which Xu joined to arrange a suitable task for him and help him to do it. But Xu's performance greatly surprised the teacher:

> Of course, I was still worrying about him. I am afraid that Xu, who doesn't engage in anything, dislikes trouble and would find an excuse to refuse. However, the next day when I met Xu in the corridor, he said to me complacently: "I collected them and handed them in. It was too easy, and I found lots of things."

As for Xu's performance in the classes, firstly the frequency of his interaction with the teacher and other students increased. Secondly, the homework completed by Xu such as the inquiry report was outstanding. In the inquiry report about Dongxiang (a minority 东乡族), Xu had collected the related information of more than 4000 words through the internet and used the framework offered by the teacher to classify and coordinate the information into an integrated report and made it into a word file. Thirdly, Xu mentioned that he had learnt a lot from the inquiry learning activities, "I feel it is interesting. The lessons taught by the teacher are abundant in content, and easier. You will not feel too tired. The content is ample and extensive … I can learn about various aspects." Xu also favored the inquiry learning activities, especially the collaboration with classmates and collective show. "For example, I can get knowledge that I do not know from my peers and vice versa."

At the same time, the teacher reflected on the reason for Xu's performance.

Progress evaluation

After one month of action, everyone including Xu himself all noticed the change that had happened to him. In the teachers' reflective journal she wrote that: "I found he had obviously changed. He wouldn't sleep in the classroom, and he liked to walk beside me and try to seek a topic to discuss with me. He is also more passionate to me than before."

Inclusion is not only a pedagogical issue, but also a right issue and a values issue. As the teacher was implementing pedagogical initiatives in her lesson, her attitude to students with disabilities and inclusive education was changing as well. A sense of empathy gestated in her heart. As she said:

> Sometimes when I saw him, I would suddenly have a small feeling of regret. Because I ignored him too much before, now I talked to him even more than in the past two years … I think he would feel lonely in his heart. Although his classmates wouldn't tease him, but often joke

with cynicism ... He always stands aside when taking photos, because he doesn't know where he should stand ... I totally understand him.

Her confidence in treating and teaching students with disabilities also increased; she said "I think the most important thing is that you should understand them first, and you will teach more suitably when you know them more. Those children have their own potential."

Her confidence comes from the successful experience in this two-round action research. According to Guskey's statements about teacher change (1986), teachers' change in belief and attitude would not happen until they saw the learning performance of students. The confidence also comes from the knowledge-of-practice that the teacher constructed in the process of problem clarification, planning, action, and evaluation. In the action research process, the teacher not only reflected her own teaching practice and the performance of Xu, but also absorbed the knowledge of inclusive education, the characteristics of students with intellectual disabilities, and inclusive pedagogy from reading books and meeting with the partner from university.

Discussion

Mainstream educators in China have to contend with large class sizes, limited educational resources, and an exam-oriented education. Teachers must find ways to include children with disabilities in regular classrooms, despite these systemic constraints. Some of the previous literature has approached the issue of inclusion as problems in changing teacher attitudes. But what teachers need to know urgently is how to work for inclusion. The teacher here had the same confusion and expectations: "[LRC] needs more research, maybe no more suitable ways. But now I feel there are a lack of strategies and means." According to Vlachou and Barton (1994, p. 105), "calls for teachers to promote more inclusive educational priorities will be viewed as an additional burden, if, for example, they feel insecure, lack encouragement and are provided with little serious, sustained and adequately resourced staff development". Findings from the interviews with the teacher's colleagues also mentioned that teachers have reservations about including students with SEN in their classrooms since they feel that they are not well prepared.

In this collaborative action research for inclusive education, the research team helped the teacher to clarify problems, to design an action plan, to implement the program, and to evaluate the process. The educational researcher became a critical friend of the teacher. The teacher became an active learner and a knowledge constructor, consistent with what Cochran-Smith and Lytle (1999) describe as knowledge-of-practice.

There are three paradigms of teacher development: teacher development as knowledge and skill development; as self-understanding; and as ecological change. This involves more than changing a teacher's behavior. In this action research, the PL of the teacher was a process of seeking self-understanding, including reflecting upon her attitude and belief about education. In O'Hanlon's (2003) discussion about the interrelationship between action research and inclusion, she argues that for education practice to become inclusive it must first become reflective. In this action research project, keeping a reflective journal and reflective interviewing aided the role of critical self-reflection for personal transformation. The effects of self-reflection and the support from a critical friend, allowed the teacher to achieve greater PL as well as solve many of the problems with Xu in her classroom. At the same time, good teaching of students with disabilities who are included in general education classrooms is the same as good teaching for all students. The teacher also said that she learned how to analyze the characteristic of different students and how to facilitate children to reach their potential from the process of treating Xu.

In such a standardization education context as is found in China, there are many barriers to the implementation of inclusive education. If the government wants to implement inclusive education, it has to provide teachers not only with new knowledge and new competences, but also with adequate human resources and physical support to enable this. Utilizing a collaborative action research approach as used here seemed to have enormous benefits and should be seen as one possible way forward for improving the PL of teachers engaged in the LRC philosophy.

References

Arends, R. I. (2004) *Learning to Teach* (6th edn), Boston: McGraw-Hill.
Carrington, S. and Robinson, S. (2004) "A case study of inclusive school development: A journey of learning", *International Journal of Inclusive Education*, 8(2): 141–53.
Clough, P. and Barton, L. (1995) "Introduction: Self and the research act", in P. Clough and L. Barton (eds), *Making Difficulties: Research and the Construction of Special Education Needs*, London: Paul Chapman, pp. 1–15.
Cochran-Smith, M. and Lytle, S. (1999) "Relationships of knowledge and practice: Teacher learning in communities", in A. Iran-Nejar and P. D. Pearson (eds), *Review of Research in Education* (24), Washington, DC: AERA, pp. 249–305.
Darling-Hammond, L., French, J. and Garcia-Lopez, S. P. (2002) (eds) *Learning to Teach for Social Justice*, New York: Teachers' College Press.
Deng, M. and Guo, L. (2007) "Local special education administrators' understanding of inclusive education in China", *International Journal of Educational Development*, 27: 697–707.
Freire, S. and César, M. (2003) "Inclusive ideals/inclusive practice: How far is a dream from reality? Five comparative case studies", *European Journal of Special Needs Education*, 18(3): 341–54.
Guskey, T. R. (1986) "Staff development and the process of teacher change", *Educational Researcher*, 15(5): 5–12.

Ministry of Education of China (2007) "The major statistical indications and analysis of the national education development in 2007". Online. Available at: http://www.moe.edu.cn/edoas/website18/54/info1209972965475254.htm (accessed 27 April 2009).

National People's Congress (1982) *Constitution of People's Republic of China*, Beijing: The National People's Congress.

Noffke, S. E. and Zeichner, K. M. (1987) "Action research and teacher thinking: The first phase of action research on action research project at the University of Wisconsin–Madison", paper presented at the Annual Meeting of the American Educational Research Association, Washington, DC, April.

O'Hanlon, C. (2003) *Educational Inclusion as Action Research: An Interpretive Discourse*, Maidenhead: Open University Press.

Vlachou, A. and Barton, L. (1994) "Inclusive education: Teachers and the changing culture of schooling", *British Journal of Special Education*, 21(3): 105–7.

Yan, L. (2008) "An investigation of Beijing's preschool teachers' perception on inclusion", *Studies in Preschool Education*, 161(5): 17–21.

Chapter 24

A model professional learning program for enhancing the competency of students with special needs

Pennee Kantavong and
Suwaree Sivabhaedya

Learning outcomes

- Understand a model for teacher training for enhancing competency of students with autism, attention deficit/hyperactivity disorder (AD/HD) and learning difficulties (LD) in an inclusive classroom.
- Become aware of the application of parallel lesson plans.
- Acknowledge sociocultural issues regarding inclusion.

Introduction

In Thailand, growing numbers of students are being identified as having autism, AD/HD and LD. To meet the educational and social needs of these students, *The Constitution of the Kingdom of Thailand, B.E. 2540* (Public Relations Division, 1997) and the *National Education Act of B.E. 2542* (Office of the National Education Commission, 1999) set forth the legislative requirement for the State to provide special education to people with special education needs (SEN) by considering their equal rights and opportunities to receive basic education. These legislative Acts also acknowledged that the State is responsible for organizing appropriate education for these groups of students based on their abilities. Despite these legislative mandates, however, reports from the Ministry of Public Health suggest that there is still a lack of education support for these students, especially when it comes to educating them in inclusive classrooms.

A significant barrier in achieving these legislative goals has been the lack of education provided to teachers, administrators, parents and the general public related to understanding the educational and social strengths and challenges of these students and the different ways educators and parents can collaborate to help enhance their learning so they can succeed in inclusive classrooms.

The professional learning (PL) program model presented here was an attempt to help professionals and parents implement inclusion effectively. Since inclusion is a relatively new concept in Thailand, we do not have sufficient trained teachers in the fields of special education and the majority of teachers do not understand or have enough knowledge to work with students with special needs. Importantly, we do not have assistants in inclusive classrooms. In order to carry out effective implementation of inclusion we need a great deal of involvement from various parties, e.g. teachers in school, principals, parents, the community, outside institutions as well as policy-level organizations. Many countries that are like Thailand are experiencing similar challenges as they aim to develop inclusive education.

The program

The PL program, which was differentiated for teachers, administrators and parents, involved a range of activities. The teachers were trained on five consecutive weekdays. This was followed by three months of working on planning and teaching materials. Presenters were available to assist teachers via phone or email. At the end of the three months the presenters went to the teachers' classes and observed and reflected with them on the process. The parents and administrators participated in one full day of professional learning.

Some of this was provided for all teachers, administrators and parents together:

1 A whole-group session addressing the concept of inclusive education and intervention attended by teachers, administrators and parents.
2 Guest speakers presented to the whole group on interventions for people with autism, LD or AD/HD. Parents were provided with a handbook for helping their children at the end of the day.

While some was presented just to teachers:

1 Teachers were asked to choose a specific disability workshop related to students with autism, AD/HD or LD. Forty-seven teachers chose the LD workshop and viewed a video related to cases of students with learning disabilities. Nineteen teachers selected the autism workshop and learned about brain exercise activities and 41 teachers selected the AD/HD group and viewed a video and attended lectures about AD/HD.
2 The project provided six hours of learning activities on content, curriculum and IEP development for the LD and autism groups, while the AD/HD group learned about behavioral modification and communication techniques.
3 All groups participated in differentiated six-hour workshops on the development of parallel lesson plans: a learning and teaching strategy designed to guide teachers in accommodating a range of learners in inclusive classrooms. Sets of teaching materials were displayed and procedures for developing and implementing parallel lessons were modelled. Each group developed at least three sets of teaching materials and lesson plans; presented their lesson plans and teaching materials

to the rest of their group members; and received immediate feedback from the presenters and participants.

4 Teachers were provided with a three-hour presentation on how to communicate with parents and ways to develop social skills. After the presentation teachers attended a group of their interests for the in-service program. Because of their roles in implementing instructional approaches to actual classrooms and reflecting on these through action research, teachers were trained in every angle including curriculum analysis and development, instructional approach, how to select and develop innovations, lesson plan development and action research.

At the end of the five-day training, the teachers received handbooks and were asked to spend three months developing their own teaching materials and parallel lesson plans.

Program participants

One hundred and seven school teachers, 18 administrators and 68 parents from 16 schools (eight from Suphanburi province and eight from Khon Kaen province) were selected to participate. The teachers received five days of training and the school administrators and parents received one day.

Curriculum

The professional learning program, developed by a team of 14 researchers and consultants, was based on a needs assessment completed by the program participants and a review of the professional literature.

Participants selected a specific disability category and received parallel lesson plans related to effective interventions for that disability category. The conceptual framework for the content of the PL program for the different interest groups focused on the following intervention techniques.

Intervention techniques for students with autism (e.g. Arayawinyoo, 2003):

- Behavioral strategies
- Task analysis
- Prompting
- TEACCH (Treatment and Education of Autistic and Related Communication-handicapped Children)
- PECS (Picture Exchange Communication System)

Intervention techniques for students with AD/HD (e.g. Salend, et al., 2003):

- Classroom environment accommodations
- Behavioral strategies

- Games/play
- Task analysis
- Basic skill
- Speech and language
- Problem solving, organization and study skills
- Meta-cognition
- Creativity
- Providing immediate feedback.

Intervention techniques for students with LD (e.g. Arayawinyoo, 1999):

- Task analysis
- Highlighting
- Providing immediate feedback
- Peer-mediated techniques.

To help overcome this barrier, this chapter presents a PL program designed to enhance the competency of teachers, administrators and parents in supporting students with SEN.

Program evaluation

A classroom observation was conducted as a following-up evaluation after three months. Researchers visited schools twice to provide feedback and share reflective problems with teachers. Forty teachers volunteered to demonstrate how they implemented their parallel lesson plans and teaching materials in actual classroom settings. The best practices were also selected from the parallel lesson plans. Finally, a collaborative meeting between school administrators, parents and teachers was organized to discuss the PL program. The results of these program evaluation activities are presented below.

Knowledge and understanding development

Participating teachers reported that they felt they could practically use the knowledge gained from the training to enhance their work with students with a range of disabilities. They also noted that they learned techniques to help students with autism. Several teachers commented on the value of the directed learning experiences which provided them with the opportunity to practice and develop new instructional skills.

Both teachers and parents reported that they tried to implement TEACCH and PECS techniques to enhance students' social skills. Though time did not allow in-depth data collection related to the development of these skills, teachers and parents both agreed that their students gained more social skills.

Parents also indicated that their participation in the program enhanced their confidence in helping their children develop new skills. Some parents asked for further advice about government financial support since they had to spend a lot of money in taking care of their children. Some parents reported that they gained more hope when learning about methods of intervention from the project. The school administrators expressed satisfaction with the PL and encouraged their subordinates to participate in this project. Teachers and parents asked the researchers to continue to help them learn new pedagogical techniques.

Results from classroom observations showed that the PL program helped teachers reflect on the ways they could improve their instruction, which was beneficial for students. As for parents, their behavior changed after the training and they felt hopeful that there were people out there to give them guidance on how to assist their children. According to interviews conducted before the training, most of the parents showed an interest in the training because they wanted to help their children. After the training, many of the parents reported that they had implemented the knowledge gained. For example, with the assistance of the manual and the PL program, some parents played learning games with their children which helped their children develop necessary skills.

The outcomes support the work of Ainscow *et al.* (2006) who stated that the success of inclusion is based on schools holding certain characteristics or a culture of understanding and good relationships with students. To achieve these, it must begin with the school principal, then involve teachers and parents.

Lesson learned

In order to organize the PL program to increase the knowledge of teachers in arranging learning activities to help enhance competency of children with autism, AD/HD and LD, the researchers studied and analyzed theories and the needs of participants to find ways of helping them to enable their students to succeed in inclusive classrooms. As a result, teachers were all interested and fully participated in every activity all through the five-day training.

From teachers' reflections as well as researchers' observations, it was found that the teachers working in inclusive classrooms had well-prepared lesson plans with clear explanations. They also applied various strategies such as buddy techniques using games and feedback (Reid, 1999), which were taught during the PL program. As for the classrooms with students with LD, students, teachers and parents tried to use games and story-telling techniques. Teachers divided one lesson plan into many lesson plans but with smaller sequential steps. They also motivated students by using diagrams and pictures, giving positive feedback, as well as encouraging students to participate in asking and answering questions in their teaching. Highlighting was also used for reading-skill development.

The test scores of students with special needs in the experimental group increased, though there was no significant difference between the pre- and post-test scores. There were, however, distinctive results in the development of teaching and learning activities as evidenced by the following.

Active participation by teachers

Teachers were active in developing their lesson plans and reflected on their teaching and participated in meetings after the researchers' visits and observations. Teachers asked questions and informed the researchers that the researchers' feedback after observing them was helpful in offering them clarification of lesson planning and the application of teaching techniques. In addition, teachers gained more confidence and motivation in applying their knowledge to assist students with special needs, though this might mean that they had more work to do. They also found that their students without disabilities also enjoyed and benefited from the learning activities provided to accommodate students with special needs.

Increased parental support

Parents realized the importance of teaching. Because of their social and economical status, some parents could not help their children, even though they received a manual and learned some games from the PL program. The underlying reasons were that they did not have time to read, they were illiterate or not very proficient in reading. After the PL program, they gained a greater understanding and more positive feelings towards their children. Before the training, they reported feeling very stressed when their children did not perform well at school or behaved badly and differently from other students. The knowledge gained from the training encouraged them to be more patient and sensible. For example, a mother of a child with LD noted that games helped them talk to each other more than before and that learning games could draw attention from her child, so she could teach him how to read and write. This mother, however, felt that she wanted to learn more since she only gained guidelines from the PL program, but when she had problems, she could not do much due to lack of knowledge. This reflected that even though parents gained a small amount of knowledge, suggestions and intervention techniques, they were willing and tried to help their children as much as they could. Most importantly, nearly all of the parents who participated in the PL program felt that it made them realize that they were not alone, or abandoned by society.

Improved social awareness

Creating social awareness, giving knowledge and encouraging understanding between teachers and parents are all important aspects for the PL. The "Loving and Care" notebook was created and introduced for teachers to use as a mean for communication. Lim and Quah (2004) pointed out that students with LD are often given fewer opportunities to develop important thinking and study skills. Teachers and parents who participated in the PLP gained knowledge and understanding about students with special needs. It did not matter whether the parents were employed or unemployed or if they were of a highly respected occupation or not. Not only teachers and parents, but also school administrators received the training. School administrators were one of the key factors in the accomplishment of inclusive classrooms since they could give support and guide the way to sustainable development of inclusive classrooms.

Teachers reflected that Thai teachers extended kindness to students with special needs. But they did not know how to handle the problems and organize the lessons and activities for students with special needs. Participation in this project was useful for them as it helped them understand aspects of working with students with special needs.

At the same time, other teachers at their schools should be aware and understand the importance of giving help to these groups of students. They should also have knowledge and understanding in order that the development and arrangement of inclusive classrooms occur within a smooth and supportive atmosphere. In this research, almost one-third of the teachers from almost all of the experimental schools were trained. In some schools, every teacher participated in the project. This assured us that we were on the right track to begin the process in helping students with special needs in schools.

Recommendations

Some recommendations for the future at a school, institutional and policy level are as follows:

School-level support

1 Develop teachers' knowledge of inclusive classrooms so that every teacher understands characteristics of students with special needs and to make it easier to help children in these groups.
2 Promote the application of various teaching and learning activities so that teachers realize the difference between and understand the strengths and challenges of all of their students. This will lead to the arrangement of teaching and learning activities that are appropriate for various groups of students.

3 Realize the importance of inclusive classrooms despite the fact that it is a rather complex issue and difficult to manage. The accomplishment of inclusive classrooms depends largely on this factor since support from outsiders can help teachers to learn about and access the different types of support necessary for each type of student.

4 School administrators should seriously participate in the developmental process of inclusive education because they are the direct supervisors of teachers at school, so they should have knowledge and understanding and be able to help the teachers. Their leadership in the arrangement of inclusive education can encourage teachers at school to seriously participate in the development of inclusive education.

5 Include plans to develop teaching and learning to help students of special needs in the year plan of the school.

Outside institutions/institutions of higher education support

1 The development of inclusive education will be successful and yield satisfactory outcomes if there is an implementation of collaborative action research or "evidence-stimulated reflection" as referred to by Ainscow et al. (2006). The collaborative action research provides opportunities for every party involved in the research to evaluate, reflect, analyze and understand each other's problems. This will lead to collaborative thinking in order to find practical solutions and mutual drive that will result in a concrete process in helping students with special needs.

2 The collaborative action research will be very useful when experts and researchers from various fields are involved in the project in order to be partners in sharing and learning from one another. This means that everyone will have the opportunity to have access to the information from the perspectives of researchers as well as teachers who act as practitioners.

3 Teacher's colleges and institutions should offer compulsory courses in inclusive education or special education. According to Ainscow et al. (2006) teachers' understanding of inclusive education affects the success of intervention towards these groups of students. Teachers' opinions about students with special needs are usually influenced by their viewpoint and attitude based on their own culture and values.

4 Encourage exchange of viewpoints and understanding beyond the scope of those working at schools. Copland (2003) suggests that systematic research that involves every party will result in leadership in creating changes. It will also facilitate the participation of communities into the process of development. This will establish the school culture and lead to a sustainable process of intervention.

5 Provide knowledge to teachers and parents by offering PL. It should be provided continuously and include as many schools as possible.

Policy-level support

1 The government should foster the policy of an equal right to a better quality of inclusive education for all students. Toward this end, the government should establish a working unit to be responsible for identifying and supporting students with special needs in general schools.
2 Promote the development of a parent's manual for helping their children. Publicize this widely since there are many parents who do not have time to participate in training, but they should be given an opportunity to understand how to assist their children. The manuals can at least help them gain a basic understanding and intervention for their children.
3 Promote the organization of schools' networking to develop inclusive education. Teachers with appropriate qualifications should be selected as pilot teachers in the network in order to give advice to neighboring schools and receive suggestions from others. Nevertheless, the idea of school networks must be established systematically with research-based organization using the approach provided in this research in order to have outstanding teachers who can actually be leaders for the network. This method will lead to a sustainable development of the intervention even after the completion of the research project.
4 Publicize documents relating to policies on education for people with special needs. Conferences and PL programs should be held continuously and nationwide to raise public awareness of and help foster positive attitudes towards people with special needs.
5 Establish and develop a database that provides information on sources of intervention for people with special needs, including diagnosis and screening tests, knowledge and training organizations as well as schools that can be a model for exchanging ideas on how to organize inclusive education.

Conclusion

The five-day PL program for enhancing the capacity of students with special needs such as autism, AD/HD and LD in inclusive classrooms, considered the appropriate approach to help teachers be successful where there were no teaching assistants and proper teaching materials. Intervention techniques, teaching materials and parallel lesson plans were introduced. Teachers gained hands-on experiences which led to their increased confidence in developing their own work. The classroom observations conducted by the research team created good collaboration between teachers and researchers. As for those teachers who did not demonstrate their teaching for feedback and evaluation, they at least gained some knowledge and understanding related to helping students with special needs in inclusive classrooms.

The one-day training session for school administrators and parents not only provided them with knowledge and understanding but also raised the awareness of the importance of good school leadership and the value of participation from parents. The notebook for parents worked as a means of communication between teachers and parents.

References

Ainscow, M., Booth, T. and Dyson, A. (2006) *Improving Schools, Developing Inclusion*, London: Routledge.

Arayawinyoo, P. (1999) *Learning Disabilities*, 2nd edn, Bangkok: Wan Kaew Pub (in Thai).

Arayawinyoo, P. (2003) *Methods of Teaching Autism Students*, Bangkok: Rum Thai Press (in Thai).

Copland, M. A. (2003) "Developing principles problem-framing skill", *Journal of School Leadership*, 13(5): 529–48.

Lim, L. and Quah, M. M. (2004) *Educating Learners with Diverse Abilities*, Singapore: McGraw-Hill.

Office of the National Education Commission (1999) *The National Education Act of B.E. 2542*, Bangkok: Prigwan Graphic Publication.

Public Relations Division (1997) *The Constitution of the Kingdom of Thailand, B.E. 2540*, Bangkok: Secretariat Office of the Parliament.

Reid, R. (1999) "Attention deficit hyperactivity disorder: Effective methods for the classroom", *Focus on Exceptional Children*, 32(4): 1–20.

Salend, S. J., Elhoweris, H. and Van Garderen, D. (2003). "Educational interventions for students with ADHD", *Intervention in School and Clinic*, 38(5): 280–8.

Chapter 25

Upskilling all mainstream teachers

What is viable?

Kuen-fung Sin, Kok-wai Tsang,
Chung-yee Poon and Chi-leung Lai

Learning outcomes

- Understand the wide range of challenges in upskilling mainstream teachers for inclusion.
- Identify the viable components specific for organizing courses of inclusion for mainstream teachers.
- Acquire a repertoire of feasible strategies to address areas of concern for teachers regarding inclusion.

The three-tier intervention model in student support

The adequacy of support for students with special education needs (SEN) in ordinary schools is debatable as it is always considered as a kind of struggle for resources and manpower. In Hong Kong, a three-tier intervention model with increasing levels of support is used to define the appropriateness in meeting the diverse needs of students with SEN. It is suggested that in Tier 1 support, quality teaching, in terms of appropriate differentiated teaching, is recommended to support students with mild learning difficulties in class. In Tier 2 support, the arrangement of "add-on" intervention will be appropriate to meet the needs of students with persistent learning difficulties. In Tier 3 support, more intensive support, special accommodations or specialist support are expected for cases of children with more persistent learning difficulties (Education Bureau, 2007).

In line with this intervention model, a five-year teacher professional development framework in integration was launched by the Education Bureau in 2007. It is expected that about 10 per cent of teachers in each school would complete the Basic Course on Catering for Diverse Learning Needs (30 hours). Participants learn theories and strategies in curriculum, teaching strategies and assessment accommodations so as to provide Tier 1 and, to some extent, Tier 2 support. For leadership training in SEN, at least three teachers in a school must attend the Advanced Course (90 hours) which includes study about students with special needs, school-based attachment experience and a school-based project. The participants are prepared to plan and arrange the Tier 2 support in schools. In addition, Thematic Courses on children with specific types of need (60 hours), e.g. Autism Spectrum Disorders (ASD) or Attention Deficit/Hyperactivity Disorders (AD/HD), are provided covering in-depth training in these areas. After these courses, participants are able to manage students with more severe learning difficulties at Tier 3 support level in schools.

In 2007–10, these programs were commissioned to the Hong Kong Institute of Education. The annual intake of teachers reached 2000 in 2007 and 2008. Because of their diverse professional needs, the operation is always challenging and demanding and raises many questions. For example, how do these courses prepare teachers competently for providing support in the three-tier intervention model? In what ways will the course design and activities help to achieve the expected goals? The following core areas have been identified as the key outcomes from the courses as they have the practical value for upskilling the mainstreaming teachers.

1 Learning the concepts of inclusion.
2 Examining knowledge about supporting students with special needs.
3 Mastering the instructional techniques for diversity.
4 Sharing successful experiences.
5 Reflecting on their beliefs in teaching.
6 Participating in professional dialogue.
7 Using community resources.
8 Disseminating research outcomes.
9 Advocating a whole-school approach (WSA).

Learning the concepts of inclusion

Inclusion involves quality education for students with SEN who can benefit from education in ordinary schools. SEN is generally considered as a continuum of diversity which can be appropriately catered for with differentiated teaching and support in learning (Education Bureau, 2007; Ainscow, 1999; Forlin and Lian, 2008). It is evident that the concepts of inclusion have not been firmly rooted in many Hong Kong schools (Tsui et al., 2007). Although teachers follow closely the guidelines or indicators for inclusion (Booth and Ainscow, 2000; EMB, 2004) in reviewing and formulating school-based inclusive policy and practice, they plead ignorance about inclusion. For example, the majority of teachers have little knowledge of the Code of Practice on Education that was derived from the Disability Discrimination Ordinance (Equal Opportunities Commission, 2001). According to the Code of Practice, it is assumed that all schools should exert effort in developing the procedures to prevent and eliminate disability discrimination. However, cases of neglect, refusal and discrimination against students with disability are reported in schools by the media or reports from time to time (CSNSIE, 2003; Tsui *et al.* 2007; Office of the Ombudsman Hong Kong, 2009). The respect for the rights and dignity of students with a disability is also less emphasized in schools. In 2008, the government of Hong Kong responded to the United Nations Convention on the Rights of Persons with Disabilities (Labour and Welfare Bureau, 2009). At the initial stage, few actions were taken in schools to eliminate discrimination. There is still room for awareness enhancement, with particular reference to the details of the Convention below.

• Respect for inherent dignity, individual autonomy including the freedom to make one's own choices and independence of persons.
• Non-discrimination.
• Full and effective participation and inclusion in society.
• Respect for difference and acceptance of persons with disabilities as part of human diversity and humanity.
• Equality of opportunity.
• Accessibility.
• Equality between men and women.
• Respect for the evolving capacities of children with disabilities and respect for the right of children with disabilities to preserve their identities.

(Labour and Welfare Bureau, 2009, p.7)

In the courses provided in Hong Kong on studying inclusion, the rationale and core values are appropriately elaborated in the local context. With in-depth study on the theories and practices in inclusive education, participants are expected to understand inclusion critically from different perspectives, such as the comparison of psycho-medical legacy, sociological response, curricular approaches, school improvement strategies and disability studies critique (Clough and Corbett, 2000). Participants, however, usually prefer contextual exemplars to theoretical concepts in the study. Cases of direct and indirect disability discrimination, disability harassment and disability vilification, for example, are therefore used as workable exemplars to inspire teachers' reflective thinking. Consequently, the learning of the underlying theoretical constructs in inclusion is crucial but the use of appropriate strategies, such as problem-based learning or case analysis, are vital in achieving the outcome.

Examining the knowledge in special needs

Students with SEN exhibit a wide range of special characteristics, deficiencies, impairments and behavioral patterns that can lead to social, psychological or learning difficulties. The implications of their disabilities for education and rehabilitation are complicated (Rehabilitation Advisory Committee, 2007). The inter- and intra-individual differences vary case by case. Rather than examining the deficits or inadequacy, the strengths for development become the major concern in learning and teaching (Mittler, 2000). Teachers are expected to demonstrate competency in identification, needs analysis, removal of learning barriers and differentiated teaching strategies when addressing students' individual needs. Many teachers overlook this notion but focus more on individual incompetency. Therefore, in the special needs courses, teachers not only learn the terminology, definitions or diagnostic criteria of disabilities, but also acquire skills in analyzing the impact of the disabilities and the derived psychological, social and learning needs. This body of knowledge and skills can then be transferred to the examination of the needs of other diverse students, such as those with cultural differences, gifted students, and those of low socio-economic status or of ethnic minority.

Mastering the instructional techniques for diversity

Competence in catering for diversity is an essential component in teacher education. The aims of study should foster the positive attitude of teachers to all students with mixed ability as well as empower them with the skills to address the wide range of needs these students exhibit. For students at different tier support levels, many instructional techniques, supported by literature and research, are possibly recommended for classroom practice. For example, the visual cues for students with ASD, behavioral modification for students with AD/HD, literacy programs for students with dyslexia, differentiated teaching for low achievers and enrichment activities for ethnic minority students are popularly found in schools in Hong Kong (Sin, 2004). Teachers are also familiarized with the use of response to intervention models in addressing the students with SEN at the Tier 3 level. Some teachers experience success in using the training resources, derived from the theory of mind, to enhance the social cognition of students with ASD. In relation to those innovative strategies, teachers should make professional decisions in the selection process. Training, practice and evaluation are necessary but the process takes time and effort. It is difficult for the participants to master all the instructional techniques effectively for diversity in the short but intensive courses provided. Class observation, sharing sessions and try-outs are also essential for improved pedagogical practice. Sometimes, by experiencing the disabilities, teachers may know more about the difficulties that the students with SEN encounter. Their first-hand experience in simulation games or social contact with students with SEN refines their planning and teaching. The participants, therefore, cherish opportunities such as school attachment, for learning and practicing the instructional techniques for diversity.

Sharing the successful experience

Since the introduction of the WSA in addressing diversity in 2003, a lot of changes at different levels have been observed in Hong Kong schools. Many schools firstly formulated policy and practice at the school level, which was followed by the setting up of a learning support team at the organization level (Tsui et al., 2007). At the very beginning, schools focused on teacher empowerment so that teachers worked competently in writing individual education programs (IEP) and doing case work. With support from the Education Bureau and special schools acting as resource schools (Forlin and Rose, in press), some schools successfully launched projects in curriculum differentiation and behavior management. In response to school bullying, peer support programs, mentor schemes or "disability awareness programs" were identified in some schools. The introduction of co-teaching was widely launched in some cluster schools (Hui et al., 2004). Some schools also recognized the significance of home–school partnerships in learning and teaching. Parents were encouraged to take part in many school activities. More importantly, teachers attempted to use innovative strategies in their teaching. Structured teaching, visual cues, paired reading, multisensory approaches or social skills training were adopted in regular classrooms (Hui et al., 2004). It is encouraging that a lot of successful experiences have been disseminated in seminars, workshops and publications in local context (Hui and Sin, 2003). The impact of the sharing culture and partnership model is far reaching, in terms of professional growth and school development. In the course activities, on the one hand, exemplars of good practice are identified for guest talks or seminars. On the other hand, participants are encouraged to share their success or front-line experience with others through different channels, e.g. e-learning, group presentations or by case analysis.

Reflecting on the belief in teaching

Inclusion is always considered as the realization of "education for all" and the way to achieve excellence in teaching and quality education. The long-term goal is to eliminate discrimination so as to build up a harmonious community with acceptance and support. The difficulties identified in the process of implementation generally discourage teachers in Hong Kong from achieving this goal. Inadequate support, poor leadership, ineffective management, large class sizes and a wide range of special needs are all sources of frustration (CSNSIE, 2003; Forlin and Lian, 2008). Teachers have strong resistance to curriculum or instructional differentiation, in view of the enormous effort and huge amount of time for preparation. They do, though, recognize the potential value in addressing individual needs, if the intervention plan is tailor made. This "cognitive conflict" leads to their upsets and disappointment. Indeed, attitude change is the most challenging task to be dealt with in the course. It is evident that the knowledge and skills they acquire changes their misconceptions about inclusion. For example, after the in-depth study in literature and research reports, teachers are able to examine critically the issues in classroom practices and school work. In case analysis, they explore the alternative strategies in addressing the needs of the individual child. Their reflection in group presentation is always affirmative and promising. Their belief of inclusion is always made known in the reflective part of their written assignment. Therefore, for successful special needs courses, the inclusion of the objective for fostering positive attitude and change is distinctive and necessary.

Participating in professional dialogue

Professional support is particularly important at the Tier 3 support level. Partnership and dialogue are increasingly noted within the support system. Apart from the case conferences and meetings, teachers are expected to take part actively in seminars, workshops, forums or symposiums for professional or academic exchange. More importantly, these activities help them build up professional links and establish future partnerships. In the past, the specific terms, autistic spectrum disorder, dyslexia and developmental coordination disorder, were not widely known to the public. Teachers found it difficult to interpret the implications of educational assessment and followed closely the recommendations suggested by the educational psychologist or other professional. Frequent dialogue exchange during the course of study, however, clarifies these misconceptions or misunderstandings. Teachers are able to comprehend correctly the assessment results and to formulate appropriate intervention plans. In some cases, for example, with the advice from the audiologist, the teacher can find out how to use the FM receiver in class teaching or assist students with hearing impairment to use their hearing aids properly. After consultations with occupational therapists, the teachers are able to set up a barrier-free school campus or use the auxiliary aids for students with physical disabilities or with visual impairment. The resultant outcome of effective communication and partnership signifies the essence of a trans-disciplinary approach in addressing diversity (Ainscow, 1999; Hui *et al.*, 2004).

Using community resources

In most Hong Kong special schools, a team comprising a nurse, a speech therapist, an occupational therapist and a physiotherapist work collaboratively. The special schools also seek help or advice from professionals, e.g. a clinical psychologist or psychiatric doctor, or from the community. Mainstream schools, though, lack the appropriate expertise and resources in addressing their students at the Tier 3 support level that is more intensive and professional in nature. Unlike special schools, mainstream schools are not entitled to or adequately provided with all types of professional or therapeutic support. Following the introduction of a new funding mode, mainstream schools are now able to hire quality services from NGOs or professionals for supporting their students. For example, because of the availability of grants for speech training, many speech therapists started their own business offering school-based training to students with SEN in primary schools. Teachers also gain skills in the staff development workshop and benefit from advice in case conferences. Some products such as screening tools for identification and teaching kits for remediation purposes are widely used for the support of students with SEN at different levels. Furthermore, the training or support programs of some parent centers for children with ASD, the deaf and the blind are welcomed by parents and teachers. Teachers become familiar with the usefulness of the assistive technology through their visits to the rehabilitation organizations. Finally, teachers also find useful resources and tailor-made teaching materials in the special education resource centre of the Education Bureau (2009). Participants in the courses note the significance of utilizing the community resources. Therefore, in the course delivery, it is necessary to develop a collaboration partnership with local NGOs and inform teachers of the possible advice, resource, aids, services and therapies available in the community.

Disseminating the research outcome

Learning comes with action. Being practitioners, teachers are expected to reflect, evaluate and disseminate their work (Hui and Sin, 2003). In the process of professional development, it is essential to encourage teachers to identify topics of interest and areas of examination, on the supposition that before the enrollment, they have difficulties, queries or failures in addressing classroom diversity. In the need's analysis during the course, this assumption is always valid. The participants expressed their intentions for seeking feasible solutions to their queries. In order to address their concerns, the outcome dissemination in the form of a school-based project is one of the course objectives to be achieved. Participants are expected to develop strategies in integrating their learning with their classroom teaching and school support work. The outcome is disseminated in the form of an oral presentation and poster display in the program seminar. Some participants, however, in the cohorts may resist carrying out the try-out and may even challenge the feasibility and practical use of the school-based project. Their inert motives finally change after they have gained support, in terms of guidelines, consultations, resources and sharing. They are encouraged to address the issue, search for literature, identify areas of interest and plan an implementation. The outcome of their practical work is always fruitful and of practical use. For example, the implications of including students with

AD/HD on teaching and learning in the primary school setting are different from those in secondary schools. Teachers report their innovative plans for social skill training and learning support. Students with ASD always have unique characteristics and different behaviors. Home–school partnerships and strategies in addressing their needs by a WSA are well elaborated in some of the participants' projects. For example dyslexia in Chinese and English language always leads to the misconceptions of students' effort in reading and writing. After the introduction of the learning programs in phonological and morphological awareness, teachers are able to recognize the achievements of these students. Indeed, it is necessary to empower teachers with the knowledge and skills in integrating their knowledge with practice. More importantly, teachers have to plan, act and evaluate the effectiveness of their interventions. Their plans may be inadequate or flawed, but the process of action learning is significantly noted, particularly regarding the evaluation for future improvement. The school-based project, therefore, though not always welcomed by some participants, is a unique feature in the Advanced Training Course.

Advocating the whole-school approach

The current policy in Hong Kong schools is a WSA to inclusive practice. It aims at providing the full range support and care to all students with SEN in schools (EMB, 2004; Forlin and Lian, 2008). The significance of effective management and leadership has been duly recognized in many local reports (e.g. Tsui *et al.*, 2007). In connection to the course objectives, the participants, after the study, are expected to be the agents or catalysts in furthering inclusive practice within their schools. With the knowledge, skills and insights learnt in the course, they are capable of demonstrating competency in establishing inclusive practice. Participants, particularly those from primary schools, seem most familiar with the practice of the WSA in catering for diverse learning needs. It is evident that the organizational structure has been further improved in primary schools. For example, the learning support team with leadership of the head or deputy head is found to be effective in the implementation. As a school policy, identification starts early in primary one and the appropriate remedial follow-up is possible at the initial stage. With the provision of additional funding for support, teachers work as a team with the professionals. Staff, parents and students are well informed and mobilized in the process. Teachers seem to find fewer barriers to achieve the goal of a WSA.

In comparison, participants from secondary schools encounter more challenges, with a diversified resultant outcome regarding developing a WSA. There is a three-band system in secondary schools with Band 1 accepting the most academically able and Band 3 the least. Thus Band 1 schools have a small number of students with SEN who tend to have few difficulties because of support and peer acceptance. Some are reported to be of average or above average ability which leads to smooth learning adjustment. The challenges are extremely demanding in Band 3 schools, where more students with SEN are identified. Great changes at organizational, curriculum and individual levels are observed (Sin, 2001). The establishment of a connected system, the development of a whole-school curriculum and the support for students to develop to their full potential at all levels, are key components of the course of study.

Conclusion

It is an extremely tough and challenging task to organize the professional learning for teachers on inclusion in Hong Kong. Attitude change and actions taken in schools are expected to be observed after the successful completion of the courses. Unlike the pre-service teacher education courses, the levels of demand for tailor-made contents, useful front-line experiences, updated knowledge, feasible instructional strategies, practical skills in classroom practice and accessible community resources are indeed great in the content delivery. The areas of concern and tactics mentioned previously are some of the viable strategies for upskilling mainstream teachers for inclusion. Research on the effectiveness in these areas will be the future focus to further examine the critical issues.

References

Ainscow, M. (1999) *Understanding the Development of Inclusive Schools,* London: Falmer Press.

Booth, T. and Ainscow, M. (2000) *Index for Inclusion: Developing Learning and Participation in schools,* UK: Centre for Studies on Inclusive Education.

CSNSIE, Centre for Special Needs and Studies in Inclusive Education (2003) *Case Studies of Four Integrated Schools in Hong Kong,* Hong Kong: Hong Kong Institute of Education.

Clough, P. and Corbett, J. (2000) *Theories of Inclusive Education: A Students' Guide,* London: Paul Chapman Publishing.

Education Bureau (2007) *Teacher Professional Development Framework on Integrated Education* (Circular No. 13/2007), Hong Kong: Hong Kong Government.

Education Bureau (2009) *Special Education Resource Center.* Online. Available at: http://www.edb.gov.hk/serc (accessed 31 July 2009).

EMB, Education and Manpower Bureau (2004) *Catering for Student Difference: Indicators for Inclusion, A Tool for School Self-evaluation and School Development,* Hong Kong: Hong Kong SAR.

Equal Opportunities Commission (2001) *Disability Discrimination Ordinance: Code of Practice on Education,* Hong Kong: Equal Opportunities Commission.

Forlin, C. and Lian, M. G. J. (eds) (2008) *Reform, Inclusion and Teacher Education: Towards a New Era of Special Education in the Asia-Pacific Region,* London and New York: Routledge.

Forlin, C. and Rose, R. (in press) "Authentic school partnerships for enabling inclusive education in Hong Kong", *Journal of Research in Special Education Needs*.

Hui, L. H. and Sin, K. F. (2003). *Collection of action research on special needs education*. Hong Kong: The Hong Kong Institute of Education.

Hui, L. H., Sin, K. F., Ho, F. C. and Chan, H. K. (2004) "Partnership in staff development: A school-institute project in Shanghai and Hong Kong", in C. K. Lee, N. K. Lo and A. Walker (eds), *Partnership and Change: Toward School Development*, Educational Studies Series, Hong Kong: Chinese University Press and Hong Kong Institute of Educational Research, pp. 239–54.

Labour and Welfare Bureau (2009) *Convention on the Rights of Persons with Disabilities: Applicable to Hong Kong,* Hong Kong: LWB.

Mittler, P. (2000) *Working Towards Inclusive Education: Social Contexts*, London: David Fulton Publishers.

Office of the Ombudsman Hong Kong (2009) *Direct Investigation on Support Services for Students with Specific Learning Difficulties*, Issue No. 3 of Reporting Year 208/09 (26 March 2009), Hong Kong: OTOHK.

Rehabilitation Advisory Committee (2007) *Hong Kong Rehabilitation Programme Plan (2005-2007)*. Hong Kong: Health, Welfare and Food Bureau.

Sin, K. F. (2001) "Developing remedial support in Hong Kong secondary schools", in Y. C. Cheng, M. C. Mok and K. T. Tsui, *Teaching Effectiveness and Teacher Development: Towards a New Knowledge Base,* Hong Kong: Hong Kong Institute of Education & Kluwer Academic Publishers, pp. 275–96.

Sin, K. F. (2004) "Teacher education on catering for diverse learning needs", *Hong Kong Special Education Forum*, 7(1), 102–9.

Tsui, K. T., Sin, K. F, and Yu, H. (2007) *Research Report of the Inclusive Education Implementation in Hong Kong Primary Schools,* Hong Kong: HKSES and HKPERA.

Chapter 26

Future directions for teacher education for inclusion

Chris Forlin

Learning outcomes

- Understand the importance of positive attitudes in teachers towards inclusive education.
- Consider a values-based approach to teacher education.
- Appreciate the critical role of teacher educators in supporting inclusion.
- Reflect upon future directions to enhance the preparation of inclusive teachers.

Introduction

This final chapter will review the importance of a teacher's attitude in enabling inclusion and how good teacher education can help support the development of this. Consideration will be given to the adoption of a values-based approach underpinning the curriculum for teacher education for inclusion. The role of the teacher educator will be explored from the perspective of their own perceptions of inclusion and dispositions towards people with special needs. Future directions for teacher education for inclusion will be discussed.

Inclusive practitioners

When considering how to train teachers to become good inclusive practitioners, a lot can be learned from the reading of Confucian philosophy. According to Confucius, in order to become a truly excellent teacher a person will need a relaxed, assured spirit and a respectful attitude (Yu, 2009). Confucius's *Jungzi* or ideal person embodies both of these attributes, in particular exhibiting high morality and showing mutual respect for human dignity and tolerance towards others. To become a good inclusive teacher requires similar traits. How then can teacher educators facilitate the development of these qualities in their teachers? Confucius provides in the Analects a range of simple truths to allow people to make the right choices believing that "the first step on this journey is having the right attitude" (Yu, 2006, 2009, p. 32).

If possessing a positive attitude is so important in becoming an excellent teacher, then surely this should underpin all work that teacher educators do to prepare teachers for inclusion. The reader of this book will have found, but may not have realized previously, that this simple truth has been embedded in all of the programs that have been discussed here. Within each of the approaches there have been either overt or covert opportunities for reflection on personal beliefs and values regarding diversity. This has been a particularly predominant focus in the approaches recommended for initial teacher education (ITE), which have highlighted many learning opportunities that allow new teachers to develop suitable attitudes, knowledge and skills to become inclusive practitioners. Developing empathy towards those with diverse needs by providing pertinent opportunities to engage with them encourages the progress of a positive belief system and affirmative attitudes towards inclusion. A focus on authentic occasions to connect with diverse communities in a pluralistic society has been a key feature of the pre-service models in this book. In addition, great emphasis has been placed on the use of collaborative approaches such as cross-discipline preparation, partnering of universities and schools, and collaborative decision making.

Hollins and Guzman (2005) talk about the need for what they term prejudice reduction in teachers in training. A proactive approach is suggested as a means of helping new teachers reflect upon their prior experiences and develop openness to the diversity of students they are likely to encounter. Similarly, D'Cruz (2007) proposes diversity training as a means of addressing complex differences between social groups in contemporary societies. Clearly, to overcome prejudices enacted due to a lack of understanding or a lack of experience a non-threatening approach must be employed. This will provide teachers with an opportunity to engage with and learn from others who may come from different cultural, ethnic, racial and religious backgrounds or with different abilities and needs. The innovative ideas shared in this book rely on supporting teachers to develop greater empathy and understanding through situations which are designed to reflect authentic opportunities without making contacts overly confronting and certainly not negative.

A values-based approach

Inclusive education requires teachers to accommodate the needs of a wide range of students within diverse classrooms. It expects that teachers will be prepared to cater for all children in their classes regardless of the learners' ability, ethnicity, cultural, linguistic or social differences. It assumes that they will hold inclusive attitudes and values and be prepared to adopt inclusive practices. To do this a multiplicity and complexity of competencies are required by teachers (Pearce and Forlin, 2005). Good inclusive teaching, though, goes beyond demonstrating achievement of a given set of competences or standards as invariably outlined by governments, as it requires the values dimension to be made explicit and to permeate all aspects of teacher preparation (Moran, 2009). To move towards an inclusive approach similarly requires a school to proactively plan for diversity and to see difference as a means of acknowledging and responding to this. Staff development is, inevitably, an essential component of this move and should similarly focus on a values-based approach by including awareness training, knowledge and skill development. There are many constraints placed on teachers such as a lack of time to engage in professional learning (PL); inflexible curricula; being required to be involved in too many systemic initiatives at once; as well as the difficulties they encounter in coping with students from diverse backgrounds and with diverse learning needs (Forlin, 2006). Suitable PL, consequently, needs to consider all of these and provide occasions that allow teachers to reflect upon their role as supporters of inclusion and consider alternatives that will allow them to achieve this.

A strong advocate for school-based approaches for preparing teachers for inclusive practice, Ainscow (2003) argues that PL needs to be context specific and directly related to teachers' work. To develop an effective inclusive school culture Ainscow posits that it must be led by school leaders who have a strong vision for moving practice forward; who are prepared to engage collaboratively with colleagues; who value individual input; are sensitive to colleagues' professional views and personal feelings; and who "... model not only a willingness to participate in discussions and debates, but also a readiness to answer questions and challenges from staff members ... [and] enable staff to feel sufficiently confident about their practice to cope with challenges they meet" (2003, p. 30). Thus, professional learning (PL) needs to be targeted, appropriate, practical and above all else flexible, so that teachers can feel confident in being able to access training at a time and place that best meets their needs. This book has addressed the challenge of organizing suitable PL for teachers by recounting models that utilize both modular and online learning approaches, develop productive collaborative school–university partnerships and engage teachers in decisions about their own learning.

Teacher educators

The examples provided in this book are all underpinned by the expectation that teacher educators essentially want to prepare teachers for inclusion and that their own attitudes are also positive and supportive. Is this always the case? A typical career path into teacher education might be via grounding in school teaching, followed by school or district-based administration roles, further PL through university study, and finally employment as a teacher of teachers. A lack of formal induction into this role makes this transition difficult for many novice teacher educators. Teaching practicing and pre-service teachers is a completely different skill to teaching in schools and requires a "deep understanding of teaching and of oneself as teacher educator" (Swennen and van der Klink, 2008, p. 221).

For many teacher educators they themselves may have not experienced inclusive classrooms. Many will have attended traditional schools that catered for homogenous groups of students who were monolingual and monoethnic in their culture. Teacher educators also tend to be drawn from academically high achieving or grammar schools where contact with peers with learning difficulties may have been minimal (Lambe, 2006). In addition, for some educators their own schooling may have occurred many years ago and they may be out of touch with the reality of standing in front of a class of students who represent a different cohort from their own practice. How can they then provide suitable learning experiences as educators of teachers for inclusive classrooms which embody multiculturalism and diverse contexts, catering for students with a wide range of diverse needs likely to impact on achieving good educational outcomes?

According to Cushner (2006), teacher educators should first consider how they position themselves regarding diversity before engaging with others. Faculty staff who have not been significantly engaged in classrooms for more than ten years may believe that they are poorly placed to prepare teachers for the changed dynamics of teaching involved in an inclusive philosophy in the new century. In some instances inherited conservative assumptions and lack of personal participation in transformative learning experiences may be at odds with an inclusive way of thinking. By personal reflection teacher educators can better understand how their own experiences have influenced the development of their identities and how this may shape their attitudes towards and subsequent interactions with people from diverse backgrounds and influence their expectations from others.

Traditionalism versus inclusion

A central tenet of Palmer's work in 1998 about what he refers to as *The Courage to Teach,* was that "good teaching cannot be reduced to technique" (p. 179). Palmer suggests that teachers who apply new pedagogy to their teaching are frequently challenged by the traditionalism of their students, parents and colleagues. By transposing his ideas into the inclusive school movement, an insight into a fundamental difficulty for teacher educators proffering the idea of inclusion with teachers can be obtained. While teachers may be comfortable with a conventional examination-oriented curricula that provides the outcomes desired by parents and administrators, especially in an increasingly competitive world, such pedagogical approaches do not allow for the engagement of students who are working at a slower pace or at a different level to their peers.

Epistemological dissonance

An inclusive approach may be quite contradictory to the ingrained philosophy of many teachers and stimulate a sense of fear that they may be unwittingly challenged by their employers and their students' parents. Teacher educators, therefore, need somehow to transcend this barrier if they are to change the attitudes of teachers to accept and value the integrity of an inclusive teaching philosophy. This is not a simple task as while promoting positive dispositions towards inclusion and a willingness to provide suitable accommodations to enable all children to be included, educational systems often remain unchanged, expecting teachers to achieve the same levels of academic outcomes for students regardless of the students' different abilities and needs.

Transposing a new paradigm onto a long-standing traditional educational system that is reluctant to change its basic structure, disinclined to allow alternative pedagogies to be employed, and unwilling to accept that all students while being included in the same class cannot be expected to achieve the same level of learning outcomes, leads to epistemological dissonance posing an impossible undertaking. As suggested by McIntyre (2009), the concept of inclusive pedagogy is "disruptive to the status quo in many schools and will no doubt be an uncomfortable idea for many school staff" (p. 607). To enable teacher education to achieve better success in the application of the ideas promoted for inclusive practitioners will require greater links to be established with schools and opportunities for more collaboration between the two institutions to ensure that inclusive initiatives learnt during pre-service training may be implemented successfully during teaching.

Coupled with greater accountability by teachers for student outcomes by demanding they increase students' scores on standardized tests to "prove" that they are demonstrating yearly progress, these demands can have a negative effect on a teacher's desire to be inclusive. Without radical educational reconstruction that acknowledges that inclusion while accommodating the needs of diverse students also requires accepting and valuing different outcomes, preparing teachers for inclusion has to rely on developing positive dispositions, providing teachers with a repertoire of skills and strategies and trusting that teachers will be able to implement at least some of these in their classrooms. Retaining an examination-oriented outcome for education does not align well with inclusion which by its very nature relies on accepting different outcomes and valuing them as important as traditional examination results. Such a model continues to promote an integrated approach and many teacher educators find that even after they have provided inclusive training, teachers are still unable to implement many ideas due to the expectation by schools for all students to achieve similar outcomes.

Raising the status of teaching

A recent review of the teaching profession in the UK, *Teachers matter: Recruitment, employment and retention at home and abroad* (Burghes *et al.*, 2009), identified a range of issues related to the professionalism of teaching and retaining professionally competent teachers. The review identified five areas of major concern: (1) the standards needed to enter teaching are too low, (2) teacher dissatisfaction is due to too much bureaucratic intervention, (3) teachers have to perform a myriad of administrative tasks, (4) there is inadequate teachers' pay and lack of an incentive framework, and (5) rates of attrition are high. While these concerns may well not be universal as many educational systems have expended enormous budgets in recent years in upgrading the professionalism of teaching, at least some of them will apply in most jurisdictions.

In order to tackle these perceived concerns relating to retaining good teachers a number of recommendations were made. Regarding teacher education the most noticeable was the proposal that the minimum standard of entry into teaching should be raised significantly and that mentoring under the supervision of experienced teachers should be provided for all new teachers. Both of these have implications for teacher education for inclusion. At the pre-service level, raising the academic standard may not necessarily result in more positive attitudes towards including learners with diverse needs. Such an approach will by default accept participants who have attended more elite schools that are less likely to have included students with special needs. In addition, increasing the focus on becoming subject specialists rather than generalists even at primary school may also make teachers more focused on achieving high learning outcomes for their subjects and less willing to include students who are unlikely to achieve these. The mentoring of newly qualified teachers, similarly, will require due diligence to ensure that they are placed with teachers who support the philosophy of inclusion and preferably those who have been practicing it. This may be difficult to achieve. Hence, teacher educators may need to work even harder to engage trainees in developing a committal to inclusion.

Planning cycles

Inclusion requires teachers to be able to respond to the individual needs of all children who appear in their classes. It assumes that they have sufficient knowledge and skills to be able to do this and that their attitude towards inclusion is positive. How can teacher educators ensure that their preparation courses are appropriate to enable teachers to be suitably prepared and that PL courses are meeting the actual needs of teachers?

One of the major challenges faced by teacher educators is that their courses are usually developed on a minimum four-year program planning cycle. Yet changes in classroom diversity are shifting much more rapidly. Sudden downturns in economic status as experienced over the past few years, increased levels of poverty, migration from disadvantaged countries into more advantaged ones, all occur very rapidly and classroom diversity can change within very short periods of time. Teacher educators who are locked into an inflexible planning cycle invariably do not have the capacity to respond immediately to the changing needs of teachers, yet this is critical if they are to ensure that their courses are up to date and can meet the current needs of teachers in schools. Inclusion requires teachers to respond to constantly changing educational environments and to do so with high levels of civic awareness and educational values of equity and social justice. In future, teacher education courses must, for that reason, consider how a degree of flexibility can be built into their planning that will allow them to respond more quickly to the rapidly changing diversity of school populations and prepare teachers for the shifting needs of children.

It is also essential to continue to reiterate that pre-service teacher education is only providing a basic training program to allow new teachers to commence their careers. It is a difficult task to determine what knowledge and skills can be realistically expected of new teachers considering the breadth of the curriculum and the continual addition of new knowledge and discipline areas that are suddenly deemed necessary by education systems. Pre-service teacher education can only be expected to provide a strong foundation as a sound groundwork for further development through ongoing PL. Key areas have been identified in the literature as being important to beginning teacher success in an inclusive classroom (Loreman, in press). Such aspects include an understanding of inclusion and respect for diversity; collaboration with teachers, parents and all stakeholders; developing a positive social climate; applying inclusive pedagogies and instructional planning; undertaking meaningful assessment, and participating in lifelong learning. The achievement of such skills may enable new teachers to be competent enough to achieve some success initially in inclusive classrooms but these will need to be supplemented with further learning throughout their careers as the need arises.

Conclusion

In conclusion, I shall return to Confucian philosophy. Confucius said "If one learns from others, but does not think, one will be bewildered. If, on the other hand, one thinks but does not learn from others, one will be in peril" (Analects 11) (于丹, 2006, 165頁). This book challenges teacher educators to both learn and think. It supports them in doing this by providing a rich source of ideas that they can employ to maximize training opportunities for preparing teachers for inclusive classrooms. Reflect upon these and select wisely.

References

Ainscow, M. (2003) "Using teacher development to foster inclusive classroom practices", in T. Booth, K. Nes and M. Stromstad (eds), *Developing Inclusive Teacher Education*, London: RoutledgeFalmer, pp. 15–32.

Burghes, D., Howson, J., Marenbon, J, O'Leary, J. and Woodhead, C. (2009) *Teachers Matter: Recruitment, Employment and Retention at Home and Abroad. The Report of the Politeia Education Commission* (ed. Lawlor, S.), London: Politeia.

Cushner, K. (2006) *Human Diversity in Action: Developing Multicultural Competencies for the Classroom*, 3rd edn, Boston, MA: McGraw Hill.

D'Cruz, H. (2007) "Working with 'Diverse Bodies, Diverse Identities': An approach to professional education about 'diversity'", *International Journal of Inclusive Education*, 11(1): 35–57.

Forlin, C. (2006) "Inclusive education in Australia ten years after Salamanca", *European Journal of Psychology of Education*, 21(3): 265–77.

Hollins, E. and Guzman, M. (2005) "Research on preparing teachers for diverse populations", in M. Cochran-Smith and K. M. Zeichner (eds), *Studying Teacher Education*, Mahwah, NJ: Lawrence Erlbaum Associates, pp. 477–548.

Lambe, J. (2006) "Student teachers' perceptions about inclusive classroom teaching in Northern Ireland prior to teaching practice experience", *European Journal of Special Needs Education*, 21(2): 167–86.

Loreman, T. (in press) "Essential inclusive education-related outcomes for Alberta preservice teachers", *Alberta Journal of Educational Research*, 56(1) (Summer 2010).

McIntyre, D. (2009) "The difficulties of inclusive pedagogy for initial teacher education and some thoughts on the way forward", *Teaching and Teacher Education*, 25(4): 602–8.

Moran, A. (2009) "Can a competence or standards model facilitate an inclusive approach to teacher education?", *International Journal of Inclusive Education*, 13(1): 45–61.

Palmer, P. J. (1998) *The Courage to Teach*, San Francisco, CA: John Wiley.

Pearce, M. and Forlin, C. (2005) "Challenges and potential solutions for enabling inclusion in secondary schools", *Australasian Journal of Special Education*, 29(2): 93–105.

Swennen, A. and van der Klink, M. (2008) *Becoming a Teacher Educator: Theory and Practice for Novice Teacher Educators*, London: Springer Verlag.

Yu, D. (2009) *Confucius from the Heart: Ancient Wisdom for Today's World* (trans. E. Tydesley), UK: Pan Macmillan Books (original work published 2006).

于丹 (Yu) (2006) 。于丹論語心得。北京：中華書局。(Confucius from the Heart)

Index